JEANS

★

JEANS

★

A CULTURAL HISTORY OF
AN AMERICAN ICON

★

James Sullivan

GOTHAM BOOKS

GOTHAM BOOKS
Published by Penguin Group (USA) Inc.
375 Hudson Street, New York, New York 10014, U.S.A.
Penguin Group (Canada), 90 Eglinton Avenue East, Suite 700, Toronto, Ontario M4P 2Y3,
Canada (a division of Pearson Penguin Canada Inc.); Penguin Books Ltd, 80 Strand, London
WC2R 0RL, England; Penguin Ireland, 25 St Stephen's Green, Dublin 2, Ireland (a division
of Penguin Books Ltd); Penguin Group (Australia), 250 Camberwell Road, Camberwell,
Victoria 3124, Australia (a division of Pearson Australia Group Pty Ltd); Penguin Books
India Pvt Ltd, 11 Community Centre, Panchsheel Park, New Delhi – 110 017, India;
Penguin Group (NZ), cnr Airborne and Rosedale Roads, Albany, Auckland 1310,
New Zealand (a division of Pearson New Zealand Ltd); Penguin Books (South Africa) (Pty)
Ltd, 24 Sturdee Avenue, Rosebank, Johannesburg 2196, South Africa

Penguin Books Ltd, Registered Offices: 80 Strand, London WC2R 0RL, England

Published by Gotham Books, a division of Penguin Group (USA) Inc.

First printing, August 2006
1 3 5 7 9 10 8 6 4 2

Copyright © 2006 by James Sullivan
All rights reserved

Gotham Books and the skyscraper logo are trademarks of Penguin Group (USA) Inc.

Library of Congress Cataloging-in-Publication Data

Sullivan, James, 1965 Nov. 7–
Jeans : a cultural history of an American icon / by James Sullivan.
p.   cm.
ISBN 1-592-40214-3 (hardcover)
1.   Jeans (Clothing)—History.   I. Title.
GT2085.S85 2006
687'.1—dc22   2005035698

Printed in the United States of America
Set in Goudy
Designed by Jennifer Ann Daddio

Photo opposite title page courtesy of Dorothea Lange/Library of Congress

To

MONICA,

who put our boys in blue jeans

CONTENTS

★

"To write about fashion, to discuss its impact and importance, always means to transform the fleeting and transitory into the statue-like and permanent, if only through black letters on a white sheet of paper. Fashion as a topic remains embroiled and disputed because of its alleged lack of substance. . . . Yet herein lies fashion's most absorbing fascination: it challenges us to transpose transitoriness, also the hallmark of modernity, into a medium of high regard."

—ULRICH LEHMANN,
TIGERSPRUNG: FASHION IN MODERNITY

"Know, first, who you are; and then adorn yourself accordingly."

—EPICTETUS

JEANS

★

INTRODUCTION:

★

The Perfect Fit

In an obscenity of riches, one humble rag was the star attraction. At Project, a trendy new fashion-business trade show making its Las Vegas debut in February 2005, denim was ubiquitous. The retail world at that moment was monomaniacal for premium blue jeans. Customers for whom casualwear had achieved an improbable pinnacle of glamour were suddenly not just willing but eager to spend $200 and more on a perfect-fitting pair of jeans, and boutique designers—seemingly a new one launching every week—were only too eager to accommodate them.

In the middle of a convention-floor maze of fancy new jeans hanging from pipe racks, one tattered denim scrap lay out for display in a weathered wooden chest. The remnant, having survived a century or so and likely salvaged from an old mine shaft, was little more than the shorn-off waistline, four or five inches wide, of a crude pair of workman's blue jeans. Just about the only feature that remained intact was the brand label—"The Stronghold," a West Coast supplier established in 1895. The rag had cost its new owners fifteen hundred dollars.

The Project show featured many of the most hailed designers of the recent denim phenomenon—Scott Morrison, the meticulous craftsman of Earnest Sewn; Chip and Pepper, the flaxen-haired Foster twins; Jason Ferro, a well-carved all-American boy who parlayed his experience with Guess and Levi's into a much-discussed new line, Los Angeles Denim Atelier. Amid so much frothy new talent, the resurrected Stronghold line was a stark anachronism, like a dignified cadaver wheeled onto a dance floor. The effect was enhanced by the old-timey portrait photographer hired to be on hand by entrepreneurs Michael Cassel and Michael Paradise, licensors of the long-dormant Stronghold brand.

Cassel was the guy who once bought the rights to Von Dutch, making the name of the late car customizer synonymous with trailer-trash chic by building a little empire of lowbrow foam-and-mesh truckers' hats and artfully destroyed, audaciously priced jeans. Now the two Michaels were launching the new Stronghold, turning out precise vintage reproductions of the old Stronghold, a workwear division of the early Los Angeles apparel suppliers Brownstein, Newmark, and Louis.

The original brand, defunct by the 1950s, never achieved much name recognition outside southern California. Most workwear companies around the turn of the century were regional, bound by shipping impediments and the difficulty of setting up a distribution network that could reach thousands of miles

from the home office. Even Levi Strauss & Co., the acknowledged granddaddy of the jeans business, was all but unknown
on the East Coast until well into the twentieth century. But
the original Stronghold was familiar to Hollywood; Charlie
Chaplin appeared in one ad for the company. With Los Angeles, the playground of celebrity, establishing itself in recent
years as the "premium denim capital of the world," as Cassel
put it, reviving the oldest L.A. denim brand seemed as sound a
proposition as any in the suddenly elbow-to-elbow, money-
crazed world of fashion blue jeans.

Stronghold's original "waist o'alls" likely cost the customer
somewhere in the neighborhood of a dollar fifty a pair back in
1895. The new Stronghold's reproductions, perched near the
very top of the steep pyramid that shaped the contemporary
denim market, would set back a well-heeled buyer anywhere
from $200 to $550. True fanatics, the owners promised, could
hunt down a limited-edition "super-collectible" pair for as
much as $2,000. The collection, Cassel said, would combine
the exclusivity of couture "with an Americana feel."

All blue jeans, whether they are rough as sidewalk or bur-
nished to a hand as fine as cashmere, share an "Americana"
feel. They may be cut and sewn in Japan, Vietnam, or Hong
Kong, using denim from mills in Mexico, India, Italy, or
Turkey and synthetic indigo dye from Germany or Brazil. Yet
wherever its origins, a pair of blue jeans embodies two centuries' worth of the myths and ideals of American culture.
Jeans are the surviving relic of the western frontier. They epito-
mize our present-day preoccupations—celebrity and consumer

culture—and we'll likely be wearing them long after the business suit, say, has been relegated to the dustbin of fashion.

"The most successful celebrities are products," wrote the cultural critic George W. S. Trow. "Consider the real role in American life of Coca-Cola. Is any man as well loved as this soft drink is?" No mere man, certainly, but we love our blue jeans that much more. Blue jeans—not soft drinks, or cars, or computers—are the crowning product of American ingenuity. They are timeless—flawlessly designed, yet infinitely versatile. They are mass-produced on an epic scale, yet each pair tells its own story. Most of all, blue jeans work on our behalf. They cover our asses.

Indigo-dyed denim, originally worn by men who dug mines, cut timber, herded cattle, drove railroad ties—workingmen, in other words, who built a civilization from a wilderness and had no use whatsoever for the cycles of fashion—has been a foundation of the fickle clothing industry for more than a half century now. Side-zip jeans for women were popular in the 1950s, when five dollars was considered a preposterous price to pay for denim pants. Twenty years later, skeptics were dumbfounded when people flocked to department stores to pay thirty or forty-five dollars for dressy jeans with designer labels stitched to the rear pockets. In the early 1990s, "lifestyle" brands such as Diesel and Lucky tugged the industry to the brink of the hundred-dollar barrier. Today, for many compulsive shoppers, there is no apparent ceiling. "I don't balk at five hundred dollars for a pair of shoes," one woman told *The New York Times* at the height of the latest denim craze. "Why should I balk at that price for jeans that are special?"

For decades, genteel designers have been effusive in their

praise for the lowly blue jean, which has its origins in European sailors' trousers and peasant overalls. "I wish I had invented blue jeans," said Yves Saint Laurent, sometimes credited as the first to bring denim to the runway. "They have expression, modesty, sex appeal, simplicity—all I hope for in my clothes." Bill Blass declared Levi's "the best single item of apparel ever designed." Even Charles James, the brilliant couturier whose intricate silk and satin creations epitomized the wholly impractical fine art of fashion, recognized his country's hardy contribution to cross-cultural modes of dress. "Blue denim is America's gift to the world," he said.

Levi Strauss & Co. patented the modern, mass-produced prototype in 1873, reinforcing the pockets—two in front, one in back—with copper rivets. In 1890, the year the patent expired, the company added a fourth pocket, the little watch pocket, to the original design. By 1905 there were two back pockets on the 501XX, the archetypal Levi's button-fly trouser, and this basic riveted, five-pocket jean has been the industry standard ever since. Thousands of manufacturers around the world have copied it.

It's a perfect pattern. Blue jeans are for men and women alike, for all body types. They stand up to hard work and rough play. They can imply either democratic parity or the aristocratic hierarchies of status. Around the world, blue jeans have obliterated every demographic distinction—age, ethnicity, income, education—in becoming the common casual uniform. And in our own headlong, irreverent culture, jeans have a deep and venerable past that is loaded with meaning. For vintage collectors and fashion-forward designers alike, jeans are steeped not just in the multiple dips of indigo dye, but in a rich sense of history. Whether we called them overall pants or "blue drillin's" or dungarees, blue jeans have been an indispensable part of our culture almost as long as we've had an American culture. First they built the country's infrastructure, then they populated it with a collective identity.

For half a century blue jeans have helped define every youth movement, and every effort of older generations to deny the passing of youth, in this youth-obsessed and obsessively renewable country. Fifty years ago America invented the concept of the teenager, and it's no coincidence that the enduring character of blue jeans—claiming independence and the right to self-expression—can be traced to the same time. "Our Models Can Beat Up Their Models," taunted advertisements for Levi's during the 1990s. Some of the ads featured a defiant, sneering image of the actor Marlon Brando from the 1953 motorcycle melodrama *The Wild One*. Brando's cinematic insolence, along with the uncorked emotions of James Dean in films such as *Rebel Without a Cause* and *East of Eden* (both 1955), demonstrated how youth could define itself in opposition to its elders. It was an attitude that proved invaluable, and endlessly recyclable, to the sellers of consumer goods of all kinds. Work pants, once unremarkably utilitarian, were recast in that era as dramatic, glamorous. More than that: they were dangerous.

Every subsequent youth movement, from hippie to hip-hop, has claimed blue jeans for itself. And every generation since mid-century has grown into maturity in them. Jeans have been worn by soldiers and protesters, headbangers and heart-throbs, vagrants and presidents. They have been worn on campus and in prison, on horses and Harleys, to the opera and the mosh pit. Paul Bunyan wore jeans. So did the Marlboro Man

and Howdy Doody, Jackson Pollock and Andy Warhol. From Marilyn to Madonna, Lead Belly to Snoop Dogg, "American Gothic" to *The Simple Life*, denim embodies American creativity and rebellion.

It transcends fashion. Designers have a tendency to describe the construction of a pair of jeans in terms that evade the bounds of their own discipline. Making a pair of jeans, especially in this age of hand-washed, individually abraded premium brands, is an art form. It's akin to architecture, they say, or woodworking, or sculpting. And to wear them is to express a kind of philosophy, in that the classic pair of blue jeans might carry more implications about the American consumer than anything else we consume.

This book is a history of denim clothing, but it is also an American cultural history, just enough to fit in a riveted hip pocket. It is a review of the national ethos—our diligence and ethics, our bravado, and our wildest dreams—an ethos which, in the global era, has infiltrated even the most far-flung cultures. Denim is a great social equalizer, and an even better paradox. We all wear blue jeans; they are often called the American uniform. Yet we are never more ourselves than when we are wearing our own favorite pair.

ONE

★

The Sans-culottes:
Before the Blue Jean

There is an old proverb: He who has pants, has freedom. The bifurcated, tube-legged, full-length trouser, a European peasant garment embraced by settlers in the untamed New World, has always suggested many kinds of freedom, including convenience, mobility—and suggestiveness. Pants drew attention to body parts that other garments were designed to conceal. The Mormon leader Brigham Young was appalled when men's trousers were first outfitted with front buttons in America in the 1830s. He called them "fornication pants."

Today, with baggy prison-style blue jeans having turned underwear into outerwear and slinky low-rise jeans revealing the rear-view peep show sometimes called "the other cleavage," Young's complaint is both quaint and familiar.

Such bodily self-awareness has contributed to a long and

rich history of pants representing a threat to the status quo. Pants have been worn by working-class revolutionaries, women campaigning for equality, and youthful agitators exploiting the generation gap. The best-selling and most volatile garment of them all, the indigo-dyed denim trouser known as the blue jean, has outfitted convicts, slaves, hobos, bikers, protesters, punks, and gangstas. Originally designed as utterly unremarkable workwear, blue jeans have become a ubiquitous presence in the culture wars of modern America. Yet their legendary durability has also earned them the veneration of the surviving outlaw.

The children of the 1950s and '60s, the first to wear jeans as a social or political statement, are now approaching retirement, still wearing their jeans. Blue jeans contain all our multitudes—young and old, rural and urban, labor and leisure, high life and low. If jeans are the clothing of America, then Brigham Young had it exactly right. Whether button-fly or zippered, jeans are "fornication pants." Though they may say something different for each of us, the basic message is twofold—either "fuck you," or "fuck me."

While human beings from east and west have worn rudimentary trousers from ancient times, widespread acceptance of the custom is only about as old as the United States. Baggy pants were worn beneath caftans by warriors of the ancient Germans, Persians, and Gauls. The Greeks and Romans, at first dismissive of this "barbaric" practice, later adopted protective leggings for their own soldiers. Men in the Middle Ages generally wore tunics and hosiery, though a loose style of trouser of the time, tied at the ankles, would evolve into the formal knee breeches of the post-Renaissance era. By then full-length trousers were widely considered a lower-class garment, perhaps appropriate for hard labor but decidedly unfit for the parlor. The term *pantaloons*, originating in England around 1600 A.D., was indiscriminately applied to various styles of garments covering the lower extremities. Contempt for "pants" is apparent in the commedia dell'arte, in which the stock character Pantalone is an old fool in trousers.

But the practicality of ankle-length pants would eventually supersede the snobbery of aristocratic fashion. Around the fifteenth century, sailors from India and Italy took to wearing cotton, linen, or wool-blend bell-bottoms, which were easily rolled up when the decks got wet. A little later, farmers in the Mediterranean countries began wearing pants in the field. By the time of the American Revolution, pants were fast becoming the norm in the brambles and thickets of the New World. Lord Carlisle, visiting the colonies in 1779, wrote in a letter from Delaware, "The gnats in this part of the river are as large as sparrows; I have armed myself against them by wearing trousers, which is the constant dress of this country."

In the early 1800s, pants became faddish perhaps for the first time when Parisian intellectuals began wearing them as a show of solidarity with the disenfranchised masses in rural France. This "back to nature" movement would help inspire the French Revolution—the upheaval that pitted the sans-culottes, the champions of the trousered working class, against the aristocrats in their knee breeches. "Thus any male who considered himself liberal and radical adopted trousers, preferably as tight as could be," wrote the clothing historian Diana de Marly. It was not the last time a fashion trend would feed a social gesture. Brashness starts with a swagger, and a swagger begins in the loins.

Yet for the next two hundred years the vast majority of men wearing work clothes remained men performing physical labor, not intellectualizing it. In 1824 the Parisian tailor Pierre Parissot caused a stir when he began selling ready-to-wear work clothes such as smocks, overalls, and duck-cloth trousers to the city's laborers in his shop on Quai aux Fleurs. Seventeen years later, one observer estimated that there were 350,000 men in Paris, "at least 100,000 of whom were doomed for life to the worker's blue, wearing nothing but overalls or plain smocks."

As work clothes evolved over their long history of underpinning (and sometimes undermining) the prevailing culture, one textile in particular has become synonymous with resistance: denim. In April 1786—almost a century before Levi Strauss and Jacob Davis patented their iconic riveted work pants in 1873—the *Providence Gazette* reported that a German redemptioner, an immigrant repaying his passage to the New World with a period of voluntary servitude, went on the lam wearing a "blue and white Kersey shirt and Sergedenim Breeches."

The name *denim* is presumed to derive from the phrase *serge de Nîmes*, the trade term for a cotton-wool blend first introduced in Nîmes, southeastern France, around the sixteenth century. But details of denim's origins are vague at best. Historians are uncertain whether a *serge de Nîmes* commonly recognized in sixteenth- and seventeenth-century England was a French import or a locally produced textile given the cachet of a French-sounding name. Further complicating the matter, another workwear fabric, this one a fustian (a blend of cotton, wool, and/or silk), was first produced in the sailors' port of Genoa, Italy, around the same period. It was named for its place of origin, Anglicized as *jean*, a word which the Oxford English Dictionary dates to 1567. (Some accounts suggest that the term *blue jeans* may be an interpretation of *bleu de Gênes*.) A popular, relatively cheap import in England—port of London records show considerable shiploads arriving from Italy in the late 1580s—jean was soon being woven in huge quantities in the booming cotton county of Lancashire.

There were marked differences between the denim and jean of the era. Denim was a heavier, much tougher twill. Unlike jean, which was woven of two dyed threads, denim had the distinctive appearance it retains today—a colored warp, usually dyed with indigo, crossed with an undyed (white) weft. The two fabrics were, however, used in the production of many of the same dry goods, leading to the eventual interchangeability of the terms.

With the coming of mechanization in the eighteenth century and the abundant natural resources of its colonies in India and North America, both of which were blessed with ideal conditions for growing the cotton plant, England built an enormous textile industry. The heavy twill of denim proved well suited not only for workwear but for goods such as upholstery, mattress ticking, and awnings as well. Similar cotton products included drill, a coarse fabric that would lend its name to one variety of prototypical blue jeans ("blue drillin's"), and duck or canvas, which was ideal for tent cloth and sails. Another name for work pants, dungarees, apparently descends from a coarse calico, often brown, that originated in the village of Dungri, in present-day Mumbai (Bombay), India. Like duck, dungaree cloth was often used for sails. Mariners were known to recycle tattered sections of sail into their "slops," uniforms including bell-bottoms.

Some accounts have suggested that the sails of Christopher Columbus's ships were made of Genoan fustian—jean cloth—though sailing experts contend that the explorer's sails were more than likely flaxen. In his diary entry of October 13, 1492, Columbus noted the offerings of the ancestral Bahamians, the first people he and his crew encountered in the New World: "They brought balls of spun cotton and parrots and spears and other trifles . . . and they gave all for anything that was given to them." While the author of *The History of the Cotton Manufacture in Great Britain* (1835) surmised that native North Americans had been making and wearing cotton garments for centuries, it was the European immigrants who brought jean cloth and denim, the cotton materials that would one day be sewn into trousers that could hold up like Indian buckskins.

Less than a decade after the *Mayflower* landed near Plymouth Rock in 1620, an invoice showed that "11 yards of wt. English jeans" were supplied to the Massachusetts Bay Company Store. In 1650, "19 peecs Jeines fustian" were imported into Boston. By the 1760s, jean was said to be the primary output of the colonists' first mill, the United Company of Philadelphia. Denim was becoming common as well. A supplier's advertisement in a Norwich, Connecticut, periodical from 1783 touted a variety of cotton fabrics including "Ribdenims . . . Thicksetts, Corduroys . . . Denims, Jeans, Jeanetts, Fustians . . ." And in 1789 *The Salem Mercury* recounted a tour of a Beverly, Massachusetts, textile mill, the first to use machinery in New England, welcoming President George Washington. "He was shown . . . about a dozen looms upon which they were weaving cotton denim, thickset, corduroys, [and] velveret," the newspaper reported. In his diary, Washington noted, "The whole seemed perfect, and the cotton stuffs which they turn out, excellent of their kind."

Present-day marketing experts have nothing on their forebears, who knew how to entice buyers with fashionable interpretations of what one newspaper referred to as "newfangled denim." John Hargrove's *The Weavers Draft Book and Clothiers Assistant*, published in Baltimore in 1792, included eight variations on jean fabric and three more for denim, including "dice" denim and "balloon" denim. An 1849 sales catalog for the New York outfitters Lewis & Hanford featured blue jean trousers and a "Fancy Mixt" jean, as well as vests, jackets, and topcoats in jean material dyed black, white, blue, chestnut, and olive. And in 1864 the wholesalers H. B. Claflin & Co. advertised a wide array of denims, including "New Creek Blues" and "Madison River Browns." The names suggest a romantic preoccupation with the rustic to rival the artful copy in today's most well-bred clothing catalogs.

Over the years jeans have been manufactured in white, black, brown, green, and just about every color on the spectrum. Yet it is no accident that their predominant color has always been, and remains, blue. "The deeper blue becomes," wrote the artist Wassily Kandinsky, "the more urgently it summons man towards the infinite, the more it arouses in him a longing for purity and, ultimately, for the supersensual."

The essential blueness of blue jeans has always been an integral part of their enduring appeal. Like the garment, the color blue is subject to multiple interpretations. It's said that blue was the last color to be recognized by the evolving human eye. Perhaps that helps explain why blue has held such mystery for us for so long. Many ancient and medieval cultures attributed magical qualities, both benign and evil, to blue. It is the color of the Virgin Mary and the so-called "blue laws" of Puritan New England, of the blue-blooded aristocracy and the blue-collar working class. And blue is the color of the imagination.

One of the few hues that can be perceived as both light and dark, blue defines our many moods. It is the eggshell shade of a baby's blanket and the stern authority of the uniforms of the police, umpires, and many military troops. The appeal of blue is near universal, spanning geography, culture, age, gender, and disposition. Though it is a comparative rarity in living nature—blueberries, the blue jay, forget-me-nots—blue is the color of both the sky and the sea. It covers the whole earth.

"It is curious that in English the word *blue* should represent depressing as well as transcendent things; that it should be the most holy hue and the color of pornography," wrote Victoria Finlay in *Color: A Natural History of the Palette*. "Fantasy, depression, and God are all, like blue, in the more mysterious reaches of our consciousness."

Psychologists attribute to blue an array of emotions and attitudes unmatched by any other color. Irving Berlin celebrated "Blue Skies" in his lovely ode to optimism. Yet the young Pablo Picasso was wracked with grief over the suicide of a friend during his so-called Blue Period, when he painted the doleful blue-smocked laborers of Paris. Sky blue is generally considered to be masculine, connoting distance, dignity, and the search for heavenly states. Ocean blue, on the other hand, can be interpreted as feminine: nurturing and reflective.

Most significantly, blue reassures. In India, it is the color of the Fifth (or Throat) Chakra, which governs the art of communication, the ability to convey one's innermost truths. Creating the illusion of truth telling, of course, is the prime objective of advertisers. Capitalizing on this connection, an overwhelming 70 percent of international corporations use blue in their company logos, from IBM ("Big Blue") and the Ford Motor Company (whose founder, Henry Ford, believed blue and white to be the colors of order and morale) to Wal-Mart and Napster. In 1995 Mars, the chocolate company, invited the public to vote on a new color for its M&M's. Blue won in a landslide. To be "true blue" is to display a profound sense of loyalty. According to one theory, the old expression is rooted in the dependable blueness of the sky. But other etymologists trace the phrase to the ancient concept of a blue dye that will not run. One early version of the saying "true as Coventry blue," referred to the highly regarded dyes of that English industrial city.

Blue dye, worn by rice farmers and royalty alike, has been used to distinguish clothing since the beginning of dyeing itself. Scientific analysis has shown that indigo dyestuffs were in use at least as early as the third millennium B.C. Examples of blue-dyed cloth used to wrap Egyptian mummies have been traced to 2500 B.C. A tablet owned by the British Museum features Babylonian dye recipes, including indigo, from the seventh century B.C., and the Old Testament notes in Ezekiel that "blue clothes and broidered work" were being offered by the merchants of Sheba in the sixth century B.C. There is also evidence of both the Maya and the Aztecs dyeing with indigo.

For centuries, then, workers around the globe have worn blue-dyed clothing. Precipitating the term *blue collar*, their smocks and aprons were historically dyed with indigo. Present in several plant species, including, most notably, a member of the pea family, indigo thrives—like the cotton plant—in the equatorial climates of southeast Asia, northern Africa, and Central and South America and was successfully introduced into North America during the colonial era. Along with madder red, the blue dye extracted from the leaves of the *Indigofera tinctoria* plant of India and Africa (in the Americas, *Indigofera anil*) was the most prevalent of the early vegetable dyestuffs. Traditionally, the shrublike indigo plant is soaked in liquid, then the plant material is removed and the liquid is beaten to instigate the oxidation process. The indigo dyestuff gradually settles at the base of the container to form a paste. Blue dye in Europe, drawn from the temperate indigo plant known as woad, or pastel (*Isatis tinctoria*), a member of the mustard family, also dates to antiquity. From its earliest documentation, the complicated process and startling results of blue dyeing often overwhelmed observers. In Icelandic myth, woad is associated with the goddess of death. Caesar noted in his *Commentaries on the Gallic Wars* that marauding Britons painted their bodies blue, possibly with woad, "that they might appear more horrible in battle."

Traveling in the thirteenth century A.D., the Venetian explorer Marco Polo documented indigo cultivation in Java, Ceylon, and India. Vasco da Gama's establishment of a shipping route to India in 1498 led to the import of indigo by the governments of Spain and Portugal, which classified it as a spice. First used in Europe primarily as an artist's pigment, the dyestuff was coveted by traders for its highly concentrated value, comparable to that of nutmeg or opium. Indigo was often pursued at the expense of all other goods; seven ships representing the Dutch East India Company in 1631 were said to have returned from the Spice Islands with 333,000 pounds of indigo worth five tons of gold. (The trade would retain its value in the

New World: in the antebellum South, landowners could trade indigo for slaves, pound for pound.)

But woad, indigo's inferior cousin, was a pillar of the European economy, and it had powerful champions determined to stop the new import. The Spencers, ancestors of Diana, princess of Wales, built their fortune on woad. Pierre de Berny, a Toulouse woad merchant, grew so rich on the "blue gold" that he guaranteed the huge ransom demanded by the Holy Roman Emperor Charles V when his troops imprisoned the French king Francis I in the battle of Pavia. In France, the pastel blocks made from woad pulp were called *cocagne,* and *pays de cocagne* still describes a land of plenty. One early writer called the woad-rich French province of Languedoc "the happiest and richest" region in Europe.

The merchants of such areas saw indigo as a grave threat, and they demonized the plant. Beginning in 1577, the Germans instituted restrictions against "the devil's dye" that would last a century. For much of the 1600s, English investigators were authorized to burn any indigo they could find. The French took the ban much farther, issuing royal edicts that called for the execution of illicit indigo traders. Oddly, woad had been similarly demonized in the thirteenth century. As clothing preferences moved from reds to blues, Germanic madder merchants tried to defend their business by enlisting stained-glass artisans to portray blue devils in their work.

The campaign against indigo lasted for the better part of two centuries. Throughout Europe weavers were led to believe that the dye was harmful to their product. The insinuation that indigo was "poisonous" to fabrics played on a long history of suspicion toward the blue dye, which was difficult to extract and mystifying to those who could not comprehend the process.

Like so many other misunderstood phenomena, indigo dyeing was assumed to be some kind of magic, a dark art. For one thing, the fermenting process yielded a putrid stench not unlike that of a decaying body. The Dutch claimed that those who handled the plant were likely to suffer sexual impotence, "accompanied by a temporary semilameness of the lower limbs." In cultures that did work with indigo, the unpredictable dyestuff was often invested with human qualities. There was widespread belief that bad moods and arguments could adversely affect it. In Morocco, if the indigo would not fix, families deliberately spread malicious lies, or "blackness," believing that would solve the problem. In remote parts of Indonesia, where village dyeing is still performed exclusively by women, those who are menstruating are forbidden to work with the dye pots, for fear that their blood flow will cause the dye to run.

Ultimately, however, the superior colorfastness of indigo made it inevitable that the dye would be adopted across Europe. As early as the 1640s, the Caribbean islands were producing more indigo than India, and slave labor made the price of New World indigo highly competitive with that of woad. The rise of South Carolina as a fertile source of indigo can be attributed to the perseverence of one remarkable woman. Eliza Lucas, born in Antigua to an English army officer, came to the American mainland in the 1730s, where she took control of three plantations the family inherited from her grandfather. Eliza's father, still stationed in the islands, sent various seeds for the young woman to plant. "I have greater hopes for the indigo than any of the rest of the things I have tried," she wrote to her father. After four years of drought and other difficulties, she achieved a successful harvest. Later famous as the mother of the eminent political figures Thomas and Charles Cotesworth Pinckney, Eliza Lucas gave South Carolina its first substantial economy when she distributed indigo seeds to fellow landowners. By 1755, the colony was exporting five hundred tons of indigo yearly.

With European imports suddenly booming—England alone imported five hundred tons from its colonies in America and India in 1770—planters throughout the New World were quick to turn to indigo. During the 1780s, there were so many landowners obsessed with the great profits of indigo around Rio de Janeiro—four hundred, by one estimate—that the region suffered severe food shortages.

But domination was short lived. By the end of the century, the indigo trade had reached its pinnacle. Following the American Revolution (during which colonial troops wore heavy winter coats dyed with indigo) and the loss of her American colonies, England turned to colonial India to produce indigo. The move caused a drastic depression in American prices. Within a matter of years, indigo was effectively replaced as a major source of revenue for southern growers by a crop with which the dye was destined to become inextricably linked: cotton. By the Civil War, Georgia and South Carolina were the only two states still producing indigo in significant quantities. Meanwhile, planters in Central and South America began to replace their indigo with coffee beans, which would soon become their leading crop.

In India, the dyestuff remained a source of contention despite the Hindu belief that blue, the color of Krishna, represented good fortune. While profit-seeking British landowners in the Bengali region planted as much indigo as possible, their farmers fought for the right to grow more rice. When in 1860 an order was handed down making it illegal to grow rice on any land that had previously harvested indigo, the peasants staged protests that came to be known as the Blue Mutiny. A postal worker named Dinabandhu Mitra wrote a wildly successful play called *Nil Darpan—The Indigo Mirror*—depicting the colonial Brits as tyrannical brutes. The play helped stir unrest throughout the provinces. It was not the last time indigo played a role in the opposition to British rule; in 1917 Mahatma Gandhi staged his first act of civil disobedience in Bihar on behalf of the indigo growers there.

Exactly when indigo-dyed denim cloth was first fashioned into a kind of trouser resembling today's jeans, we may never know. His only regret, Yves Saint Laurent liked to say, was that he didn't invent jeans. He needn't have worried. No single clothier can lay claim to that achievement. Jeans were not invented—they evolved democratically, like so much Americana. Just as Abner Doubleday has been credited with "inventing" the game of baseball, or Jelly Roll Morton claimed to have fashioned jazz from a more primitive kind of urban rhythm, it is not precisely accurate to call the wholesaler Levi Strauss the creator of blue jeans. But Strauss was a certifiable pioneer in one important respect: He knew how to turn a commodity into a legend.

TWO

★

Tug-of-War:
"Those Pants of Levi's,"
and the Competition

San Francisco in the mid-nineteenth century was a hell of a place to start a business. The port city, originally called Yerba Buena, sprung up at a furious pace, a hub for the anxious hordes of miners flooding the Sierra Nevada foothills during the great California gold rush. From a tiny trading settlement that included pelt hunters, wayward sailors, Spanish-speaking immigrants, and a shipload of Latter-day Saints in the mid-1840s, the base quickly became a tent city, and then a brick-and-iron forest of shipping and commerce. By 1852 there were thirty-six thousand residents crowding the northeast corner of the peninsula, just inside the magnificent aquatic portal of the Golden Gate, where San Francisco Bay meets the Pacific Ocean.

Newcomers surged onto the docks of the settlement's

wharves with every ship's arrival in the wake of the gold rush, each one bringing the high hopes of a fresh start into an eager venue. One of those newcomers made a name for himself that is world renowned today. Born in Buttenheim, Bavaria, on February 26, 1829, Levi Strauss made the passage to America in 1847 with his mother, Rebecca, and his sisters Fanny and Mathilde, two years after the death of his father by tuberculosis. In New York the young man joined his half brothers, Jonas and Louis. The brothers, earlier arrivals in the New World, were already operating a dry-goods establishment in lower Manhattan.

Six years after his emigration, Levi Strauss set out for the West, seeking expansion opportunities for the family business. Like so many other enterprising men and women of the time, he sailed to Panama, where he crossed the isthmus and boarded another steamer bound for California. The young entrepreneur disembarked inside the Golden Gate on March 14, 1853. (For years employees of Levi Strauss & Co. used letterhead dating the company's existence to 1850. Company historian Lynn Downey theorizes that the discrepancy may be due to faulty newspaper reporting, or perhaps a company employee fudging the inaugural year sometime in the late 1940s in order to align more neatly with the California centennial in 1950.)

Strauss, then twenty-four years old, set up a dry-goods supply house on Sacramento Street, moving within a few years to a bigger warehouse just up the road. Because many records were lost in the great San Francisco earthquake and fire of 1906, documentation for the early decades of Levi Strauss & Co. is unfortunately spotty. In lieu of more paper evidence, the company's past has become a repository for tall tales and dubious anecdotes, some of them possibly embellished by long-ago salesmen, others by the vagaries of old newspapers and bio-graphical resources. By some unsubstantiated accounts, the founder may have sometimes traveled into the foothill towns with his wares. Whether he ventured out or stayed put in San Francisco, almost everything in northern California was at a premium. Prices in the city were so high that the standard of currency was said to be the twenty-dollar gold piece.

"There was plenty of gold but very little to buy—a classic supply-demand crisis," wrote J. S. Holliday in his gold rush study, *The World Rushed In*. According to the author, the Monterey businessman Thomas O. Larkin was among those advised to bring goods of all kinds, such as blankets and clothing, to the Sierras as quickly as possible. Larkin's agent warned that the printer and Latter-day Saint Sam Brannan—by then a store owner at Sutter's Fort in the Sacramento Valley—"had purchased almost $12,000 worth of such supplies, hence the shortage and high prices. Then the agent urged Larkin: 'If you can have it done within a month, you had better have a large lot of pants made up of flannel, jeans [jean cloth], osnaburg, and cotton goods.' "

It is here that the formidable Levi Strauss legend has its deepest roots. Countless chroniclers have repeated the claim that Strauss immediately recognized a shortage of durable trousers in the gold "diggings," where men, many of whom had left respectable vocations back east in the hope of striking it rich, wore the same heavy clothing under the hot California sun, day in and day out. Not only were their clothes worn threadbare, but a water shortage forced many miners to drink fetid water, which inevitably led to chronic diarrhea. Under those conditions, Levi Strauss is said to have encountered a man in the foothills who told him his tent cloth was a poor investment.

"Shoulda brought pants," this apocryphal prophet supposedly said. "Pants don't wear worth a hoot in the diggin's."

Various versions of the tale have Strauss hustling to the nearest tailor, where he had the man fashion a pair of work pants from his canvas tent cloth, or even stitching them together himself, by the light of a campfire. Charming as such lore may be, it's not true. Strauss did sell work pants to the miners not long after his arrival in California—in fact, the Levi Strauss & Co. archive includes an invoice dated March 17, 1859, for a transaction with merchants named Hardy & Kennedy in Auburn, California, for three dozen pairs of "jeans pants," total sale $45. In those early years, however, Levi Strauss was strictly a wholesaler. He did not begin manufacturing denim work pants until 1873.

Despite the San Francisco earthquakes of 1865 and 1868—the latter damaged the company's newest headquarters on Battery Street—by the 1870s Levi Strauss & Co. was well established as a leading dry-goods supplier to the coastal frontier. The growing business had become a partnership of five, including Jonas, Louis, and Levi and their San Francisco brothers-in-law, David Stern and William Sahlein, when in 1872 the company's namesake received a fortuitous offer.

Jacob Davis was a struggling tailor, a failed investor in coal, tobacco, and brewing who had recently settled his family in Reno, Nevada. Davis was making tents, wagon covers, and horse blankets when he was struck with an idea. The local laborers were constantly complaining that their pants were not tough enough to withstand the wear and tear they subjected them to, especially in the pockets. The tailor is said to have been approached by the wife of a hefty woodcutter, who was having particular difficulty finding trousers that would not come apart at the seams. (Some accounts attribute the folksy nickname Alkali Ike to this figure; others call him a prospector who may have had trouble keeping his pockets intact as he stuffed them with gold nuggets.) Working on a horse blanket, Davis realized that the same copper rivets he used for the straps on the blankets might be useful for reinforcing pants pockets. Using undyed duck cloth purchased on credit from Levi Strauss & Co., Davis outfitted the woodcutter with the strongest pants he could conceive. He sewed four more pairs for drop-in customers in the next month. Soon he had a steadily growing business, as word got around among the laborers of Reno that Davis was making a superior product.

Though he quickly recognized the earning potential of his innovation, Davis was not eager to pay a patent fee, having failed with two previous patents involving steam-powered machinery. He wrote to Strauss, from whom the tailor had begun buying blue denim as well as off-white duck cloth to make his waist-high overalls. Sending along two sample pairs of the pants, he offered the wholesaler a half-interest in the proposed riveted pants business in exchange for the price of the patent application. While the original letter no longer exists, the LS&CO. archive does include a transcription typed at a later date, presumably from memory. It's an odd little document written in a phonetic approximation of the immigrant tailor's heavily accented English.

"The secratt of them Pents," it reads, "is the Rivits that I put in those Pockets, and I found the demand so large that I cannot make them up fast enough. I charge for the Duck $3.00 and for the Blue $2.50 a pear. My nabors are getting yealouse of these success and unless I secure it by Patent Papers it will soon become a general thing." The $68 required to apply for a

Trade show, 1898

patent would be considerably less burdensome for someone of Strauss's stature than for himself, Davis suggested. "The investment for you is but a trifle compared with the improvement in all Coarse Clothing."

The government rejected their first two applications, noting that the tongues of soldiers' boots had been reinforced with rivets during the Civil War. Finally, on May 20, 1873, Levi Strauss & Co. was awarded patent number 139,121. Strauss soon brought Davis to San Francisco, where the tailor supervised the cutting of cloth for the production of the new riveted trousers. In the custom of the clothing industry's domestic system of the time, the piece goods were then delivered to in-home seamstresses, who sewed them together and added the rivets. This system soon proved inefficient, however, and Davis

JAMES SULLIVAN

was given the task of overseeing the opening of a new factory in downtown San Francisco. It was the first manufacturing venture for Levi Strauss & Co.

From the beginning, LS&CO. used denim made by the Amoskeag Manufacturing Company of Manchester, New Hampshire, reputedly the best denim in the world. That sort of commitment to quality was the distinction on which Levi Strauss & Co. would stake its name.

Amoskeag's reputation for making the finest in "coarse cotton goods" reached back as early as 1851, when the company featured denims, ginghams, and flannels at the Great Exhibition of the World's Fair in London. That a representative of the upstart Americans would earn praise among much more sophisticated competition—showing mattress tickings and material for homely work clothes, no less—was cause for grumbling. "The surprise and chagrin of the Old World manufacturers may be imagined," wrote a historian for the mill in 1915, "when the award of the first and only prize was given to the Amoskeag Manufacturing Company."

The Amoskeag Manufacturing Company was incorporated in 1831 on the site of Benjamin Prichard's 1804 cotton mill at Amoskeag Falls, a formidable source of water power on the same Merrimack River that drove the huge mills of Lowell and Lawrence, Massachusetts, thirty miles or so to the south. Named after Manchester, England, the world's largest textile city, Manchester, New Hampshire, ballooned from a population of 877 in 1830 to 70,000 in 1910. In time the Amoskeag Manufacturing Company would itself be the world's largest textile producer, encompassing thirty major mills and eight million square feet of floor space scuffed by the boots of seventeen thousand employees. In 1906 the *Manchester Union-Leader* reported that the firm was producing four million yards of cotton goods a week.

The enormous millyard inspired the kind of mythmaking that would one day come to dominate the blue jeans industry it helped spawn. Presidents and campaigning politicians routinely visited to inspect this colossus of American manufacturing, a "total institution," as one historian wrote, "a closed and almost self-contained world," which at its apex covered almost a mile of riverfront. One of those candidates, Abraham Lincoln, arrived in Manchester during the election season of 1860 at the invitation of Ezekiel Straw. Straw, who would one day become governor of New Hampshire, ran the daily operations at Amoskeag on behalf of the millyard's Boston-based financiers. He dispatched a machinist named Edwin P. Richardson to escort their guest through the facility. Richardson's heavy work clothes and his "begrimed" face and hands made him self-conscious. "When Mr. Lincoln held out one of his great hands to clasp mine," he recalled, "I shrank back." Lincoln, it was reported, would have none of it. "Young man," he said, "the hand of honest toil is never too grimy for Abe Lincoln to clasp."

Richardson asked for a moment to change into something more presentable, but again Lincoln waved him off. "Young man," he said, "go just as you are."

Competitors began making similarly riveted garments almost as soon as "those pants of Levi's," as some unidentified miner is said to have dubbed them, hit the market. In its first year of manufacturing the company sued two rivals, San Francisco's

A. B. Elfelt and San Jose's Kan Lun, for patent infringement. The name of the latter competitor suggests the extent of the Chinese immigration of the period, which would soon create hysteria among the West Coast workforce. The Panic of 1873 and the prolonged drought of 1876–77 would precipitate a backlash against Chinese immigrants who were willing to work for brutally low wages, especially in the garment industry. The so-called "nativism" of the era, in which American-born citizens objected to job competition from foreign immigrants, erupted in San Francisco's Chinatown into several days of rioting in July 1877. Like so many of his fellow businessmen of the time, Strauss—already considered a paternal figure in the city—employed white "American" labor, and made a point of saying so during the immigrant controversy.

The situation would carry historic ironies for Levi Strauss & Co., which would one day earn a reputation for its carefully considered social conscience, including its insistence on opening fully integrated sewing plants in the Jim Crow South. In recent years the American apparel industry has lost the vast majority of its domestic manufacturing jobs to cheaper workforces overseas, especially in the Far East. Levi Strauss & Co. was one of the last garment makers to fully embrace the move toward lower wages in the global marketplace, and in the 1990s it would pay for its loyalty—some would say its stubborn loyalty—to United States workers.

In 1875 Strauss purchased the Mission and Pacific Woolen Mills, one of the oldest mills on the West Coast. Their woolen blanketing was used to line Levi's denim and duck clothing for outdoor laborers. "These goods are specially adapted for the use of farmers, mechanics, miners, and working men in general," the company advertised.

Sometime around 1890 the company assigned a lot number, 501, to its signature "waist overalls." The original 501XX would prove to be a timeless design—copper rivets, button fly, heavyweight denim—with the exception of a few nineteenth-century features that were eventually phased out, such as suspender buttons and a cinch belt, or "buckleback," in the rear. From the beginning the 501 was adorned on the rear pocket with the so-called "Arcuate" design, a pair of adjoined arches sewn with orange thread to match the rivets. Although not officially trademarked until 1943, the pocket stitch is nonetheless one of the oldest design trademarks still in use in the United States. Today, Levi's classic 501 blue jean is widely acknowledged as the best-selling garment of all time.

In 1886, Levi Strauss & Co. began sewing a leather tag onto the rear waistband of its pants. As it still does today, the panel featured a crudely drawn artist's rendition of two men leading a pair of horses in opposite directions, trying in vain to tear a pair of Levi's hitched between them. While the "Two Horse Brand" patch would become one of the company's most enduring symbols (along with the arcuate design on the back pockets and, beginning in 1936, the "Levi's" red tab on the seat of the pants), it had plenty of rivals.

Which brand came first remains a matter of conjecture. What we do know is that many of them used copycat labels featuring the tug-of-war theme, claiming superior durability by depicting two powerful forces grappling over a pair of jeans. Possibly devised so that illiterate immigrants could recognize the foremost selling point of the garment, the tug-of-war image may well have started in the East and moved west, like American expansion itself. The waistband tag on the denim trousers of the New York company Sweet-Orr, for instance, depicted two teams of men playing tug-of-war with the pant legs. Established in 1871, Sweet-Orr claimed to be the first commercial producer of overall pants in the country, predating Levi Strauss by two years.

James Orr returned to his hometown of Wappingers Falls, New York, near Poughkeepsie, after traveling throughout the 1850s in California, where he demonstrated Singer sewing machines and sold the overalls he made for five dollars a pair. (Quite a sum—the earliest mass-produced overalls of the 1870s generally retailed for about seventy-five cents apiece.) Like Levi Strauss, Orr, sometimes called "the Father of the Overall Industry," had his own personal legend embedded in the brand identity. A company history, written for Sweet-Orr's seventy-fifth anniversary in 1946, maintained that Orr had been among the forty-niners panning for gold in the Sacramento Valley. In the diggings, the anonymous author suggests, "dazzling dust sparkled" at Orr's feet. "He stooped down to grasp it—split the seat of his pants." And he determined to make a better trouser.

Back in Wappingers Falls, the man future employees would call "Uncle Jim" secured the financial backing of his nephews, Clayton E. and Clinton W. Sweet (the latter the future founder of Sweet's, the enormous reference work of product data sheets), and together they established Sweet-Orr. With six young women initially comprising their workforce, the company began making its "pantaloon overalls" in July 1871. When the staff stockpiled nine hundred pairs before selling any, the locals began whispering about "Orr's Folly." So the entrepreneur hit the road, traveling to Pennsylvania and Ohio and bringing back orders for three thousand pairs. Sweet-Orr sewing machine operators at the time assembled each article from start to finish, rather than concentrating on one aspect—the inseam, say, or the rear pockets—on an assembly line. They were paid about seven cents per garment.

The company's influence on subsequent manufacturers seems evident. An advertisement from around 1880 extolls the merits of Orr Pantaloon Overalls, the buttons of which "are put on so strong that it is impossible for them to get away from the garment." Also around this time Sweet-Orr began controlling the shrinkage of its product in a process it called Ace of Spades, decades before the introduction of Sanforizing. The company was also first in the garment business to adopt the Union label. During the 1880s Sweet-Orr pants accompanied American miners traveling to South Africa for that country's gold rush. The company quickly established an export division which was so successful that for years South Africans used the Sweet-Orr name when referring generically to any brand of workwear, like Levi's.

"All Goods Warranted Never to Rip," declared the company logos. Any six men who were able to pull apart a pair of the company's pants, "properly witnessed," were each guaranteed a new pair. One Wappingers Falls historian says that Sweet-Orr was using its tug-of-war trademark as early as 1876, when the company took part in the Philadelphia Centennial Exhibition. That would have predated the introduction of the Levi's "two-horse" patch by ten years.

In the infancy of company branding in America—Campbell Soup was founded in 1869, and Quaker Oats became the first cereal maker to register a trademark in 1877—other denim businesses soon created their own versions of the tug-of-war insignia. The Boss brand, one of the first in Los Angeles, featured two elephants trying to rip apart their pants. Samson workwear depicted the biblical strongman pitted against a lion.

ALL GOODS WARRANTED "NEVER TO RIP"

ORR'S PANTALOON OVERALLS

EASY FITTING PANTS & WORKING SHIRTS

MANUFACTURED BY **SWEET, ORR & CO.** HOUSE EST.ᴮᴰ 1871.

Courtesy of Jeff Spielberg

The logo for an Indiana company called Harrison & Harrison featured two dogs. Because of the breed—they were English bull-baiting dogs—vintage denim collector Jeff Spielberg speculates that the image was inspired by the garment trade in England, where the haute couture House of Worth, founded in 1858, may have been first in the apparel business to affix labels to its clothing. The tug-of-war theme proliferated in the Bay Area, where Nonpareil, a brand of waist-high overalls produced by Murphy Grant & Co.—a local company cofounded by Levi Strauss's good friend Adam Grant—advertised its product with two trains.

The strongest regional competition for Levi's, however, probably came from Can't Bust 'Em, the denim workwear brand of Eloesser-Heynemann, a rival wholesaler said to be the first importer in San Francisco, founded in 1851. Produced as early as 1880, Can't Bust 'Ems were sometimes described as the best-selling line of work clothes on the West Coast. The company's "industrial apparel," it advertised, was perfectly suited for nearly any job that involved manual dexterity (and some that did not), from "Bakers, Barbers, Bartenders, Bottlers, Brewers, Butchers, Blacksmiths, and Brassworkers" to "Sailors, Stevedores, Stockroom Clerks, Stonemasons, and Steelworkers." From 1901, the year when California garment workers organized, the company was the first on the West Coast to display the union label. The Can't Bust 'Em brand was later recognized for its rooster-in-overalls logo ("Something to Crow About"), introduced after the 1906 San Francisco earthquake and fire, when the company relocated much of its manufacturing to the Sonoma County farm town of Petaluma.

While jeans-style workpants were undoubtedly manufactured before Strauss and Davis secured their patent—as noted, Strauss himself sold them as a wholesaler—the great improvement of the copper rivets helped usher in a demand for all-purpose workwear that quickly led to a profusion of competitors in the industry. By the time the Levi's patent expired in 1890, dozens of regional firms were poised to launch their own workwear lines. They typically manufactured overalls, overall pants, and, in many cases, the short-cropped work jacket, sometimes made of red flannel, sometimes denim, archaically known as the wamus (or waumus, or wampus).

"Don't Say Overalls, Say Ironalls," suggested one brand. Seattle had Blackbear; Dallas had Dixie King; Baltimore, the Iron King Overall Company (after the nickname of magnate Andrew Carnegie). Railroad men and construction workers in Boston wore DubbleWare. Little Rock was home to the Tuf-Nut brand. Wordplay was rampant. Overalls appeared on the shelves of general stores with names such as Kumfort, Cuvverem, and Dozfit. Some of the puns were more effective than others. Surely the makers of the Asanox brand intended to recall the old adage "Strong as an ox," rather than the alternative—

"Dumb as an ox." Many of the companies were great sources of only-in-America stories. For instance, Henry Carter, of Lebanon, New Hampshire, was called "the Merchant Prince" for his unparalleled showmanship. Hauling samples of his many wares, including jewelry, knives, perfumes, stationery, and all kinds of clothing in brightly painted wagons pulled by impressive teams of "coal-black" horses, Carter made his mark by selling bib overalls that blanketed the Northeast beginning around 1870.

Other companies, such as Wisconsin's OshKosh B'Gosh, founded in 1895, would become similar sources of regional pride in an era when distribution was largely restricted by the railroads. Detroit's Larned, Carter & Co., makers from 1897 of the Headlight brand, which was marketed as a railroading uniform, called themselves the "World's Greatest Overall Makers." "Full Seat, High Waist, Wide Legs," they boasted. "There's Comfort in Every Wrinkle." In the 1920s A. B. Larned would serve alongside Stanley A. Sweet and Oscar Berman, president of the Crown Overall Manufacturing Company, as part of a joint committee in conjunction with the United Garment Workers of America. The committee was set up to investigate the exploitation of prison labor for private profit. According to its findings, the workwear industry was in grave danger from prison labor contractors producing "millions" of overalls, work shirts, and other pieces annually, undercutting the union labels. The problem was so rampant that some manufacturers earnestly declared their products "Not Prison Made."

In Texas, entrepreneurs C. N. Williamson and E. E. "Colonel" Dickie led a group of investors who established the U.S. Overall Company in 1918, later renaming it Williamson-Dickie. A major supplier to the United States armed forces during World War II, today the Dickies brand bills itself as the world's largest manufacturer of workwear. In 1889, a young Michigan dry-goods salesman named Hamilton Carhartt invested five hundred dollars in a rented loft space. Equipping it with two sewing machines and bolts of denim, he began producing "O'Alls" (as his buttons read) specifically designed, like the Headlight brand, for railroad workers. Carhartt was the embodiment of the rock-solid integrity often ascribed to denim by astute marketers. "My business was not started to do the gainful thing alone," he once said, "but the just and honest thing, gainful if possible."

Like every other "pure" cultural product of America, be it (African) jazz or (European) apple pie, blue jeans have mongrel origins that can be traced back across oceans and traditions. Bib-front overalls, often considered to be a precursor to jeans, were a common workingman's garment by the time they became prevalent in America in the early nineteenth century. No one knows where or when the first pair was sewn. But overalls, like trousers, were familiar in the new country from its inception. They were mentioned in the *Journals of the Continental Congress* in 1776: "A suit of cloaths [sic] shall be annually given each of said officers and soldiers, to consist . . . of two linen hunting shirts, two pair of overalls. . . ." In 1802 a Mrs. Ruth Henshaw of Leicester, Massachusetts, recorded a journey to Virginia on which she took nine pair of overalls "to make for the Negroes." As Henshaw's diary suggests, overalls—trousers with an attached apron or chest piece supported by shoulder straps—were crude, home-sewn garments. Sometimes they were as simple as a shirt and a pair of pants stitched together. Often they were intended to be worn as protection

James Goodwyn Clonney's "In the Woodshed," 1838

over the workman's more formal everyday clothing, as depicted in James Goodwyn Clonney's 1838 painting "In the Woodshed."

At Old Sturbridge Village, the reenactment of 1830s New England life located in central Massachusetts, a few of the farmers wear white duck-cloth overalls patterned after an actual pair dating from the period. White cloth, says Sturbridge costume coordinator Christine Bates, was commonly used by working people at the time because it could be bleached when soiled. The prototype was discovered, along with many other exceptional examples of nineteenth-century work clothes, in a trunk in the attic of another village employee, Daphne Stevens.

The Bullards, Stevens's ancestors, descended from two

brothers who arrived in America from England in 1635. Stevens says that the duck-cloth overalls likely belonged to her great-great-great-grandfather or one of his sons. Sturbridge curators have dated the garment to 1840, based in part on its similarity to the overalls worn in Clonney's painting.

Overalls were practical not just for farmers or butchers, but for mechanics, fishermen, carpenters, bricklayers, and employees of any other industry that was hard on clothing. In 1848 G. W. Simmons of Boston advertised their overalls "and Overall Pants" in a catalog under the heading "LABORING MEN, MECHANICS, TEAMSTERS, &C." They cost between thirty-seven and fifty cents a pair. The United States Army issued white canvas bib overalls to its laborers in the engineer troops during the 1850s, and in 1867 the secretary of war documented the distribution of thirty-one thousand pairs of overalls to depots and arsenals. Some urban American bohemians of the 1850s, a decade in which both men's and women's fashions took an idiosyncratic turn, fancied wearing work clothes. One such individual was the poet Walt Whitman, whose coarse overalls, red checked shirts, big cowhide boots, and signature round felt hats were "a kind of caricature of working-class garb," according to his biographer David S. Reynolds. One Whitman friend called the writer "a poseur of truly colossal proportions, one to whom playing a part had long before become so habitual that he ceased to be conscious that he was doing it."

Over time, overalls came to be seen as play clothes for children as well as work clothes for adults. As in the timeless portrayal of Huckleberry Finn, Mark Twain's barefoot orphan adventurer, they could represent the endearing side of wayward, rascally youth. Huck wore his overalls with the apron hanging from one strap, an irreverent gesture that would be reprised more than a century later, in the 1980s and '90s, by hip-hoppers such as the Beastie Boys and Tupac Shakur. The look might also imply a genuine lack of sophistication, as in the case of Li'l Abner, the hillbilly manchild of Al Capp's long-running satirical comic strip of the same name that ran from 1934 to 1977.

If overalls in Whitman's day were part of an aesthetic anti-fashion statement that suggested free will, they were also the costume of bondage. When elderly former slaves were interviewed for the Federal Writers' Project of the 1930s, one, Anna Peek, remembered that "the men wore pants known as apron pants. The cloth was known as jeans." And a man named Sabe Rutledge recalled his earliest memory of his grandfather: "He have on no pants, but something kinder like overalls and have a apron. Apron button up here where my overall buckle and can be let down. All be dye with indigo."

In a land of plenty where manual labor now constitutes driving the forklift at Wal-Mart, bib overalls, for better or worse, recall the physical exertion that once defined America—the endless cycle of working someone else's land, or the thankless grind of machining, coal mining, or felling timber. In *Let Us Now Praise Famous Men*, his classic account of three poverty-stricken Alabama families during the Depression, James Agee rhapsodized about their overalls, homely, mass-produced goods that aged, shaped, and faded into "marvels of nature." With their white stitching and chipping blue pigment, Agee observed, overalls were "a blueprint . . . a map of a workingman." In the preface, the photographer Walker Evans gently chided the writer for adopting the rough garb of his subjects. Like Whitman before and countless sympathizers since, Agee was guilty of a "knowingly comical inverted dandyism," as Evans put it.

One of the most forthright names in the business over the past century belonged to H. D. Lee. Lee, a tailor's son with eight siblings born in 1849, learned to fend for himself after his father's premature death, by some accounts competing as an amateur, bare-knuckle boxer. Moving from his native Vermont at age sixteen, Lee became a night clerk in a hotel in Galion, Ohio, where he drew the attention of a wealthy local banker named Chris Crim. Crim lent the young man three thousand dollars to start his own business, selling knitting machines. Soon after, Crim lent Lee fifty thousand dollars to buy an oil distributor. In 1886 Lee contracted pulmonary tuberculosis, forcing him to sell his business to the Rockefellers, who would merge it with Standard Oil. Studying during his recuperation, Lee decided that his business interests would be best served in the burgeoning West, where he could also avail himself of the clement weather and the natural hot springs.

Against his doctor's orders Lee moved to Kansas, taking along several business associates. In Salina, having identified a scarcity of grocery suppliers, he established H. D. Lee Mercantile, specializing in packaged foods such as coffee, tea, and spices. The great success of the operation encouraged Lee to expand, and he opened a cold storage division and a flour mill, the latter of which turned out products featuring the Admiral and American Eagle brands. (The company did not divest itself of its food division until 1950.) "I really did not appraise the full size of the field," Lee said of the business opportunities afforded by westward expansion, in a 1917 interview with *The Kansas City Star.* "It's bigger, better, than we expected, a field susceptible of great and rapid development in almost any line."

Lee was widely admired for his business acumen. In 1900, he began serving as chairman of the National Wholesale Grocers Association. He was also appointed treasurer of the American Tobacco Company, for which he conceived the green rebate certificates soon found in most packages of cigarettes. When two hardware retailers from Salina, Charles L. Schwartz and Norb F. Schwartz, approached Lee to request help in extending their business ventures, Lee recalled the financial support he'd received during his own lean years. He bankrolled the two men with a hundred thousand dollars, and together they launched the Lee Hardware Company. Despite a 1903 fire that razed the H. D. Lee Mercantile Company building, by 1911 Lee was growing again. The garments he had been selling in the hardware store came from unreliable suppliers whose product Lee found lacking in craftsmanship. Typical of this free-ranging entrepreneur, he reasoned that he could do better. He went into the workwear business, breaking ground on a facility producing overalls and overall pants, starting with a simple overalls design the company called the "Jumbo" brand.

Once established, Lee's workwear division began marketing a coverall the company dubbed the Union-All. The name was not a reference to the labor unions; it simply described the design, a union of shirt and pants. Designed to be slipped on over everyday clothes like a jumpsuit, the Union-All was initially intended for automobile drivers, who found themselves routinely climbing out to change tires or turn crankshafts in those primitive days of auto travel. Lot No. 201 was the blue denim Union-All; Lot No. 202 was its khaki twill variant. Here is where the Lee legacy takes on some embroidery, like so much blue jeans folklore. As the tale goes, Lee's chauffeur, John Helmsey, suggested the design after complaining about the grease and grime he had to contend with each time the car broke down. Like Levi Strauss's "invention" of blue jeans in the miners' camps, Lee's Union-Alls story appears to be a liberal interpretation of the facts, perhaps the work of a zealous early public relations executive. Though Helmsey was a trusted confidant who was bequeathed five thousand dollars in Lee's will, internal company memoranda indicate that the idea most likely originated with a letter Lee received from an enterprising Detroit auto mechanic.

Whatever the details, the fact remains that, following a brief period of uncertainty, the Union-All became a profound success. After selling just 118 dozen pairs in the first year, by 1915 Lee was selling roughly 8,500 dozen annually. The line made Lee a household name in workwear. "A suit of Union-Alls under the seat of every auto," the advertisements urged. Babe Ruth signed on as a spokesman. In 1927 Lee introduced the Amazing Hookless Fastener, answering the complaints of field workers and others who were tired of fumbling with their button flies when nature called. The company ran a contest to find a name for the gimmicky new feature. The winning entry: the onomatopoetic Whizit. Today, it's known as the zipper.

There was at least one other whimsical promotion in this otherwise sober-minded company. In 1920 Lee salesman Chester Reynolds supervised the distribution of miniature pairs of over-

(Courtesy of Lee Company)

alls at county fairs. Contriving an idea for the remainder of the batch, Reynolds dressed a number of doe-eyed dolls in the tiny duds. When a window display at Dayton's department store in Minneapolis created an instant furor over the dolls, the company began producing them as a mascot it dubbed Buddy Lee. Sold for $2.50 apiece, the line of hand-painted dolls in authentic hand-sewn costumes quickly grew to include an engineer, a cowboy, and an athlete in an old-fashioned leather football helmet and letterman's sweater. There was also an all-purpose tradesman design licensed to companies including Pepsi and Coca-Cola. Today, early Buddy Lee dolls sometimes command $250 or more at auction. Though the mascot was retired in 1960, Lee reinstated Buddy Lee in 1998, rolling out a bobblehead version. In a renewed effort to attract younger customers, the company aired television commercials pairing Buddy Lee with teen heroes such as Sarah Michelle Gellar (*Buffy the Vampire Slayer*). It also landed product placement on TV shows such as *Dawson's Creek* and *Dharma & Greg*, with cast members wearing Buddy Lee T-shirts.

The Buddy Lee revival featured the Can't Bust 'Em slogan, borrowed from the workwear line of the same name. Each new Buddy Lee replica was inscribed "Lee Dungarees: Can't Bust 'Em, Est. 1880," lending the impression that Lee's workwear dated as far back as the Can't Bust 'Em brand. Rather, the slogan became Lee property in 1946, when the firm purchased the parent company of the Can't Bust 'Em line, Eloesser-Heynemann. The transaction also gave Lee possession of the Boss of the Road trademark and its bulldog mascot, properties of Eloesser-Heynemann since 1932, when the San Francisco company bought out its own longtime competitor, Neustadter Brothers.

Levi Strauss died in 1902, a multimillionaire, a highly regarded philanthropist, and, from what we can tell, a contented man.

"Levi died a bachelor," says company chairman Bob Haas, the founder's great-great-grandnephew and the central family figurehead of Levi Strauss & Co. for the past two decades. "Some lore would say his sister wanted him to stay a bachelor so her four sons, the Stern brothers, could inherit his business." According to family legend, Haas says, Levi's sister knew how to assure her sons' ascension: "She made sure he was supplied with plenty of women who were somewhat below his standing, unsuitable for him to marry. I don't know if that's true or not."

The founding father, Haas says, was hungry for success in his younger years, but he cushioned his later days by taking champagne lunches with other captains of San Francisco industry at the posh St. Francis Hotel.

"Things were slower in those days," Haas remarks with a wry smile.

THREE

★

Dudes: Selling the
Western Frontier

"Cowboys are cash," the painter and sculptor Frederic Remington once remarked. Remington and his confidants, the pioneering genre novelist Owen Wister and the future president Theodore Roosevelt, are widely acknowledged for mythologizing the western frontier. In Remington's dynamic bronze casts and oil paintings, Wister's fiction, and Roosevelt's essays, together they ushered the national notion of the West from its hard reality toward the realm of romance, and commercial packaging.

All three men were easterners whose enthusiasm for the great frontier exceeded their formative experience with it. Although the young Remington once presented himself at the offices of *Harper's Weekly* decked out in a cowboy costume, he typically traveled through the frontier in urbane attire that often left him mistaken for an Englishman. He painted many of his famous studies of bucking broncs and prairie-roaming cowpunchers from a distance of thousands of miles, in his "czar-sized" studio in New Rochelle, New York. Roosevelt, a sickly, asthmatic child who later kept turtles, snakes, and lobsters in his dormitory at Harvard, fixed his lifelong passion for the West during a two-year stint (1884–1886) as a rancher in the Dakota Badlands, a respite following the devastating deaths of his first wife and his mother on the same day.

Wister, born in Philadelphia in 1860, gathered the material for his novel *The Virginian* as he made his way out west seeking a temperate climate for his own poor health. Published in 1902, the book almost single-handedly invented perhaps the greatest American archetype of all—the lone figure of the fearless, irrepressible, duty-bound, yet nomadic westerner. The narrator's opening description of the "Horseman of the Plains," set in a train station at Medicine Bow, where the Virginian is casually teasing an older man about his fancy "weddin' gyarments," set a standard for cowboy worship with its breathless, barely contained homoeroticism: "Lounging there at ease against the wall was a slim young giant, more beautiful than pictures. His broad, soft hat was pushed back; a loose-knotted, dull-scarlet handkerchief sagged from his throat; and one casual thumb was hooked in the cartridge-belt that slanted across his hips. He had plainly come many miles from somewhere across the vast horizon, as the dust upon him showed. His boots were white with it. His overalls were gray with it. . . . But no dinginess of travel or shabbiness of attire could tarnish the splendor that radiated from his youth and strength. . . . Had I been the bride, I should have taken the giant, dust and all."

Uncle Hughey, the older man, is exasperated by the Virginian's needling. "This country's getting full of kids. It's doomed," Hughey moans, anticipating countless complaints to come.

The Virginian was an instant success, selling three hundred thousand copies in its first year. It was soon produced as a stage play, and in 1914 it became one of the early full-length Hollywood Westerns, directed by Cecil B. De Mille. The tale's broad popularity helped build an appetite throughout the entertainment industry for dashing loners in big hats who charm the ladies and challenge amoral men. Not until the western states effectively completed their long transformation from pure barrenness to suburban sprawl, in the second half of the twentieth century, would the public begin to tire of the template. *The Virginian* has been remade at least four times since De Mille's version, with Gary Cooper and Bill Pullman, among others, in the title role, and the book was the basis for a long-running television series of the same name (1962–1971).

But the everyday truths of the West were less glamorous, less operatic, than the triumvirate of Remington, Wister, and Roosevelt and their many successors—including such genre artists as John Ford, Gene Autry, and Zane Grey—would have us believe. Mining, cattle ranching, and the methodical planning of towns and cities in once-vacant fields were often thankless, grueling jobs. Rarely did they require the chivalry and gunplay that Hollywood quickly imagined as the life of the horseman. Remington, whose illustrations often accompanied the books and magazine articles of Roosevelt and Wister, admitted as much in a letter home to his wife. "Shall never come west again," he wrote on one excursion late in his life, which ended in 1909. "It is all brick buildings—derby hats and blue overalls—it spoils my early illusions."

The artist Frederic Remington in his youthful cowboy phase, 1880s

While functional denim clothing, like the other cumulative details of the West, was more typically mundane than provocative, the idealized West remains a bottomless resource for the denim industry. The late critic Robert Warshow was perhaps best known for his characterization of the classic American westerner as portrayed in the movies. For him, the western hero is a melancholy loner, indifferent to home life, a man who never seems to change his clothes. The gradual shift toward a kind of shabby realism in Hollywood Westerns—"the loose, worn hang of clothing, the wrinkles and dirt of the faces" (and Warshow was writing more than a decade before the arrival of Clint Eastwood's grimy spaghetti Westerns)—represented not the freedom of the frontier but "its limitations, its material bareness, the pressures of obligation." Violence, Warshow maintained, is not the real crux of the Western. Style is—the image of a man who contends with violence.

By the latter part of the nineteenth century, many western ranches had begun taking in well-to-do vacationers, some seeking fishing and hunting excursions, others a momentary escape from the urban tumult. Railroad travel made the untamed world of Lewis and Clark newly accessible to big-city dwellers and wealthy foreigners alike. Already, industrialization was taking its psychological toll. The naturalist John Muir noted that thousands of "tired, nerve-shaken, overcivilized people are beginning to find out that going to the mountains is going home; that wilderness is a necessity." By the 1920s "dude" ranching was thriving; the National Dude Ranchers' Association was established in 1926. There is some evidence that the term *dude* initially implied no disrespect toward the visitor. But over the years it became associated with the hapless easterner, "comically encumbered with useless knowledge, ignorant of the basics, too crippled with theory to act," as the historian Garry Wills wrote. When the Depression hit the West, many more ranch owners began advertising as getaway destinations in East Coast publications. Some, such as Larry Larom's Valley Ranch outside Cody, Wyoming, were operated by former easterners who had grown to love the West.

Dudes themselves, or at least the female variety, were unapologetic about their maladjustment, if George Cukor's 1939 film classic *The Women* is a reliable indication. In it, a circle of acerbic socialites go on holiday at a dude ranch in Reno, "the American cradle of liberty"—home of the quickie divorce. Mary Boland as the matronly Countess DeLave is comically attired in her stiff, high-waisted dungarees, accessorized with studded leather bands covering her forearms and a long rope of pearls dangling around her neck.

By the time the film debuted, however, many Park Avenue women had already been initiated into the exotic world of roughing it. In 1935, the same year Levi's introduced its "Dude Ranch Duds," part of its Lady Levi's campaign, *Vogue* and *Mademoiselle* became two of the first fashion magazines to acknowledge the trend among women toward genuine cowboy attire. *Mademoiselle* instructed its readers that "blue denim saddle pants" were the one type of trouser appropriate for wearing in the West. "True western chic was invented by cowboys," noted the author of the *Vogue* article. "The moment you veer from their tenets, you are lost." The well-heeled crowd heeded the warning: In New York, Abercrombie & Fitch began stocking Levi's 501 waist overalls and other western apparel by mail order, prompting the West Coast manufacturer to place its first ads in Manhattan newspapers. The apparel industry was coming to understand that image making might prove to be even more durable than the claim to durability itself.

The rough-hewn mythology of western life was the core concept behind Wrangler, the Greensboro, North Carolina, dungaree brand that rose after the war to join Lee and Levi Strauss & Co. as the Big Three of all-American jeanswear. C. C. Hudson was a Tennessee farm boy who took his first job away from home, in Greensboro, in 1897, at age twenty. The job was in an overall factory, where he sewed buttons for twenty-five cents a day. When the plant floundered and liquidated, Hudson pooled his money with a few associates, including his brother, Homer, to buy several of the sewing machines, and together in 1904 they formed the Hudson Overall Company. Initially operating out of an old church in downtown Greensboro, the company produced most of its inventory by the domestic system. But the success of the business quickly outgrew that arrangement, and in 1919 Hudson built the company's first plant. Railroad workers partial to Hudson's overalls gave the boss a locomotive bell as a token of their appreciation. Hanging in the company's sprawling new factory on South Elm Street, the bell soon became covered with a fine coating of blue dust from the denim cuttings. It inspired a new name for the company—Blue Bell.

Blue Bell's rapid ascent to dominance in the overalls industry was the result of some astute business practices. Since 1908 Hudson had faced stiff regional competition from the Jellico Clothing Manufacturing Company of Jellico, Tennessee. When Hudson became Blue Bell in 1919, Jellico relocated to Middlesboro, Kentucky, changing its own brand name to Big Ben. Four years later, with C. C. Hudson in poor health, he negotiated a merger with his friend Robert W. Baker, president of Big Ben. With Big Ben buying Blue Bell for $585,000, the two companies officially merged as Blue Bell on January 1, 1926. Baker would remain president at the combined Greensboro headquarters until 1936, by which time Blue Bell was recognized as one of the largest workwear manufacturers in the world. That year Blue Bell merged with another competitor, the Globe Superior Corporation of Abingdon, Illinois, the alliance combining companies that had each achieved annual sales of $5 million. But the Blue Bell executives were not content to simply assimilate the competition. They took the initiative to improve their product. In 1936, the company introduced Sanford Cluett's new Sanforizing process to the denim for its Super Big Ben overalls. By mechanically stretching the cotton fibers before washing and drying, thus creating a preshrunk fabric, aftermarket shrinkage was reduced to 1 percent—a boon especially to rural farmers and laborers, who were accustomed to buying their clothing through mail-order catalogs.

Acquisitions continued in 1943 when Blue Bell purchased Casey Jones, a workwear company based in Virginia and Maryland. With Casey Jones came the rights to a dormant line of blue jeans called Wrangler. Recast as an authentic western-style jean, Wranglers were reintroduced as a Blue Bell signature product in 1947. Rodeo Ben, a well-known Philadelphia tailor who helped promote western chic with his fancy duds for the singing cowboys Gene Autry and Roy Rogers and many top rodeo stars, was enlisted to help design the new Wrangler "Cowboy Cut." Features such as higher hip pockets, which held a wallet better on horseback, and wider belt loops, to accommodate oversized western-style belts, were added. And they worked. The 13MWZ—Men With Zippers (another feature that appealed to outdoorsmen)—was an immediate success with riders. Future Pro Rodeo Hall of Famers Jim Shoulders—known as the "Babe Ruth of Rodeo," a sixteen-time world champion—and Freckles Brown made endorsements, establishing instant credibility on the rodeo circuit for the brand. A half century later, Wrangler recycled old images of the rodeo greats for an ad campaign that declared, "Since 1947 cowboys have been putting on our jeans. Since 1947, bulls have been trying to get them off."

But denim did not immediately dominate the stock image of the frontiersman. Folkloric legends such as Davy Crockett and Daniel Boone wore buckskin, not overall pants. Perhaps taking cues from such stagy road shows as Buffalo Bill Cody's Wild West—a vaudeville in the dust that grossed a million dollars in 1893 alone, drawing six million spectators—the Hollywood cowboy of the earliest Westerns was more often than not a range-riding fussbudget in fringe, elaborate embroidery, and silk bandannas. At the same time, however, extensive efforts were made on some movie sets to accurately depict the real-life clothing styles of the settlements. Tom Mix—the "Beau Brummell of the West," a man said to require an entire train car just for his wardrobe—wore a denim work shirt as part of his onscreen attire as early as 1916, playing a ranch hand in a movie called *Local Color*. In *Mr. Logan, USA* (1920), Mix wore one of the first western-style shirts with arrow stitching, tucked into a pair of jeans.

For some actors, a dandified cowboy was just playing dress-up. "One of the many things you have to thank the movies for is that they have about banished the old 'stage' cowboy," said William S. Hart, nicknamed "Two-Gun Bill" after one of his earliest roles. "The real cowboy clothes are all made for utility, not for effect." The folksy philosopher Will Rogers, who got his start in vaudeville as an expert cattle roper, customarily wore denim pants, a cowboy shirt, and a neckerchief. "After his bath in the morning he put on a clean shirt," recalled his wife, Betty, years later, "and that bath and that shirt had to last him through the evening, no matter what came up." For formal occasions, he changed into a double-breasted blue serge suit and a bow tie.

But while denim was an essential component in the wardrobes of many of Hollywood's first saddle stars—Hart, Hoot Gibson, Hopalong Cassidy—it was John Wayne who truly popularized the authentically weathered look of the outdoorsman. Wayne's inspiration, in turn, was the film star Harry Carey, a former playwright and son of a sewing machine company president. Carey, whom Will Rogers once called "the most human and natural of the Western actors," adopted a rugged, realistic style of western costume in silent films beginning in 1910, setting a standard for many of his contemporaries.

Wayne, born Marion Morrison in Winterset, Iowa, in 1907, and raised primarily in suburban Glendale, California, grew up in an unhappy home. A class officer in high school and a representative to the Southern California Shakespeare Contest, he had to cultivate the plainspoken rectitude that would consume his screen image. "Wayne hated horses, was more accustomed to suits and ties than to jeans when he went to the movies, and had to remind himself to say 'ain't,' " wrote Garry Wills in *John Wayne's America*. But a commanding physical presence, so aptly suited to the great outdoors, was Wayne's by birth—"his large rolling walk was baffled by four walls," Wills noted—and it was enhanced by his no-nonsense costuming when he became a leading man.

Playing the Ringo Kid in Ford's 1939 masterpiece, *Stagecoach*, the emerging star wore seasoned Levi's 501s featuring both a belt and suspender buttons, with five inches of cuff turned up at the boots. For real-life cowboys, cuffs were practical, often used to hold a pack of cigarettes or, when traversing dry, flammable brush, as ashtrays. For Wayne, the cuffs were artful. "Western stars traditionally identified themselves with elaborate signals worked out through their costume, devices to make people conscious that this hero lived in an entirely different social system," wrote Wills. "William S. Hart wore leather and tough fabrics layered around him almost like body armor. . . . Wayne also had some costuming tricks—his placket-front shirt, dark and semimilitary. But his signals were sent by the body under the clothes, which was far more semantically charged than they were. His pants were folded up at the cuff, to reveal the gracefulness of his footwork."

Wayne's son, Michael, once recalled family vacations on southern California's Catalina Island. These retreats would typically precede the actor's departure for his next film shoot. In what became something of a family ritual, the children would help Wayne bundle up his newest denim clothing. Together they would tie the bundle to a pier and toss it in the ocean. After a few days, the clothes were ready for retrieval. "We thought everyone did that to their clothes," said Michael Wayne.

There was another, more familar ritual in buying denim pants. To achieve a comfortable fit, the wearer submerged himself in water, maybe a bathtub or a river, for a few hours, shrinking the fabric to his own body. While the advent of shrinkage control relieved the customer of this obligation, many remained loyal to the old do-it-yourself routine. Lee, a pioneer in the use of Sanforizing in the 1920s, took the snug look to a new extreme in the '30s, when the rodeo champion Turk Greenough visited the company officers in Kansas City with his wife, the fan dancer Sally Rand. How could Lee improve its western brand, Lee Riders (introduced in 1935), with the working cowboy in mind? As the story goes, Rand tore the leg seams of the sample pair her husband was wearing, pinning them as tightly around his thighs as she could. "They should fit like wallpaper to a wall," she advised. (Rand, who had become an overnight sensation performing her fan dance at the 1933–34 Chicago World's Fair, went on to stage "Sally Rand's Nude Ranch"—"a dude ranch a la 1939"—at the Treasure Island World's Fair in San Francisco. Her female dancers dressed in cowboy hats, gun belts, boots, and not much else.)

Chester Reynolds, the Lee salesman who came up with the Buddy Lee mascot, was instrumental in identifying Lee with cowboy culture. He represented the company in its efforts to help establish the Rodeo Cowboy's Association, and he went on to found Oklahoma City's National Cowboy Hall of Fame (since renamed the National Cowboy & Western Heritage

Museum). Adopting the slogan "The Jeans That Built America," Lee helped familiarize midwesterners with the western look, and the company even took on Levi Strauss & Co. on its own turf, opening a branch in San Francisco. Lee had a history of taking the initiative. Among the company's innovations were the elimination of hip-pocket rivets, which had a tendency to scratch saddle leather; and a national advertising campaign in 1946 in *Life* magazine, enticing shoppers to "Bring the Romance of the West to the East." In 1939, the year of the company's fiftieth anniversary "Jubi-Lee," Lee claimed to be the country's biggest manufacturer of workwear, with $6.4 million in sales.

(Courtesy of Lee Company)

While Lee grew, the men behind Levi Strauss & Co. were reevaluating their priorities. After the death of the founder in 1902, Levi's nephews, Jacob, Sigmund, Louis, and Abraham Stern, took over the operation. But they had little interest in the business. "They had a pretty cozy arrangement," says current LS&CO. chairman Bob Haas, Sigmund Stern's great-grandson. "As long as there were always one or two of them around, the others could be off, taking the transcontinental railroad and the steamship to Europe. The business in those days was largely run by lieutenants."

One of those was Simon Davis, son of Jacob, the tailor who invented the riveting process. Simon Davis succeeded his father as Levi's factory manager, operating the Valencia Street plant that would remain a Levi's showplace until it was shut down in the late 1990s. In 1912 the company introduced Davis's pet project, the Koverall, a one-piece denim jumpsuit for children. A gold medal winner for excellence from the San Francisco Mechanics Institute, Koveralls—"The Kind of Klose That Keep Kids Kleen"—were the first Levi's product to be sold nationwide. In one of the more successful advertising campaigns of the 1910s, Davis's three-year-old daughter, Estelle, was featured as the Koverall Girl. The line prospered, inspiring imitators—in 1916 Levi Strauss & Co. sued J. C. Penney for trademark infringement.

Despite the impressive launch of the Koveralls, the Stern brothers were restless. Abe would die in 1912, a victim of food poisoning, and Louis had health problems; as the 1920s approached, Jacob was preparing for retirement. Having no descendants mature enough, or interested enough, in succeeding the operation, Sigmund Stern was mulling a liquidation. With his daughter Elise set to marry an industrious young man named

Walter Haas, an heir to the Los Angeles–based Haas Brothers grocery chain, Sigmund invited his son-in-law-to-be to come aboard. Walter, whose older cousin, Charles, was president of Haas Brothers, knew he was destined to hit a ceiling as vice president with the grocery. Here, potentially, was a better opportunity. Walter Haas joined Levi Strauss & Co. in January 1919.

Almost immediately Haas faced a tough financial crisis. From forty cents a pound in 1920, the price of cotton plummeted to six cents a pound within a year. The market was saturated, and southern textile manufacturers were paying their workers as little as ten to fifteen cents an hour. As a result, the wholesale price of Levi's waist overalls dropped from thirty-five dollars per dozen in 1920 to eighteen dollars in 1922. "We had a ship bringing us two hundred bales of denim," Walter Haas once told a company historian, "and I was hoping the ship would go down without loss of life because it was insured at full price."

Heeding customer complaints about the high cost of Koveralls—a dollar a pair—Haas conducted a thorough review of production. He found that while the core product, the company's waist overalls, brought in a 15 percent profit, the cost of Koveralls advertising and the added legwork of national sales and distribution made the children's clothes a liability. Rather than raising the price, he chose to deemphasize the Koveralls line, which was eventually phased out around 1940.

Simon Davis was incensed, and he quit in protest. After some years working for LS&CO.'s local competition, Neustadter Brothers, around 1935 Davis founded a workwear company he named after his youngest son, Ben Davis. The younger Davis, a professional saxophonist, consulted a pattern from Neustadter

Brothers, makers of the Boss of the Road brand, to design the new company's original denim jeans. Inspired by Boss of the Road's bulldog mascot and the Can't Bust 'Em rooster, Davis chose a cartoon gorilla logo that exists today on Ben Davis workwear.

Davis's acrimonious departure from LS&CO. was a cause of consternation for the aging Sigmund Stern, but it also confirmed Walter Haas as the caretaker of the company legacy. "Sigmund was essentially faced with losing this person who was the glue of the company," says Bob Haas, by putting his faith in his "wet-behind-the-ears son-in-law. He chose blood over money, shall we say." At the time, Levi's was not yet a household name. The organization, though well grounded, was not even dominant in the West. In 1929, the year of the stock market crash, sales totaled $4.2 million, 70 percent of which was attributed to waist overalls. According to Ed Cray, author of *Levi's: The 'Shrink-to-Fit' Business That Stretched to Cover the World*, those sales accounted for 10 to 15 percent of all workwear sales on the West Coast. "To be honest, at first we didn't look beyond the cowboy-miner-laborer market in California, Arizona, Nevada, and maybe Colorado and Utah and, in a minor way, Oregon and Washington," said Daniel Koshland, Haas' brother-in-law and the company's longtime treasurer (and future president).

The Depression hit Levi Strauss & Co. like most other businesses. By 1932, sales had sunk to $2.1 million, half the figure for 1929. But as the financial picture slowly began to improve, the company seized upon its geographic advantage, promoting the link between the folkloric western rancher and Levi's 501XX denim. Advertising manager Dick Cronin diligently worked the rodeo circuit, hosting hospitality suites and outfitting winning riders with Levi's clothing. For the 1939 World's Fair in San Francisco, Cronin put together a wildly popular attraction, a mechanical bull-riding exhibit that he would credit with impressing the Levi's name upon enthusiastic visitors from the Midwest, the Deep South, and other previously untapped markets.

By then the Wild West had emerged as a conventional fixture of popular culture. In Hollywood, the B Western was ubiquitous. Studios were typically reluctant to finance big-budget Westerns, or "outdoor dramas," as they were sometimes called, but the genre was ideally suited to the short-feature slots, the second titles of double bills. Stock characters (good guy/bad guy) and conflicts (nature versus progress, savagery versus culture) provided the framework for hundreds of series Westerns, with recurring casts and continuing plot lines similar to the television series of the not-too-distant future. The "singing cowboy" model made stars of Gene Autry, Rex Allen, Tex Ritter, and others, adding not just music but light comedy and romance to the formula. (Several of them, including Autry and Roy Rogers, launched their own lines of denim clothing.) And the critical and box office success of two 1939 Westerns, John Ford's *Stagecoach* (the film that elevated Wayne, in his cuffed 501s, from "B" to "A" status) and Henry King's *Jesse James* (with Tyrone Power, Henry Fonda, and Randolph Scott), led to a Golden Age of Hollywood Westerns that would endure through the 1960s. In the '30s, however, much of the country's leisure class and the eastern intelligentsia were just acquainting themselves with the romantic possibilities of a backdrop that was instantly recognizable to rural Americans.

By the 1950s, the rodeo was one of the last bastions of active cowboy culture. The disappearance of the actual lifestyle whetted the collective imagination for all things western. The early years of television were saturated with Westerns, a few of which—*Gunsmoke*, 1955–1975; *Bonanza*, 1959–1973—spanned generations. Young boys of the 1950s were routinely depicted as half-pint versions of their cowboy heroes, suburban pistol-poppers in checkered shirts and bandannas, chin-strap hats, spurred boots, and blue jeans.

The famed advertising man Leo Burnett remade Marlboro cigarettes—a relic of Victorian England originally marketed in America to women ("a tearoom smoke," as Burnett once said)—with his invention of a durable American icon: the Marlboro Man. What is our most masculine figure? Burnett asked his staff on a retreat at his farm south of Chicago. The nominees included the cabdriver, the sailor, the marine, the pilot, and the race car driver, until someone suggested the obvious choice: the cowboy. Burnett chose as his model an image he recalled from a 1949 *Life* magazine cover, a Texas ranch foreman named C. H. Long. A succession of imitators were tried until in 1963 the agency discovered Carl "Big-un" Bradley, a genuine Texas rancher, who would inspire generations of chiseled Marlboro Men to come. Dressed head to toe in denim, hat pulled down tight to shield his eyes from the glare of the sun, the mustachioed Marlboro Man "is what we have for royalty, distilled manhood," wrote James B. Twitchell in *20 Ads That Shook the World*. "One look at him and you know: no Ralph Lauren jeans, no 401(k) plans, no wine spritzers, nothing with little ducks all over it, just independence, pure and simple."

That mystique, lionizing the rugged individualist who wouldn't dream of wearing anything "with little ducks all over it," continues to drive the blue jeans industry today. The fictitious western hero can be endlessly sold, as Frederic Remington observed. But he can't be bought. "Some things you don't do for the cash," drawls Robert Mitchum's Jeff McCloud in *The Lusty Men*, Nicholas Ray's masterful yarn about the hard life of the rodeo released in 1952 (three years before the director's quintessential blue-jeans drama, *Rebel Without a Cause*). At the end of the movie, dying after puncturing a lung in an ill-advised return to riding, McCloud makes a claim for immortality. "Never was a bronc that's never been rode. Never was a cowboy that's never been throwed," he growls. "Guys like me last forever."

FOUR

★

Modern Pioneers:
At Work and Play

The people at Farmer jeans, a tiny, three-year-old Los Angeles brand, believe that a little dirt is good for your denim. They recommend "dry aging" your jeans—wearing them without laundering for weeks (or months), until they begin to crack. With the first wash, "the character of your body will show up," promises thirty-seven-year-old founder Peter Lang Nooch.

While that sounds like something James Agee might have written about his Alabama sharecroppers, you won't find Farmer jeans in the hardware store, hanging on peg hooks near the pitchforks and the wheelbarrows. With retail prices hovering around the two-hundred-dollar mark, Farmer sells 80 percent of its product to women—women shopping primarily in exclusive boutiques. As Lang Nooch sees it, his loyalty to the modest concept of the five-pocket jean is precisely what makes him stand out in the mind-boggling world of contemporary upscale denim. He's not so much designing clothing, he says, as reinterpreting a classic.

"Fashion is frivolous," says this affable, outspoken fellow with big dark eyes and a little goatee. "You put rags on people. I look at girls' asses all day."

Girls' asses have been shaping the blue jeans business for decades. The original notion for "designer" jeans grew out of the unisex movement of the late 1960s and early '70s, when men and women alike grew their hair long and slipped into each other's jeans. And the skyrocketing prices of recent years were fueled by female customers willing to pay a premium for a stylish blue jean with a contoured fit. Tim Kaeding is creative director of the cult jeans phenomenon Seven for All Mankind, one of the first brands to break the hundred-dollar barrier in the late 1990s. Seven only branched into men's jeans after establishing itself as a leader among women, he says.

"Historically, when you think of jeans, you think of guys," says Kaeding. Until the 1970s, denim manufacturers only sporadically tailored jeans for women. The deliberately unfashionable look of a young woman wearing a man's jeans was so prevalent, the industry gave it a name—the "boyfriend" look.

For women, breaking the taboo of wearing pants was a long, arduous haul. The Bible calls for distinctly gendered clothing in Deuteronomy: "The woman shall not wear that which pertaineth unto a man, neither shall a man put on a woman's garment; for all that do so are abominations unto the Lord thy God." In seventeenth-century England citizens could be hung for wearing the clothes of the opposite sex. Even in the Wild West of the rodeo, where trousers might have been considered a necessity, most performing women wore corsets and skirts, following the lead of Annie Oakley. (Calamity Jane, however, wore buckskin trousers without apology: "Look, I wear men's pants and [they] let me move around when these females in petticoats had to ask for help," she once wrote to her daughter. "You must excuse your mother, Janey, she knows she's strange and badly raised.")

Through the ages there have always been staunch supporters of a woman's right to wear "men's" clothing. The suffragette Elizabeth Cady Stanton described her prime motivation on the subject in 1869: Nonspecific apparel, she argued, would protect women from the unwanted advances of "brutal" men. "The true idea is for the sexes to dress as nearly alike as possible," she wrote. "When we have a voice in legislation, we shall dress as we please, and if, by concealing our sex, we find that we, too, can roam up and down the earth in safety (not seeking whom we may devour), we shall keep our womanhood a profound secret."

By the early years of the twentieth century some were no longer inclined to keep a secret of their affinity for traditionally male clothing. Famously assertive performers, from the stage star Sarah Bernhardt to screen idols Greta Garbo and Marlene Dietrich, cut provocative profiles in silk slacks and riding pants, inspiring ordinary women to do the same. Helen Holmes, the original star of the short-film action series called *The Hazards of Helen* (1914–1917), wore railroad overalls for stunts involving high-speed trains and motor cars. Some physically active women began wearing trousers for increased mobility; emancipators wore them as a symbol of their defiance of male domination. But denim signified nothing so much as hard labor, making overalls and overall pants doubly taboo for women, who were still routinely discouraged from doing "men's" work. It would take a fictitious character, the patriotic poster girl Rosie the Riveter, to decisively clear the way for women in jeans.

Women were not complete strangers to work clothes prior to World War II. The radical journalist Anna Louise Strong argued for a woman's right to wear overalls in the factories, where loose-fitting outfits were often hazardous. During the First World War, women newly hired to work in munitions plants dressed in coveralls that were quickly nicknamed "womanalls." Lee manufactured a khaki version of its popular Union-Alls sized for women as early as 1914. Levi Strauss & Co. made its own version, "Freedomalls," available in 1918.

"Women! There's Great Convenience in Overalls for Housework," read an advertisement in a 1917 issue of *McCall's* for Stifel, a Wheeling, West Virginia fabric company dating back to 1835. Known for its signature hickory stripes and geometric patterns, the company specialized in printed calicoes, drills, and denims. The ad promoted "Miss Stifel Cloth," a lightweight cotton twill.

Between the wars, however, women were often discouraged from factory work. Not only was tending heavy machinery considered a man's job—the mere presence of women among men was seen as a distraction too. But while the scarcity of jobs for able-bodied men during the Depression only worsened the prejudice, the drastic depletion of the workforce brought on by massive conscription during the Second World War changed that abruptly. Women boosted the war effort by taking jobs on assembly lines in lumber and steel mills, shipyards and foundries. Six million mothers and daughters went to work between 1940 and 1944, and government-sponsored ad campaigns urged them to feel proud of their contributions. "Ma's Making Bombers!" hollered the headline of an article reprinted in a 1942 *Reader's Digest*. "This woman is a modern pioneer," declared the voice of Katharine Hepburn in *Women in Defense* (1941), a ten-minute short film written by the first lady, Eleanor Roosevelt.

In Norman Rockwell's celebrated rendering of Rosie, she is a broad young redhead with a shapely silhouette, with the stout legs and well-developed biceps of a football player. With her cherubic face smeared with grime, she is taking a sandwich break. Her deep blue overalls are loosely cuffed above red socks and penny loafers, one of which rests on a battered copy of Hitler's *Mein Kampf*. The image ran on the cover of the *Saturday Evening Post* on May 29, 1943. It was an instant conversation piece. Rockwell, in a newspaper article printed that week, sheepishly noted a mistake: Rosie has a pair of protective goggles resting on her forehead and a shield tipped back on her head. "I don't think riveters use both," said the painter. "It was silly of me."

The creation of the Rosie the Riveter archetype lent unprecedented glamour to a dowdy pair of overalls, accessorized perhaps with a bandanna wrapped around the head and a pair of saddle shoes on the feet. The model for Rosie was a nineteen-year-old telephone operator from Arlington, Vermont, named Mary Doyle. By the time the *Post* cover hit newsstands, Rosie the Riveter was already a folk hero. In February, a singing group called the Four Vagabonds had released a popular song named for her. A *Rosie the Riveter* movie hit theaters in 1944. Real-life women were feted as local Rosies in the press. When Rose Bonavita and her partner drove a record number of rivets into the wing of a Grumman Avenger torpedo bomber on the grave-yard shift for Eastern Aircraft in Tarrytown, New York, her hometown paper proclaimed her "Peekskill's Rosie."

(Courtesy of the National Archives, photo no. 86-WWT-46-22)

Operating a bolt-cutting machine

Despite all the fanfare, however, warnings about the im-propriety of women in the workplace persisted. In Seattle, one newspaper voiced a typical reservation, urging women not to "go berserk over the new opportunities for masculine clothing and mannish actions." That attitude persisted in some circles well into the 1950s, when the author of a book called *Wife Dressing* warned, "Don't look like a steamfitter or a garage

mechanic when what you are, purely and simply, is a wife."
The writer did, however, grudgingly allow that dungarees were
sometimes acceptable for heavy chores.

By wartime, some in the cultural vanguard—men and women
alike—had grown accustomed to wearing dungarees by choice,
not just for practicality. Some intellectuals began wearing
them in Socialist solidarity with the working class. Wearing
denim was seen as an empathetic gesture toward the less privileged. In classic American novels such as John Steinbeck's *The
Grapes of Wrath* and Robert Penn Warren's *All the King's Men*,
denim signified low station. "His blue jeans were pale at knee
and seat," Steinbeck wrote of the headstrong farmer Muley
Graves, "and he wore an old black suit coat, stained and spot-
ted, the sleeves torn loose from the shoulders in back." Warren's novel, published in 1946, details the political ascendance
of a Louisiana country boy named Willie Stark, loosely based
on the real-life career of Governor Huey Long. Stark climbs
the ladder of taste as his career unfolds, graduating from "overalls which hung down around his can as though he were little
Droopy-Drawers" to seersucker suits. Upon becoming a lawyer,
Stark could hang his old overalls "on a nail and let them stiffen
with the last sweat he had sweated into them."

Writing of his tramping experience in 1933's *Down and
Out in Paris and London*, George Orwell described the surprising camaraderie among desolate men in rags. The clothes he
wore, he wrote, were a faded brown coat, a cloth cap, and a
pair of black "dungaree trousers." "It gives one a very strange
feeling to be wearing such clothes. I had worn bad enough
things before, but not at all like these, they were not merely

dirty and shapeless, they had—how is one to express it?—
a gracelessness, a patina of antique filth, quite different from
mere shabbiness." Yet his attire, Orwell felt, registered him as
an instant member of a heartbreaking fraternity: "Everybody's
demeanor seemed to have changed abruptly. I helped a hawker
pick up a barrow that he had upset. 'Thanks, mate,' he said
with a grin. No one had called me mate before in my life."

In Orwell's time in England, however, corduroy trousers
were more common than denim among students and theorists.
The British workwear manufacturer Lee Cooper, founded in
1908 as Morris Cooper, helped denim earn its place as a cultural mainstay in England during World War II, when citizens
were allotted clothing rations of thirty coupons apiece. While
a man's suit cost twenty-six coupons and a woman's dress sixteen, overalls were just two, and jean pants a single coupon.
The resulting ubiquity of the Lee Cooper name in England
carried the brand down the generations, with the company
capitalizing on the youth movements of the 1960s and '70s
and into the present day.

Some young Americans took to wearing jeans as an artistic
statement, or simply, in the case of a growing number of college students, as knockabout clothes. The artists of Santa Fe,
New Mexico, are sometimes credited as the first to adopt blue
jeans into their daily wardrobe, in the 1920s. By the mid-1930s,
undergraduates at the University of California–Berkeley (the
alma mater of Levi Strauss & Co. president Walter Haas Sr.)
and the University of Oregon were wearing denim as casual

clothes. Sophomores at the schools claimed the pants as their own, forbidding freshmen to wear them. LS&CO. advertising manager Dick Cronin was quick to recognize the trend, prevailing upon Oregon's governor to issue a proclamation in support of the sophomores. But collegiate affection for denim remained a largely underground phenomenon until 1944, when a photograph in *Life* magazine captured two Wellesley College women impetuously strolling down the street in jeans and sweatshirts. Proclaiming it the "sloppy" look, the magazine was inundated with letters from outraged parents and self-appointed defenders of social decency.

Despite the concern, denim was finding admirers in the realm of higher fashion. Denim is "a wonderful fabric that thrives on soap and water," declared one 1943 advertisement in *Mademoiselle* plugging a line called "Country Bumpkins," a collection of blouses and skirts in mix-and-match indigo and stripes. The same magazine featured ads a few years later promoting a line out of Philadelphia called "Queen Casuals," which included a sleeveless denim shirt with "perky 'flyaway' shoulders and unusual sailor collar," denim pedal pushers with "Zip-to-Fit" side closings, and a denim hat.

Harper's Bazaar challenged the designer Claire McCardell to create a garment with a new, unfamiliar clientele in mind— the well-to-do homemaker who was obliged for the first time in her life to prepare dinner and do her own chores, with the hired help having left her to join the defense effort. "I'm Doing My Work," read the headline of the November 1943 article that introduced McCardell's Popover, a wraparound denim housedress with oversized, rolled-up sleeves, a sewn-in potholder and quilted oven mitt, and a large pocket "big enough for matches, cigarettes, the morning mail, and the duster." "I've always wondered why women's clothes had to be delicate," McCardell once said. "Why couldn't they be practical and sturdy as well as feminine?"

Named for the popover pastry that the Hotel Algonquin was serving when the manufacturer, Adolph Klein, struck his deal with the retailer Lord & Taylor, the Popover retailed for $6.95. Though the initial run was planned for 10,000 yards of denim, enthusiastic executives at the department store quickly increased the order to 75,000 yards. Klein, nervous about sales forecasts, beseeched McCardell to come up with more denim clothing in the event of a surplus. She designed a denim suit and coat that did well on their own. But the Popover was a sensation. Within a year, more than 75,000 dresses, requiring 250,000 yards of denim, were sold, and the dress remained a McCardell staple into the 1950s. It was perhaps the greatest success in a notable career, earning the designer a citation of honor from the judges of the American Fashion Critics' Award.

McCardell specialized in innovative uses of practical, relatively inexpensive fabrics not previously considered fashionable. "For me it is American—what looks and feels like America," she said, describing her aesthetic (and sounding an awful lot like Ralph Lauren, fifty years later). "It's freedom, it's democracy, it's casualness, it's good health. Clothes can say all that."

Also in 1943, McCardell unveiled a denim coverall designed for the growing ranks of clock-punching Rosies. This piece was also featured in *Harper's Bazaar*, modeled by a slender, athletic, wholesome-looking young woman named Betty Bacall. The model's intriguing look caught the eye of the socialite Slim Keith, the original California Girl, whose own casual, "scrubbed-clean" flair made her a regular photographic subject in the pages of the magazine. (In fact, one photo of Keith in dungarees and a denim work shirt, an outfit ordered straight out of a Sears, Roebuck catalog, was instrumental in convincing many housewives to consider wearing denim.) Keith told her husband, the filmmaker Howard Hawks, about Bacall, recommending the newcomer for a part in Hawks's film *To Have and Have Not*, opposite Humphrey Bogart. The character, a frank-talking filly named Slim, was a thinly disguised portrayal of Keith herself. Now known as Lauren Bacall, the young model with "a bit of the panther about her," as Keith once put it, would go on to an illustrious career in Hollywood, and a storybook marriage to Bogart.

Although not a performer herself, Slim Keith was a role model for a generation of increasingly self-reliant women. Her gift, she recalled in her 1990 autobiography, was her "talent for individuality," yet she credited Hawks with helping her develop it. "Howard liked a no-nonsense femininity," she wrote. "His woman could be chic, she could be sexy, but you'd better believe she could also make a ham and hoe a row of beans." That was essentially the case when Keith and Hawks hosted a meeting with a young Montgomery Clift, who was being courted for a part in Hawks's epic Western *Red River* (1948) opposite John Wayne. Clift, Keith remembered, was not too keen on the idea of making an "oater"—a melodramatic Western. But he was, she recalled, smitten with his hostess: "Knowing as we now do the whole story of Monty Clift's [sexual] inclinations, his interest was ironic. Much to Monty's seeming dismay, I didn't stick around for their lunch. In jeans and a denim shirt, I went off to work in the garden." Nevertheless, she convinced the young actor to take the part.

Material shortages during the war led Levi Strauss & Co.

Iowa, 1944

to discontinue its Lady Levi's line, launched during the dude ranch fad of the 1930s. The company also made significant alterations to its 501XX blue jean. In the name of conservation it temporarily eliminated the orange arcuate stitching on the back pockets in favor of a printed facsimile, abolished the martingale (or buckleback), and replaced the copper rivets with metal washed in copper. (The crotch rivet was another casualty, but not due to the conservation effort. The fasteners had a tendency to absorb heat. Company folklore sometimes describes Walter Haas Sr. standing too close to a campfire on a retreat, then returning to the office to suggest the removal of the offending accessory.)

If the necessities of wartime helped soften the shock of seeing a woman in overalls, by the 1950s the big jeans manufacturers were acknowledging women as a potentially lucrative customer base. Levi's reintroduced women's jeans with a side zip, and Wrangler parent Blue Bell designed a line of ladies' overall pants called Jeanies of the West. In England, Lee Cooper unveiled a front-zip jean for women, drawing loud protests from some of the more priggish corners of British culture. It was Brigham Young's hundred-year-old complaint about men's front-button trousers, revived for the fair sex.

Despite the occasional outcry, denim was quietly attaining a measure of glamour. Thanks in large part to McCardell, by the early 1950s denim could suddenly be found in a dizzying variety of garments and accessories, including raincoats, shoes, purses, and umbrellas. "Local Denim Is Focus of Fashion Revolution" read the headline in the *Greensboro Record* of August 28, 1953, noting that the city's Cone Mills was the recent recipient of a windfall as "lowly" denim continued its surprising rise to favor. From the "field and factory," the article reported, denim was suddenly taking its place, "Cinderella-like, on Fifth Avenue and Fashion Lane." Perhaps wishfully, the paper wondered whether the material's ascendance to the upper end of the garment district might sound a welcome death knell for the "sloppy" look on campus: "Chances are that the old denim dungaree, levi, and wrangler will have faded pretty well out of the picture," wrote the reporter. (Note the lower-case lettering not only of *Levi*, an increasingly common occurrence at the time, but also of *Wrangler*, the local Greensboro brand that was just six years old in 1953.)

But denim wasn't simply moving toward fashion. Fashion was also moving toward denim. The critical eye was beginning to retrain itself, entertaining the idea that practical attire could be beautiful too. Not since Oscar Wilde, while on a lecture tour of the United States, had pronounced the Rocky Mountain miners with their wading boots and their wide-brimmed hats the only well-dressed men in America, had the upper crust taken such notice of egalitarian workwear.

FIVE

★

"A Hollywood-style Tough": The 1950s and the Fabrication of the Teenager

Robert Mitchum was a budding movie star in the late 1940s, a cool customer with a thick chest and a stony, heavy-lidded gaze that telegraphed his trademark contempt. Born in 1917 in Bridgeport, Connecticut, he drifted through his teen years, once escaping from a Georgia chain gang while serving a short sentence for vagrancy. As a young man he landed in southern California, where he discovered acting in an amateur theater company in Long Beach. It seemed like a much easier way to make a living than hauling loads on the docks.

During World War II Mitchum was cast in two dozen quickie pictures, mostly boilerplate war dramas, with an occasional detour into Westerns. By the time he drew a Best Supporting Actor nomination in 1945 for his work as Lieutenant Bill Walker in *The Story of GI Joe*, he had earned a reputation among gossip columnists as a loose cannon. He was "Hollywood's Bad Boy," a combustible celebrity always good for some ink. The rap was cemented in mid-1948, when Mitchum was arrested with three others at a private home for possession of narcotics. Ironically, on the morning of the incident he had been scheduled to address a group of students for National Youth Day on the subject of juvenile delinquency—presumably, how to avoid it—at Los Angeles City Hall, at the mayor's request. Mitchum had canceled.

The actor, a friend, and two female acquaintances were raided by police that night as they sat smoking marijuana in a Laurel Canyon bungalow where the women were staying. In 1948, smoking "tea" was still considered an exotic transgression, an unfathomable act to many ordinary Americans. Mitchum and his sidekick, Robin "Danny" Ford, a bartender trying to break into the real estate business, were photographed in the custody of the LAPD, wearing the all-denim uniform of the county jail. With his shirt unbuttoned to the navel and a defiant smirk on his face, Mitchum tipped back in his chair, flouting the scandal. Ever the wiseguy, he gave his occupation as "former" actor and joked to the press, "I'm sorry if my new look doesn't appeal to you. It doesn't appeal to me either."

But the look of denim was starting to appeal to more restless young men, and women. Dungarees, still the occupational clothing of many respectable professions (rancher, fireman, lumberjack), were beginning to take on an aura of disrepute. For some, they were simply an extension of childhood. Men who were boys in the 1920s or '30s, whose mothers bought

Robert Mitchum and Robin "Danny" Ford

them blue jeans through catalogs featuring illustrations of little buckaroos, began wearing them into adulthood. It was one way of announcing their aversion to the responsibilities of maturity. In Hollywood, the Western genre featured an increasing number of rough characters in denim pants and jackets, with the good guys and bad often occupying the same vast territory beyond polite society.

As Mitchum's prison photo attested, the use of denim was also widespread in the correctional system. Durable, low maintenance, and machine washable, the fabric is ideally suited to prison life. When Charlie Chaplin is incarcerated on suspicion of Communist sympathies in *Modern Times* (1936), he and some bullying fellow inmates bumble through the slapstick of a

JAMES SULLIVAN

botched jailbreak in boxy prison blues. For real-life detainees, the outfit could be demoralizing, just as it had been for slaves in the South. During the Depression, with government money sometimes too scarce to buy prison uniforms, many vagrants wore their own clothes behind bars. In Nazi Germany, denim was considered lowly enough for the concentration camps. One Dachau survivor described the terrible conditions there: "Our prison clothes were a heavy, coarse denim. They would freeze when they got wet. We were not issued hats, gloves, or underwear."

Denim is still common in many prisons as an alternative to jailbird stripes and orange jumpsuits. In Oregon, a small company called Prison Blues makes denim workwear using paid prison labor. As part of a progressive inmate work program, state prisoners have been making their own jeans, work shirts, and yard coats since 1989. Prison Blues was founded in 1997 when an Oregon ballot measure cleared the way for private-sector partnerships with the state's Department of Corrections. An early attempt to market the product with inmates drew some negative publicity, prompting Prison Blues to recast itself as American-made clothing for loggers and other reputable workingmen.

"The public wasn't too thrilled, to be honest," says John Borchert, the company's head of marketing. "They didn't want their kids to think that prisoners were cool."

There has always been a class distinction apparent in wearing denim. By the 1940s, however, the material was becoming a personal choice, not just an institutional obligation. For the first time it could be seen as a fashion. More accurately, young people wearing dungarees were making an *anti*fashion statement, as they imagined a kinship with the country's dispossessed— hobos, hardened criminals, and the heroic loners of the mythic West. A new cultural tug-of-war was taking place over the widening generation gap.

As with many culture clashes, both sides fell easily into their prescribed roles. Confronted with the grim realities of the Depression and atomic bombs, some students began to adopt a surly sort of fatalism. At the same time, the postwar sense of relief was evolving into a newfound sense of entitlement. Cars were no longer just the playthings of the wealthy, and ready access to them gave high schoolers and young adults an unprecedented mobility. For the first time, money earned from after-school jobs was not expected to be turned over to Mom and Dad but could be spent on records, clothing, and recreation. School administrators, fearing a loss of control, isolated dungarees as a sign of unrest and swiftly set prohibitions against them. The school system of Buffalo, New York, was one of many that banned jeans in its high schools. "These students are portraying what we consider bad taste in school attire and behavior," one schoolmarmish figure tells the camera in an instructional film typical of the period. Modeling for the narrator is a nervy high school couple wearing dungarees, the girl in ankle bracelets and drop earrings and the boy in a black jacket, his shirt open at the collar.

Denim mills and jeans makers struggled against that perception. North Carolina's Erwin Mills, for instance, promoted its "Bluserge" denim in trade magazine ads of the mid-1950s touting the company's "Clean Jeans for Teens" initiative, dungarees sold three to a hanger and targeted for mothers buried knee-deep in laundry. The accompanying illustration featured a smiling, well-scrubbed young man with schoolbooks slung over his shoulder, wearing a V-neck sweater, a tie, a pair of penny loafers, and crisp denim trousers.

But many parents saw jeans as the clothing of a much less wholesome kind of boy. "If you want to know the good boys from the bad boys, you can tell just by looking at them," as one Levi Strauss & Co. executive put it, describing the brand's sudden image problem. As early as 1949, the company felt compelled to defend its product with advertising—"Denim: Right for School." "It was a battle for my dad to overcome the initial negative images," says Levi Strauss & Co. chairman Bob Haas. "We were working against the stereotype in the newspaper business at that time against jeans, and specifically the Levi's brand, as shorthand for an outlier, a rogue, a criminal."

Haas's father, Walter Haas Jr., joined the company in 1939 as a graduate of Harvard Business School. After folding its old wholesale division, in 1948 Levi Strauss & Co. reached a goal long sought by Walter Haas Sr. when it achieved a net profit of $1 million for the first time. Even so, Walter junior was planning an overhaul. Recognizing the economic might of the postwar baby boom—*Life* magazine would soon report that young people were a $10 billion-a-year industry, "a billion more than the total sales of GM"—the heir apparent shifted the company's focus from westernwear toward the suburban youth market. Despite some initial resistance among elder executives, the move paid off handsomely. By the end of the 1950s, just a decade after Walter senior's dream million-dollar profit, total annual LS&CO. sales nearly tripled to $46 million, with a $2.5-million profit margin. Walter Haas Jr. was elected company president in 1958, with his younger brother, Peter, named executive vice president.

But the Levi's brand, like the rest of the denim industry, was not immune to growing pains. The makers of chinos and other competing garments appealed to parents not to dress their sons and daughters in denim. The American Institute of Men's and Boys' Wear, representing a coalition of ready-to-wear manufacturers, helped promote the movement against dungarees in schools. And the president of the Amalgamated Clothing Workers of America laid the blame for the blue jeans trend squarely at the blue suede shoes of a fast-rising rock 'n' roll star. His name was Elvis Presley.

The irony was that Presley himself was not especially fond of denim clothing. It reminded him of his working-class childhood. He even preferred not to wear shades of brown, because they, too, reminded him of workwear. But Elvis Presley Jeans were one of the earliest items of Elvis-related merchandising. They went on the market in 1956, when the singer-actor from Tupelo was in the Top Twenty almost continuously with songs including "Heartbreak Hotel," "Don't Be Cruel," and "Love Me Tender." The following year Presley wore a thick-stitched black denim jacket and jeans with a striped black-and-white shirt for the famous title dance number of his third movie, *Jailhouse Rock*, for which he was billed as the "Rebel of Song." The exuberant (if exceedingly hokey) sequence features Elvis and his fellow inmates scampering over a set styled to look like a two-tiered cellblock. Upon the film's release, black jeans became the rage of the season. Presley, who would often be cast as a guileless Li'l Abner type, here played a brooder with some genuinely unsavory qualities. Vince Everett, serving time for manslaughter, wears prison blues when he's not singing and dancing in the pen. After getting whipped for punching a guard, he staggers back to his cell with his denim jacket draped over his bare shoulders.

Other Presley roles would call for denim, such as Deke Rivers, the gas station attendant who becomes a pop star in *Loving You* (1957), or Toby Kwimper, the idiot-savant son of a family stranded in Florida in the 1962 comedy *Follow That Dream*. But Elvis, despite the allegations of the Amalgamated Clothing Workers of America, was not the idol most blame-worthy for promoting a lower standard of dress among American teenagers. That notoriety belonged in large part to the two enduring figures of male Method acting of the 1950s, Marlon Brando and James Dean.

Brando in particular instinctively understood the feral message that jeans were capable of transmitting. Working in the theater in New York in the late 1940s, years before his iconic role in the biker melodrama *The Wild One*, the young actor dressed just as he had in high school in suburban Illinois. "He knew what he had by way of allure," wrote his biographer, Peter Manso, "and would appear at the Russian Tea Room in Levi's and a white dress shirt that was visibly ripped, once with the collar torn off." Later, one playwright was astonished by the actor's "Bowery bum" attire, which included a pair of jeans carelessly belted with a length of clothesline.

Brando's first major breakthrough came with the 1947 Broadway production of Tennessee Williams's *A Streetcar Named Desire*. For the smoldering role of Stanley Kowalski, costume designer Lucinda Ballard drew her inspiration from a crew of ditchdiggers working in midtown Manhattan. "Their clothes were so dirty that they had stuck to their bodies," she recalled. "It was sweat, of course, but they looked like statues. I thought,

'That's the look I want . . . the look of animalness.' " It was an appearance that suited Brando's brute physicality well. Ballard started with the T-shirt, still considered scandalous when worn without an overshirt. She fitted the actor very tightly, dyeing the T-shirts a faint red and tearing them at the shoulder.

Brando's blue jeans were similarly snug. Ballard, Manso suggested, "invented the first pair of fitted blue jeans, changing forever not just the face of theater but American fashion. 'I thought of them as though they were garments in the time of the Regency in France,' she said, 'which meant fitting the Levi's wet, pinning them tight. I had seven pair and I washed them in a washing machine for twenty-four hours.' " After tailoring, during which Brando insisted on wearing no underwear, he leaped gleefully around the fitting room. "This is it!" he shouted. "This is what I've always wanted!"

Ballard had removed the inside pockets from the test pair, and the actor implored her to make the same alteration to the rest of the pants. "I think that Stanley would have liked to push his hands in his pockets and feel himself," he told her. Clearly, he had a grasp of the character.

Kowalski was a prototype for a new American caveman, furious with inarticulate passion, insatiable, bluntly sexual. He wasn't sure what he wanted, but he knew how to get it. "Guess I'm gonna strike you as being the unrefined type, hah?" Stanley challenges his wife's fragile sister, Blanche Dubois, when they meet. For the film version of *Streetcar*, which came out in 1951, with Ballard again in charge of wardrobes, Brando wore a more nondescript style of trousers. But two years later the actor gave Levi Strauss & Co. the best unsolicited publicity a business could imagine when he and his fellow motorcyclists wore the company's trademark 501s throughout *The Wild One*, a hopped-up set piece loosely based on the real-life 1947 "invasion" of tiny Hollister, California, by a group of rowdy bikers.

The movie, directed by László Benedek, greatly exaggerated the clash between the quiet townspeople and their boorish guests. The incident, which the town of Hollister (the self-proclaimed "Birthplace of the American Biker") still commemorates with yearly festivals, was laden with polarizing hysterics similar to other genre movies of the time, movies about alien invasions and the Red Scare. Outfitted in leather and denim, the members of Brando's Black Rebels Motorcycle Club speak in the exaggerated hepcat slang that would soon be

(© Getty Images)

identified with the cartoon image of another subset of undesirables, the beatniks. When the sheriff's daughter, the soda fountain girl who finds herself oddly attracted to Brando's Johnny Strabler, asks whether the bikers go picnicking when they're on an outing, he grimaces at her naïveté. "A picnic? Man, you are too square. You don't go any one special place. That's cornball style. You just *go*," he says, snapping his fingers.

The Wild One is no masterpiece, but it certainly made loutish behavior look like a lot of fun. Brando set the tone for future generations of aimless young Americans when a local girl, dancing to a jukebox with one of his accomplices, teases him for his sullen reserve. "Hey, Johnny," she asks, "what are you rebelling against?"

"Whaddya got?" Brando replies, delivering the film's celebrated punch line. For the children of the radical 1960s, that simple rejoinder would be remembered as the first political gesture of their youth.

Taunting Brando's stoic Strabler with a drunken grin on his face, Lee Marvin nearly stole the movie as the incorrigible Chino, a piratic character loosely based on the real-life biker "Wino" Willie Forkner. Forkner was a former World War II paratrooper who had led a small contingent from the Los Angeles chapter of a gang called the Boozefighters into Hollister for the July Fourth weekend in 1947, when the area held its annual motorcycle "scrambles." The bikers' weekend-long binge and their misbehavior—one rode his motorcycle into a barroom and left it there for the duration—was first reported in the *San Francisco Chronicle*. A few weeks later, *Life* magazine ran a photo of Don Middleton, a nineteen-year-old biker with an ample beer belly. Arriving in Hollister the day after the rally ended, the photographer improvised. He made a pile of discarded bottles and asked Middleton to pose, pie-eyed and disheveled, on his bike. The reenactment crystallized a vigilance movement against the perceived menace of marauding biker gangs, and it helped create the cultural climate—both the alarmed parents and their excitable youth—that would incite the clamor over *The Wild One*.

The din crossed oceans. In England, authorities banned the film for more than a decade. The prohibition, of course, led to a hunger among young people to see the movie, enhancing its cult status. In the movie, the Boozefighters' gang name was fictionalized as the Beetles, inspiring a certain rock 'n' roll group that would emerge in Liverpool a handful of years after the American release of *The Wild One*.

Years later, Forkner told the *Chronicle* that he and his contemporaries were mostly veterans who felt underappreciated for their service. "We were rebelling against the establishment, for Chrissakes," said Forkner, who died in 1997. "You go fight a goddamn war, and the minute you get back and take off the uniform and put on Levi's and leather jackets, they call you an asshole."

Some elders undoubtedly had a name or two for James Dean, the melancholy young actor who made a habit of playing resentful offspring. Before his premature death in a 1955 car crash, Dean ensured his lasting fame in a role that had once been reserved for Brando. In 1955's *Rebel Without a Cause*, named for the psychoanalyst's book that inspired the screenplay, Dean's Jim Stark is a misanthropic high schooler tormented by his parents' marital strife and his family's middle-class affectations. At the helm of *Rebel* was Nicholas Ray, the mercurial conjuror of disaffection who had directed Mitchum in *The Lusty Men* and Humphrey Bogart in *In a Lonely Place*. Jim Backus, who played Frank Stark, Dean's ineffectual father, once said that he thought the movie was going to be "a routine program picture . . . a sort of *Ozzie and Harriet* with venom"— until the cast and crew began to gauge the extent of the excitement surrounding their fast-rising star.

At first set to be shot in black and white, *Rebel* became a priority for Warner Bros. as the raves rolled in for Dean's debut performance in *East of Eden*, John Steinbeck's updated version of the story of Cain and Abel. That film, released earlier in 1955, was directed by Elia Kazan, Brando's mentor in *Streetcar* and *On the Waterfront*. Of Dean's Cal Trask, Kazan once explained, "Everything this kid does should be delightfully anarchistic, odd, original, imaginatively eccentric, and full of longing. He is the unexpected personified." "I don't want any kind of love anymore," Dean tells his father in *Eden*, establishing the unglued persona that would characterize all three of his major roles. "Doesn't pay off."

In *Rebel*, *The Wild One*, and dozens of similar wayward-youth melodramas of the era, Dean, Brando, and their long list of imitators helped define the concept of the generation gap, as many teens and young adults of the 1950s rejected the world their parents tried to make for them. "You live here, don't you?" Stark, the new kid in town, asks his neighbor, Judy, played by sixteen-year-old Natalie Wood. "Who lives?" she replies wearily.

Cast as the "rebel," Dean actually plays a sensitive boy forced to confront the real juvenile delinquents of his new school. The actors playing gang members were coached by Frank Mazzola, real-life leader of the Athenians, a Hollywood youth gang, who was given a role in the movie and made a technical adviser. Based on Mazzola's instructions, the cast went through more than four hundred pairs of Levi's scuffed up just so by the wardrobe department. In the stage-setting knife fight outside the planetarium with Buzz, a thuggish ringleader in leather jacket and Levi's (played by Corey Allen), Dean is actually dressed in slacks and a sports coat. Only when he accepts a challenge to a game of "chicken," driving stolen cars to the brink of a cliff, does he change into his jeans—which have been sometimes identified as Lee, not Levi's, and were a point of contention between the two rivals.

In the film's lasting image, the actor wears a red windbreaker over his T-shirt and jeans. A sympathetic, complex character amid a gang of one-dimensional hooligans, Stark's raw emotion and his disgust with the example his parents have set were an indictment of the modern family, consumer culture, and misplaced moralism. "You're tearing me apart!" he bellows drunkenly at his parents.

"His defiant stoop and despondent gaze, his hesitant mumble and tentative plea for love, canonized a new characteristic of saintliness—simply being misunderstood," wrote one of Dean's many biographers. That pose, struck in a well-worn pair of jeans, would be a perverse badge of honor for generations to come.

Vladimir Nabokov's Lolita wasn't just, like Dean, a product of postwar America. She *was* postwar America.

"She used to visit me in her dear dirty blue jeans, smelling of orchards in nymphetland; awkward and fey, and dimly depraved, the lower buttons of her shirt unfastened," as her tormented pursuer, Humbert Humbert, recalled. If with 1955's

Lolita Nabokov exquisitely satirized the inappropriate love of Old World intellectuals for the vulgar charms of America—that vacuous, uncultured playground still dithering through its formative years—then the title character was aptly appointed. Barefoot in blue jeans, "her toenails showing remnants of cherry-red polish," she drove Humbert to a pitiable frenzy. The motels and shopping plazas that define their cross-country excursion are the consummate low-culture backdrops for Lolita's jeans, sneakers, and lollipops. It's not just the girl Humbert falls for, against his better judgment.

In the movie theaters, men of all ages fell for an aspiring starlet named Marilyn Monroe, who wore rolled-up blue jeans and tennis shoes in her first A-list role, as Peggy in Fritz Lang's 1952 drama *Clash by Night*. Appearing as a tomboyish Rosie type who punches the clock in a cannery, in her first scene she flirts playfully with her budding boyfriend Joe (Keith Andes), jamming her thumbs in the front pockets of her jeans as she dares him to get physical with her. "Just let me see any man try," she taunts. Later, in the film's most famous scene, Peggy and Joe run onto the beach after a swim. When she complains about having water in her ear, he picks her up by the ankles, forcing her to stand on her hands. Laughing, she pulls her jeans up over her bikini bottom, and the two race barefoot into the open-air barroom nearby.

Though she could be Hollywood's most elegant figure, a big part of Monroe's appeal was her casual demeanor, her disregard for her own beauty. Blue jeans were a recurring costume in her short career, from the JCPenney brand she wore in 1954's *River of No Return* (opposite Mitchum) to her Levi's and Lee Storm Rider jacket in the 1961 wild-horses drama *The Misfits*, the last completed picture for both Monroe and Clark Gable.

(RKO/Photofest)

Keith Andes and Marilyn Monroe in Clash by Night

Blue jeans also played a role in *Bus Stop*, one of the actress's most beloved movies, in which she portrayed a saloon singer pursued by a rodeo cowboy. Lee Jeans was an underwriter of the picture.

Monroe was classically American, declared the great French photographer Henri Cartier-Bresson upon a visit to the Nevada set of *The Misfits*. "One has to be very local to be universal," he said. She seemed to delight in the ordinariness of her wardrobe. The Foremost brand jeans that Monroe wore with a men's-style shirt on the runaway raft in *River of No Return* cost $2.29 a pair in Penney's department stores at the time of the movie's release. Predictably, however, the value of Marilyn's costumes has risen just a bit. In 1999, the designer Tommy Hilfiger paid thirty-seven thousand dollars at a Christie's auction for three pairs of her jeans from *River of No Return*. He hung one in his office, and gave another to the pop star Britney Spears.

It's no accident that the dominant images of Brando, Dean, and Monroe still picture them in jeans. These actors were something new. They were complicated—tender and volatile and wry. They encouraged more than one generation of teens to remain true to their own complicated natures. The hard-and-fast rules of gender were no longer so hard and fast. Girls became more assertive; boys fumbled for ways to express themselves.

"I was a fat band boy who didn't wear cool jeans," wrote former president Bill Clinton of his 1950s childhood in his autobiography, *My Life*. With the movies, the pop charts, magazines, and other media cultivating (and helping to define) youth culture, for perhaps the first time kids around the country were uniformly aware of what constituted coolness, and what did not. "The trouble with teenagers began when some smart salesman made a group of them in order to sell bobby sox," complained *PTA Magazine* in 1956. A year later *Cosmopolitan* asked the half-serious question, "Are Teenagers Taking Over?" The country, the magazine suggested, was facing "a vast, determined band of blue-jeaned storm troopers, forcing us to do exactly as they dictate."

For Aggie Guerard Rodgers and her high school crowd in Fresno, California, there was only one true cult figure, and that was James Dean. "I kept a scrapbook on Dean," Rodgers recalls. "We were all obsessed with him." Many of the boys in her school, in the early 1960s, grew up emulating the deceased star, and she grew up watching the boys. She was a good girl hopelessly smitten with the guys who were up to no good, cruising the hometown boulevards in their custom deuce coupes and '55 Chevys.

"Guys that dragged the Main in the [San Joaquin] Valley all worked on their cars," Rodgers says. "They were mechanics. They didn't have anything else to do—they didn't go to college. So their jeans were always really dirty. No one washed them. They were thick with grease. They were so stiff, you could stand them up in the corner." For the sake of the girls, the guys made a point to change into clean shirts to go with their grubby jeans. Some of them wore their jeans in the street-smart style of the time, with the belt loops razored off and the waistband folded down. "It was not cool to wear a belt," Rodgers says flatly.

Not surprisingly, given her extraordinary attention to detail, she went into costume design. As luck would have it, her first interview in film turned out to be for a movie called *American Graffiti*. Set in the early 1960s in Modesto, California—just up the highway from Fresno—the movie, released in 1973, was a bittersweet look back at school days among the preppies and hot-rodders of the 1950s and early '60s. It was precisely the time and place in which Rodgers grew up. The first-time director of *American Graffiti*, George Lucas, timed his debut perfectly to coincide with a growing nostalgia for the fifties, and the movie's success launched him on a rather lucrative Hollywood career. As for Rodgers, the break led to a fruitful film career of her own. She went on to design costumes for Lucas's *Star Wars: Episode VI—Return of the Jedi*, 1985's *The Color Purple* (for which she received an Academy Award nomination), and, most recently, the film adaptation of Jonathan Larsen's Broadway sensation about modern bohemia, *Rent*.

For *American Graffiti*, Rodgers dressed two characters in denim, the very Dean-like grease monkey John Milner (played by Paul LeMat) and nebbishy Toad (Charlie Martin Smith), who desperately wants to be one of the cool guys. "Toad's pants hang the way kids' pants hang now, strangely enough," she says. "They were thick and wide in the leg, and all bunched up around the feet." The main characters, matriculating Steve Bolander (Ron Howard) and his conflicted buddy Curt Henderson (Richard Dreyfuss), are plaid-shirts-and-chinos types. These were the kids who probably grew up changing into their "playclothes"—their dungarees—after school. Howard, of course, would go on to play a very similar character in the long-running sitcom *Happy Days*. His Richie Cunningham was the quintessential freckle-faced, well-groomed American boy, a congenial counterpart to the Brylcreemed, jeans-and-T-shirt role-playing of Arthur Fonzarelli (Henry Winkler). Always armored in his leather jacket, astride his motorcycle, "The Fonz" was the pop apogee of the terminally hip archetype first shaped by Dean, Brando, Presley, and their imitators.

If Dean was a dream lover for an American girl like Aggie Rodgers, Brando and Presley helped sell postwar American attitude to young men overseas. In England, still photos from the forbidden *Wild One* provided some behavioral clues for a generation of rockabilly cats. The British rockabillies, later called rockers, borrowed their initial style from Presley. Arriving in the wake of the so-called teddy boys—the Edwardian-revival dandies of the 1950s who dressed in drape jackets, drainpipe trousers, and string ties—the rockers first hit the streets in pegged pants, spread-collar shirts, and two-tone shoes. They quickly revised their wardrobes, however, adopting the quasi-military

gang look of *The Wild One*. Many of the former teddy boys became de facto rockers, joining the biker fraternity. Elvis's jar-
ring appearance in *Jailhouse Rock* further refined the image. "The
contrast with his sleek white suit and spotless white shoes of
1956 is absolute," wrote the British culture critic Ted Polhemus.
"But somehow this was appropriate and logical: having demonstrated that he was no longer a truck driver, he is free to remind us of his roots."

Elvis may have sufficiently outgrown his roots to revisit
them, but for some country boys there was little choice. For
Johnny Cash's first public performance with his group, the
Tennessee Two, he set a dress code of black shirts and blue
jeans. "We were a band, and we thought we ought to look like
one," Cash wrote in his 1998 autobiography. "Unfortunately
none of us had any clothes a 'real' band would wear—I didn't
own a suit, or even a tie—but each of us did have a black shirt
and a pair of blue jeans. So that became our band outfit." But
his mother despised the look, and she quickly sewed some stage-
worthy outfits for the threesome.

In *Lolita*, set in the late 1940s, Humbert finds himself im-
probably immersed in the pop fantasy world of his muse. "The
Lord knows how many nickels I fed to the gorgeous music
boxes that came with every meal we had!" he moans. "I still
hear the nasal voices of those invisibles serenading her, people
with names like Sammy and Jo and Eddy and Tony and Peggy
and Guy and Patty and Rex." In the real world of American
teens, pop idols and their songwriters were acutely attuned to
the audience. The period was full of songs about sweethearts in
denim, from crooner Eddie Fisher trying his hand at rock 'n'
roll with "Dungaree Doll" to the Baton Rouge heartthrob Jimmy

Clanton, who had one of his biggest hits with the dreamy ballad "Venus in Blue Jeans"—"She's Venus in blue jeans, Mona Lisa with a ponytail."

The songwriting team of Jerry Leiber and Mike Stoller, who got their start writing R & B songs for black acts, broke into the pop mainstream with the melodramatic premature-death yarn "Black Denim Trousers and Motorcycle Boots." In the song, a "motorsickle"-riding bad boy in a leather jacket "with an eagle on the back" ignores his girlfriend's pleas not to ride, dying in a collision with a "screamin' diesel" locomotive. The original recording, featuring a Los Angeles vocal trio called the Cheers (whose members included future TV personality Bert Convy), entered the Top Ten in late 1955. Other versions included a follow-up chart hit by the western-style baritone bandleader Vaughn Monroe ("the Voice with Hair on Its Chest") and a suitably frenetic French translation ("L'Homme à la Moto") by "the Little Sparrow," Edith Piaf.

Teen recklessness was the topic of the day. "Why do you kids live like there's a war on?" pleads Doc, the fatherly candy-shop owner, just before the fatal shooting in *West Side Story*. The rival Jets and Sharks are lithe street kids whose confrontations are a lusty kind of ballet performed in various shades of tight, straight-legged jeans and work pants. In the climactic sequence of the 1961 film version, Tony (Richard Beymer) dies with his jeans on in the arms of his forbidden lover, Maria (Natalie Wood). To their elders, restlessness, dissatisfaction, and misdirected violence were adding up to an alarming trend among the young. Given that such social concerns were also a surefire source of free publicity, by the end of the 1950s Hollywood had become a virtual assembly line for the production of the so-called "teensploitation" movies.

Many of these movies featured slick-talking, finger-popping caricatures of the Beat generation, the demonized literary movement. "Jack Kerouac was responsible for selling a million pairs of jeans with On the Road," Kerouac's cantankerous, shabby-suited colleague, William Burroughs, once remarked, not without some derision. On the Road, published in 1957, did in fact generate great word of mouth for the peripatetic, experience-seeking lifestyle—what Kerouac called the "rucksack revolution"—that was emerging among the postwar generation. And jeans, wearable every day, regardless of the availability of a washing machine, were the ideal clothing for their lifestyle. Kerouac's literary circle, oddly enough, was not especially partial to jeans (although Allen Ginsberg did wear cuffed Wranglers in the experimental Beat film Pull My Daisy). Kerouac's own image was featured long after his death, in a famous 1990s ad campaign for Gap, in which various hip figures were pictured wearing khakis—Ginsberg, Miles Davis, Pablo Picasso, even James Dean.

Another Dean, Kerouac's fictional Dean Moriarty, the impetuous protagonist of On the Road, was drawn from the actual escapades of Kerouac's friend Neal Cassady, who maniacally crisscrossed the country, often in stolen cars and later at the wheel of the Merry Pranksters' psychedelic bus. "What got Kerouac and Ginsberg about Cassady," said another Beat figure, the poet Gary Snyder, "was the energy of the archetypal West, the energy of the frontier, still coming down. Cassady is the cowboy crashing." And he dressed the part. Cassady's widow, Carolyn, once said that she never knew her husband to wear anything but blue jeans, and Dean Moriarty follows suit. "Dean was wearing washed-out tight Levi's and a T-shirt and looked suddenly like a real Denver character again," Kerouac wrote.

For polite society, the look of the "real Denver character" was a badge of dishonor. "All the children in the world have gotten too big for their britches," wails a mother in *Blue Denim*, a 1959 screen production of the Broadway play of the same name, cowritten by William Noble and James Leo Herlihy (who went on to write *Midnight Cowboy*). Played by the young actor Brandon De Wilde (*Shane, Hud*), Arthur Bartley is a decent young man in rolled up "levis" (as the script indicates) who steals from his parents to pay for an abortion for his girlfriend, Janet (Carol Lynley). His budding sexuality panics him. "I'm trouble, Jan," he warns her, refusing an embrace. "I'm just this crazy goddamn body!" De Wilde was destined for an early death, at age thirty. Like Dean, he died on the road, in a car accident.

For some pop stars, too, tragedy would prove to be more than just a storytelling ploy. Gene Vincent, who wore a steel brace following a motorcycle accident in 1952, named his first album *Blue Jean Bop*, after his song of the same name. He met young Eddie Cochran, three years his junior, on the set of the 1956 rock 'n' roll movie *The Girl Can't Help It*, where Vincent and his Blue Caps performed their first and biggest hit, "Be-Bop-A-Lula." The burbling opening lines of Cochran's 1959 hit, "C'mon Everybody," identified him as an authentic member of the teen crowd he was singing to: "Well, c'mon everybody and let's get together tonight / I got some money in my jeans, and I'm really gonna spend it right."

Touring England with Vincent in 1960, Cochran decided to fly home to America over the Easter weekend to honor a scheduled recording date. En route to London from Bristol, the car carrying Vincent, Cochran, and Cochran's girlfriend,

Sharon Sheeley, blew a tire, and the driver crashed into a lamppost. Sheeley fractured her pelvis; Vincent reinjured his leg and suffered multiple broken bones. Cochran, who was thrown through the windshield, died the following day of massive head injuries. He was twenty-one years old. Vincent eventually succumbed to an alcohol problem, dying eleven years later of a bleeding ulcer, at age thirty-six.

Sheeley, a songwriter whose very first effort, "Poor Little Fool," was a number-one hit for Ricky Nelson, lived long enough to see her brief relationship with Cochran romanticized in a 1988 Levi's ad in the UK. As she told it, despite writing a song for Eddie, dyeing her hair blond, and spending money on expensive dresses, Sheeley was unable to attract much attention from the singer, with whom she had grown infatuated. Though she was invited to Cochran's 1958 New Year's Eve party at a New York hotel, she was disappointed that Cochran himself hadn't bothered to call—he sent word through their mutual manager. In a pique, Sheeley scrubbed off her makeup and yanked on a sweatshirt, tennis shoes, and a pair of Levi's before heading out to the party. That, finally, got the young rocker's attention, and their whirlwind affair began that night. "Are you in love with me, Charlie Brown?" he supposedly asked her. "You better be, 'cause I'm in love with you."

Storybook legends in the making, there was a whiff of fatalism about the rockers. Sometimes called "coffee-bar cowboys" in the UK, the rockers resented authority in much the same way as the renegades of the Wild West did. Their defiance masked their sensitivity, but it also ensured they'd be judged exactly as they took pains to portray themselves, as potential troublemakers.

Before they were introduced to the world in their matching lapel-less Pierre Cardin suits, a scrappy group of Liverpudlian rock 'n' rollers calling themselves the Beatles apprenticed on Hamburg's seedy Reeperbahn, wearing biker gear. Stu Sutcliffe, the band's momentary, ill-fated bassist, was a Dean acolyte, and he gave the group much of its early visual style. His German art-school girlfriend, a photographer and fashionable-in-black existentialist named Astrid Kirchherr, helped with the streetwise makeover. "They look beat up and depraved in the nicest possible way," wrote one female pop columnist in London on the eve of the Beatles' breakthrough, not long after Sutcliffe's premature death. In the spring of 1963, just prior to the ascent of their first number-one-charting UK single, "From Me to You," the Beatles took part in a photo session in their hometown, Liverpool. They were modeling the jeans of Lybro, Ltd. a local workwear institution. The photos were used as guidelines for a company brochure in which the rising stars were rendered as line drawings. It was reportedly the only time the Beatles officially endorsed a product during their years together.

In May 1964, fights erupted in several British seaside resort towns between local rockers and much larger crowds of visiting mods, or Modernists, the new wave of fashionable, scooter-riding young men who were buying into Carnaby Street hip. For the mods, the rockers were an outdated joke. In the most notorious of the skirmishes, some of which resulted in stabbings, two rockers were forced to jump off a seawall to the beach fifteen feet below. (The incidents would become the subject of the Who's 1973 rock opera *Quadrophenia*.) Reporting by the British press suggested that the rivalry was a simple matter of stylistic differences. That view, according to the critic Polhemus, lacks nuance: "In our age, style has become a language with the power to convey deeply rooted, complex attitudes and beliefs," he wrote. Class conflict was inherent in the two groups' contrasting wardrobes—"scruffy leather and jeans versus pristine casualwear and sharply pressed suits"—but the battles may also have signaled the mods' rejection of parochialism in favor of a newfound worldliness. They prided themselves on their continental tastes and their appreciation for black American soul music and the imported rhythms of London's West Indian immigrants. Also, as Polhemus noted, the mod–rocker confrontations suggested a cultural upheaval over "changing definitions of masculinity."

While the mods were exhibiting a fussiness over clothing traditionally associated with women, some gay men in London were gravitating toward the "butch" look of the rockers. Vacationing in France, the owner of a trend-setting Carnaby Street boutique called Vince Man's Shop observed young people wearing all-black outfits—shirts, sweaters, and jeans. He brought the look back with him to England, and it "went like a bomb," said the owner, Bill Green. "People said the stuff was so outrageous that it would only appeal and sell to the rather sort of eccentric Chelsea set or theatrical way-out types"—in other words, gay men. One scenester noted what most others had not yet openly acknowledged. "The gay crowd took to jeans," he said, "because of the closeness and tightness of them, which showed up all of the essential parts."

Both onscreen and off, jeans were becoming a self-conscious kind of costume, and the effect was increasingly campy. To be a mechanic or a rancher was one thing. To dress like one, as Dean and Brando did, was just that—playing dress-up. Not for another decade or more would denim workwear become sufficiently prevalent as recreational clothing to reclaim the ordinariness of its origins.

Denim did have some unlikely celebrity champions, wholesome favorites such as Ozzie and Harriet Nelson and Lucy and Ricky Ricardo, famous television (and real-life) couples who were photographed in crisp blue jeans. Bing Crosby, the fatherly singer and actor whose career reached back to the 1920s, became a lifelong friend of the Levi Strauss & Co. family following an incident that occurred in 1951. Crosby and a hunting buddy were on vacation in Canada when they tried to check into a Vancouver hotel. Unrecognized, they were refused service: they were wearing Levi's jeans and jackets. (A bellman eventually identified Crosby, and the two travelers were accommodated.) Upon hearing of the mix-up through one of Crosby's Bay Area neighbors, Levi's had a denim tuxedo jacket custom-made for the entertainer. Sewn into the inside lining was a panel that read, "Notice to hotel men everywhere. This label entitles the wearer to be duly received and registered with cordial hospitality at any time and under any conditions." The jacket was presented to him at the 1951 Silver State Stampede in Elko, Nevada, for which the singer was serving as honorary mayor.

Despite the Crosby episode in Canada, by the 1950s jeans were acknowledged around the world as an American icon. During World War II, American soldiers had worn their jeans on leave in France, Italy, Germany, and Japan, generating international demand among the young. Whatever impact the soldiers had, jeans were still considered a sign of crudeness. In the melancholy French musical *The Umbrellas of Cherbourg*, set in 1957, Catherine Deneuve's young Geneviève falls deeply in love with Nino Castelnuovo's Guy Foucher, an auto mechanic in greasy jeans. He is, of course, not good enough for her.

He was "the picture of a Hollywood-style 'tough' wearing blue jeans, leather jacket, cowboy boots, and sideburns." That's how *U.S. News & World Report* described Charlie Starkweather when the scrawny nineteen-year-old was arrested after his killing spree across Nebraska and Wyoming in 1958.

Were blue jeans really the clothes of delinquents, or were delinquents just partial to blue jeans? It was a conundrum that frankly panicked the workwear industry.

(© AP/Wide World Photos)

Caril Fugate and Charlie Starkweather: teenagers

"At one point, every perp was wearing blue jeans," says Norman Karr, a lifelong promotions man who worked closely with the denim industry. In 1956, responding to a dampening of blue jeans sales ascribed to anxieties over juvenile deliquency, a coalition of textile companies sponsored the formation of the Denim Council, an organization dedicated to putting schoolchildren "back in blue jeans through a concerted national public relations, advertising, and promotional effort." Appealing to mothers, the group's public relations associates encouraged fashion designers to create new denim lines for women, and they arranged "jean queen" beauty contests with retailers around the country. When the Kennedy administration formed the Peace Corps in 1961, the Denim Council outfitted the corps's first two hundred volunteers in blue jeans, securing invaluable publicity that would pay off in subtle ways for years to come.

Jeans manufacturers were experiencing a strange paradox of the American marketplace. They had a daunting image problem, yet it was precisely that image problem that gave the product its desirability among the target audience. Antifashion, as the critic Anne Hollander has written, "has often simply been the next fashion."

"The last thing you can do with a teenager is tell him he can't wear something. As soon as you do, it becomes very important in his life," says Karr, who worked with the Denim Council and its successor, Jeanswear Communications, beginning in the 1970s. Like mind-altering substances, premarital sex, or banned books, jeans were increasingly coveted *because* they were prohibited. It made for some uncomfortable dilemmas for industry fathers, many of whom were fathers at home too.

After the temporary dip in the mid-1950s, sales escalated.

"There was no way to plan for the kind of growth we were experiencing," Peter Haas told Levi's biographer Ed Cray. "Every time we'd make up a plan, it would be obsolete." In the three years from 1963–1966, Levi Strauss & Co. doubled its annual sales, to $152 million.

"It seemed impossible to me that we could sell more and more pants," said Walter Haas Sr.

★

SIX

Classlessness: The Politics of Fashion

The garment that had once been called dungarees, or overall pants, was now universally understood as blue jeans. In the summer of 1962 a Greenwich Village newcomer drawled about his jeans on side two of his debut album—"My mother was a tailor / She sewed these new blue jeans." The baby-faced folk singer had recently taken the name Bob Dylan, inspired either by the Welsh poet Dylan Thomas or Matt Dillon, the marshal on TV's *Gunsmoke*, depending on which story you chose to believe. The song, "House of the Risin' Sun," was a traditional lament based on an old English ballad, recorded by bluesmen, folkies, and Roy Acuff, "the King of Country Music." The updated lyric referred to an actual House of the Rising Sun, a house of ill repute dating to the 1860s in New Orleans's French Quarter.

Fast approaching the century mark for its famous product, even Levi Strauss & Co. finally acknowledged the notion of calling the pants "jeans." Although the term had been used colloquially for decades—all the way back in 1885, *Harper's* magazine had referred to "jeans-clad" mountaineers—the company was still referring to its classic 501s as "waist overalls" as late as the 1950s.

The aimless teenage rebelliousness of the 1950s was congealing into the social protests of the 1960s, first with equal rights campaigns, then with the outcry against the war in Vietnam. Campus discontent was a lofty kind of fad, wrote David Hajdu in *Positively 4th Street*, his life and times of Dylan, Joan Baez, and the folk movement they popularized. The movement had "a distinctly postwar American character"—it was "a mobilization in the name of political and moral principle that was also a fashion trend and a business opportunity." Universities such as Northwestern, Princeton, and Georgetown relaxed their traditional dress codes as more students joined the trend toward unpretentious work clothes. "Annual sales of dungarees had increased nearly fifty percent in 1961, and sales of dress shoes reached a historic low for the industry in the same year. . . . A million Americans were now purchasing guitars every year, and they all seemed to be sitting on college grounds in blue jeans and no shoes, strumming 'Where Have All the Flowers Gone?' and 'This Land Is Your Land.' " A few years later, in school districts where jeans were still banned, civil rights groups took up the fight against dress codes as an imposition on freedom of expression.

"Amazing," says Norman Karr. "Just for a pair of pants."

The moralists had nearly succeeded in casting an unassuming pair of blue jeans as a prime source of social ills in America.

As the 1960s began to unfold, students set about reclaiming jeans for themselves. Denim was now seen as a potent symbol of integrity, empathy for the less privileged, and a commitment to one's own true self. "Theorists of blue jeans in the sixties," the *New Yorker* fashion critic Kennedy Fraser would later write, "claimed that one's individuality was made more apparent when it was contrasted with the sameness of denim, and that the malleable clay of blue jeans brought out the touching differences in human bodies."

By the 1960s, many black Americans had shed their past in part by renouncing the clothing of their predecessors. For them, denim and overalls were unpleasant reminders of slavery days and sharecropping. Black farm boys had escaped rural poverty by moving to the industrial cities of the North, to Detroit and Chicago and other manufacturing hubs, in the mass migration of the 1940s and '50s. Denim clothing was what they had worn in the cotton fields, and they did not want to go back.

Yet during the civil rights movement of the early 1960s, the northern college students who went south to join the sit-ins soon traded their chinos, loafers, and short-sleeve Oxford shirts for the everyday clothes of the men and women they came to support. They were "powerfully affected by the most impoverished and disenfranchised Negroes," wrote Todd Gitlin in his definitive history *The Sixties: Years of Hope, Days of Rage.* "What began as strategy became identity. SNCC [the Student Nonviolent Coordinating Committee] organizers, mostly city bred, picked up the back-country look of Georgia and Mississippi: denim jackets, blue work shirts, bib overalls. . . . SNCC's clothes were physical markers of solidarity."

The placid Piedmont North Carolina city of Greensboro is perhaps best known for the historic lunch-counter sit-in that took place at a downtown Woolworth's department store in February 1960. Denied service at the whites-only diner, the African-American college students Joseph McNeil, Franklin McCain, Ezell Blair Jr., and David Richmond refused to leave their seats, triggering a six-month protest that inspired similar demonstrations across the South. The "Greensboro Four" were nattily attired in suits, ties, and trench coats, befitting their career ambitions; McNeil, for instance, was a freshman physics major at the time. But Greensboro's working-class population, both black and white, was much more likely to be clothed in working-class denim, one primary output of the city's dominant industry, textiles.

Founded in 1895, Greensboro's Cone Mills was the first southern company to crack the stronghold that the mills of Massachusetts and New Hampshire held over the textile industry throughout the nineteenth century. Brothers Moses and Ceasar Cone went into business in 1870 with their father, a Bavarian immigrant born Herman Kahn, as grocery wholesalers based in Baltimore. In 1891 the brothers, recognizing the rapid growth of the textile industry in the South, established the Cone Export & Commission Company, headquartered in New York City, where they promoted southern goods. Four years later, the brothers went into manufacturing for themselves, opening the Proximity Cotton Mills in Greensboro. The name referred to the nearness of the plant to its interrelated industries, from the North Carolina cotton fields to the abundant railways of Greensboro, a burgeoning shipping hub nicknamed "Gate City." The company's Revolution Cotton Mills opened in 1899, followed by a plant exclusively devoted to denim, White Oak, in 1905.

From the start Cone was a substantial presence, hastening the obsolescence of New England mills such as Amoskeag. In 1915 Cone signed an exclusive agreement to provide the denim for Levi's classic 501XX blue jeans, a relationship that would last almost ninety years. Just a year earlier, Amoskeag's company newspaper had touted its forty-year relationship with the San Francisco institution and its mutual benefits. Now the Levi's business had moved south. By 1923 Cone's White Oak facility could claim to be the world's largest manufacturer of denim, with 4,600 looms in operation.

Each Cone mill became the focal point of an adjoining village for employees, housing a total of eight thousand people in a thousand cottages built on brick pillars on lots seventy-five by one hundred fifty feet. Employees rented the houses from the Cones for three to five dollars a month, and the villages featured schools, churches, general stores, and two YMCAs. Until the rationing of World War I, an annual Fourth of July picnic took place on the grounds surrounding the enormous old oak tree that gave White Oak its name. With the Union Textile Band playing patriotic marches, participants in the 1910 picnic consumed one thousand pounds of ham, eight thousand frankfurters, twenty-five thousand bananas, and five hundred gallons of ice cream.

Cone family members succeeded one another as company president until 1965. They were evidently magnanimous toward their subordinates. "Away with the carping critic who has said that American life today is the lowly pursuit of the dollar, that benefaction and brotherly love are catalogued among the lost arts," reads the florid copy of the company's thirtieth-anniversary yearbook, published in 1925. The Cones claimed to be first in the American textile industry to provide medical insurance, and cofounder Ceasar lobbied on behalf of child labor reform. There were personal touches too. The company delivered hams to its employees' front doors each Christmas Eve. Loyalty and gratitude were high; over the years there were instances of longtime employees naming their sons Cone, or Levi.

The sense of community was deeply ingrained, says former Cone executive Raymond Fuquay, a garrulous native of the Piedmont region who worked his way up in various capacities for the company, including vice president of denim manufacturing, from 1960 until his retirement in 2000. In fact, the community spirit extended to rivalries within the company villages: "If you dated a girl from another village, you had to sneak in," Fuquay recalls, smiling. "They'd throw rocks at you."

Despite the Cones' benevolence, their paternalism could also have a stifling effect. As with so much industry well into the twentieth century, pay in the mills was low, conditions were dangerous, and the opportunity for advancement among the self-proclaimed "lintheads" was nearly nonexistent. Not long before Fuquay's arrival in 1960, the Cone Mills were embroiled in a tense labor dispute, with employees encouraged by the unionization of the country's coal miners and steelworkers.

"We had the National Guard out here one time," says Fuquay. "I was told, more times than one, who struck and who didn't. In all honesty, at one time this was a chain gang mentality." But the Greensboro economy was deeply dependent on the textile production of Cone and its crosstown rival, Burlington. For Fuquay, nothing in the job was more satisfying

(Courtesy of Cone Mills)

White Oak

than helping to reinvigorate a sense of community in the mills, from the floor sweepers up through the company executives. "There are a lot of third-generation employees here right now. You grow up in it."

During his infrequent visits back to White Oak, Fuquay is greeted like a beloved ex-mayor, with hearty handshakes and warm embraces. Over dinner and beer at a steakhouse near Cone's spic-and-span headquarters in a modern Greensboro office park, he would lament the erosion of the textile industry's once-enormous local impact. He recounts an old tale about a small southern town whose poverty-stricken residents have fallen into dissolution. The local preacher knows just the cure: "What this town needs is God and a cotton mill," he says.

An inveterate yarn-spinner and joke teller, Fuquay likes to talk as much about his passion for mountain music as his life-long commitment to denim. Though he was a mischievous teenager in the 1950s—"I liked Fats Domino, Little Richard, all that shit," he says with a grin—he grew into a deep apprecia-tion for the traditional music that his father, a banjo picker, played. The folk revival of the 1960s seems to have helped Raymond Fuquay define his own sense of social justice. "You used to see some guy in bib overalls and some guy from Har-vard playing the same song," he says. Today, leading an active retirement in a restored log cabin on the family farm in Rock-ingham County, he attends as many old-timey festivals as he can. "What I like is it's a classless society," he says.

That kind of democratic ideal has long been a crucial part of the blue jeans myth. The universal image of the denim-clad common man has sustained the business better than any ad-vertising campaign. If clothing is a kind of language, express-ing countless attitudes and dialects, then jeans are the great American ice-breaker, common to welfare recipients and MBAs alike. "When Alice in Wonderland stepped through the Look-ing Glass," wrote the anonymous chronicler in Cone's thirtieth-anniversary yearbook, "she experienced no more surprises, nor did she encounter a more interesting lot of folks than you will meet in stepping through and back of a yard of denim."

At the dawn of the 1960s the ready-to-wear clothing industry was just beginning to understand the ways that a preoccupation with image could impact its bottom line. Advertising directors, as Naomi Klein has noted, had been touting the concept of "branding" since the 1940s: "There was a burgeoning awareness that a brand wasn't just a mascot or a catchphrase or a picture printed on the label of a company's product; the company as a whole could have a brand identity or a 'corporate consciousness,' as this ephemeral quality was termed at the time."

Together with the automotive industry, the blue jeans trade was among the first to recognize that it was selling an idea as much as it was selling the product itself. "Identity no longer depended on pedigree like workmanship or materials, which belonged to an object's past, but was as fungible as the copywriters said it was," wrote John Leland in *Hip: The History*. "Ads did with products what protohip Americans were doing with their own identities"—reclaiming them from the dreary historical record and rejuvenating them. In the case of blue jeans, an embrace of the *appearance* of rebellion did not always mean an unconditional embrace of rebellion itself. Jeans "connoted adventure," says Bob Haas, who was himself a product of the 1950s, "being on the edge, a vicarious life [our customers] didn't have to actually experience."

Haas tells the story of a longtime Levi Strauss & Co. salesman who loved to regale his colleagues with a well-traveled tale of his personal connection to 501s. Moving with his family from the eastern seaboard to southern California in the early 1960s, he was a pariah from his first day of grammar school in his well-pressed khakis.

"People looked at him like he was a freak," Haas relates with a grin. "All the guys, particularly all the cool guys, were wearing Levi's. So he went home that night and begged his parents to get him a pair. They stiff-armed him, but he was relentless. Finally they gave in. He said it was instantaneous from that moment forward. The reserve that had greeted him when he arrived evaporated. He was embraced by the cool guys. He became one of them, and he lived happily ever after."

The jeans companies weren't just selling pants. They were selling the key to popularity. Lee advertised its products as "The Clothes You Need for the Life You Lead." In an era of dance crazes such as the Twist, the Watusi, the Loco-Motion, and the Stroll, Wrangler hired a choreographer named Killer Joe Piro to create a dance called the Wrangler Shake. The company promoted another dance called the Wrangler Stretch with a contest offering a grand-prize 1931 Rolls-Royce with a rumble seat. The Wrangler line, by then well established in westernwear specialty shops, was now focusing its efforts on suburban fifteen- to twenty-two-year-olds. "Radio advertising is concentrated on the 'rocker' stations that appeal to the young; magazine ads go in books like *Seventeen*, *Glamour*, *Hot Rod*, and *Playboy*," reported the Greensboro-area *News and Observer* in 1966. Not all of the newfangled promotions seem so shrewd in hindsight. The company tried its hand at Wrangler-branded sneakers and cologne. It also boasted a special collection of mink and chinchilla jeans. "We bicycle them all over the country for local promotions," the vice president of promotions at Blue Bell, Wrangler's parent company, told the newspaper.

In another nod to the youth market, by the early 1960s "blue" jeans were widely available in a splashy variety of colors. Black jeans were already fairly common; Frisko Jeens, once compared to the tight black leggings of the Barbary Coast Apache, were popular on the West Coast between the wars, and Wrangler had good success with black jeans popularized by William Boyd's Hopalong Cassidy, one of television's early stars. In the late 1940s Sears added "barn red" to its denim items for women, including shorts and pedal pushers.

Levi Strauss & Co. soon began offering its "Ranch Pants" for women ("the trim, tidy slack-of-all-trades") in red, gold, and pink denim in addition to light blue and indigo. An ad for Wrangler featured rodeo champion Jim Shoulders and his family—"Dad and all the boys in blue or faded blue; Mom and the girls in six happy colors." In 1959 Lee introduced Lee Westerners, dressy white jeans and jackets commonly called Lee Whites. The following year LS&CO. rolled out a line of preshrunk "sand"-colored jeans, which customers quickly (if somewhat inaccurately) dubbed "White Levi's." The company added a range of shades, and the list reads like an early draft of the J. Crew catalog, or a rich kid's crayons: loden, antelope, pewter, sage, whiskey, and black forest, as well as "white white."

White jeans were a prominent feature of the March 21, 1966, cover story in *Newsweek*, a comprehensive sociological report on "The Teen-Agers" ("A *Newsweek* Survey of What They're Really Like"). On the cover, a young woman in a cable-knit sweater, a sun-kissed dirty blond who looks like she could be Brigitte Bardot's kid sister, smiles shyly over her shoulder as she sets off for a spin on her boyfriend's motorcycle. Just above the bike's California license plate is the girl's Wrangler tag, prominently centered on the back pocket of her crisp white jeans. The cover story, noting the relative novelty of the term *teen-ager* (which had only been in use a few decades, having supplanted the earlier *teener*), took pains to reassure parents that "a solid majority" of their coming-of-age offspring "are

builders, not breakers—not hop-headed hoodlums and hood-
lettes churning up the drag strips with their hot rods, rolling in
the hay, [and] thumbing their noses at organized society." A bit
ominously, however, the piece also quoted the prediction of an
Italian magazine: "America's teen-agers make up, as we shall
see, the most pitiless, irreducible, indestructible dictatorship in
the world."

Commercially speaking, the warning was right on the button. With the baby boom generation spending an estimated
$3.5 billion in 1965 on casual clothes, the denim industry was
overhauling its emphasis from workwear to fashion. As more
young women declared themselves feminists (or at least free
spirits, like the girl on the *Newsweek* cover), wearing blue jeans
was a conspicuous reminder that the call for gender equality
was much more than mere lip service. "To the careful observer,"
wrote Alison Lurie in *The Language of Clothes*, "all these students are only identical below the waist; above it they may wear
anything from a lumberjack shirt to a lace blouse. Grammati-
cally, this costume seems to be a sign that in their lower or physical natures these persons are alike, however dissimilar they may
be socially, intellectually, or aesthetically." More women were
working, attending college, and setting out on travel adventures
of their own, and they were also gaining control over their
sexuality. The Pill, granted FDA approval in 1960, was being
used by 1.2 million American women in 1962; three years later
that number had risen to 6.5 million. Birth control and jeans
were a powerful combination for both sexes, according to the
sociologist Paul Fussell. Together these two talismans of the
emancipation era "ushered in an entirely new world of pleasure
for the young." Young women were distancing themselves from

traditional notions of propriety, and the celebration of the body that would soon result in the commotion over miniskirts and bra burnings was forecast by girls in tight jeans.

While women were making work pants sexy, inspiring ever tighter fits, many men were moving toward an expressive fashion sense that was considered a historically feminine domain. Together with the long hairstyles that prompted endless barbs—you couldn't tell the guys from the gals anymore, the Ralph Kramdens liked to complain—the floral prints, decorative patterns, and vivid colors of the so-called "Peacock Revolution" helped move fashion toward the middle ground of unisex style. "We hope these shirts destroy our image," as the traditional men's clothier Tyson Shirt advertised its splashy new patterns in GQ in 1968.

In England, a new kind of dandy was emerging. Representing the brash sound of the Carnaby Street scene, mod bands such as the Who and the Small Faces helped spark a rage for white "drainpipe" jeans and jean jackets. At the celebrity wedding of the actress Catherine Deneuve and the photographer David Bailey (the inspiration for Antonioni's *Blow-Up*), best man Mick Jagger wore a blue denim suit.

And the Beatles, ever accommodating when it came to playing dress-up, shed their fanciful Sgt. Pepper satin and their *Magical Mystery Tour* ruffles in favor of the people's fabric. On his celebrated stroll along San Francisco's Haight Street during the Summer of Love in 1967, George Harrison wore "flowered bell-bottom trousers, a denim jacket with a button reading 'I'm the Head of My Community,' and dark glasses shaped like hearts," as described by the Haight-Ashbury historian Charles Perry. Strumming a borrowed guitar at the head of an impromptu procession, the Beatle seemed startled by the anarchy he found at the crossroads of the counterculture. "If it's all like this, it's too much," he said. Later, he admitted his curious revulsion to the scene. "I expected them all to be nice and clean and friendly and happy," he said, but "they were all terribly dirty and scruffy."

For the denim industry, those same "scruffy" teenagers were good customers. On the cusp of the Summer of Love, Levi Strauss & Co.'s advertising agency cut a series of radio commercials tilted toward the increasingly eccentric listening habits of the psychedelic underground. San Francisco bands including the Jefferson Airplane and Sopwith Camel were hired to record the spots for white Levi's and the label's new stretch fabrics. The Airplane, at the time enjoying the success of the career-defining hit "Somebody to Love," contributed four cacophonous, Dadaesque ads featuring random sounds such as a balloon stretching and a duck impersonation. In another spot, singer Grace Slick ululated over a druggy, improvisational raga, droning on about how white Levi's were available in black and blue.

"My father, uncle, and grandfather were all horrified," Bob Haas once recalled in *The New Yorker*. "To them, the commercial sounded as if it came from a bunch of people who were dazed out of their minds and had gone bananas." But Bob's younger brother Wally, a teenager at the time who would later manage the Bay Area rock group Sons of Champlin, gave the transparently subversive ads his stamp of approval. Airing on local rock stations, the commercials are still remembered fondly by certain survivors of San Francisco's hippie heyday.

Some of the musicians' peers, however, were appalled at what they considered to be the Airplane's craven grab for advertising money, despite the band members' defense that they actually wore the product they so whimsically endorsed. In a letter to *The Village Voice*, the radical activist Abbie Hoffman groused, "It summarized for me all the doubts I have about the hippie philosophy." He noted that while the band was doing "its thing, over 100 workers in the Levi Strauss plant on the Tennessee-Georgia border are doing their own thing, which consists of being on strike to protest deplorable working conditions." The incident was a reminder that labor relations were less than perfect even at Levi Strauss & Co., where conscience-driven corporate policy—the hard-won integration of its Blackstone, Virginia, manufacturing plant in the early 1960s, for example—was a long-standing cornerstone of the company's self-image. That kind of attention was not what Levi Strauss had in mind, and the company moved swiftly, releasing the Airplane from its contract. The controversy convinced another Bay Area band, Country Joe and the Fish, to back out of an agreement to cut another Levi's commercial in exchange for thirty thousand pairs of factory seconds. The bartered jeans had been earmarked for the Diggers, the guerrilla-theater and community-service group that advocated the "death of money."

The stark contrast between the old-guard LS&CO. braintrust and its new target audience was sometimes difficult to process, as Walter Haas Jr. later admitted to a *New Yorker* reporter. "It bothered me at times," he said. "But, look, jeans are worn by young and old, radical and conservative. The real point is their classlessness."

To some, of course, jeans still lacked class in more ways than one.

SEVEN

★

After the
Gold Rush:
Stylizing Denim

Is it possible to express your individuality in clothing that everyone else is wearing too? Can ready-to-wear fashion exist outside the mainstream? And is shopping a political gesture? These were some of the questions facing the blue jeans business at the dawn of the 1970s, when the great whale of fashion swallowed the prophets of the counterculture whole.

Don't trust anyone over thirty, as those who had yet to reach the milestone were in the habit of reminding one another. Yet the vast majority of those under thirty were settling into their own version of a status quo. In 1971 *The New Yorker*'s Kennedy Fraser set out on foot down Fifth Avenue on a fact-finding mission. She observed that the country's young people had grown nearly as conformist as their elders. "Apart from the men in business suits," she wrote, "the largest group of people I came across was wearing blue jeans. The kids who wear them often look as tediously uniform as their fathers; tie-dyed T-shirts, headbands, and denim are, of course, blind emblems of a way of life quite as much as seersucker jackets and button-down collars."

Two years earlier, on a wet weekend in August 1969, hundreds of thousands of young people descended on upstate New York for the defining event of the generation, the Woodstock Music and Art Fair. They were armored almost unanimously against the rain and mud in standard-issue blue jeans. They "went in a tribe," as members of the tribe like to joke, "and came out a market." Nineteen sixty-nine was a pivotal year in the commodification of the counterculture. In a fifty-dollar-a-month basement rental in Elmira, New York, three high school seniors opened People's Place, a shaggy boutique selling records, rolling papers, and bell-bottom jeans. One of the owners was named Tommy Hilfiger. Across the continent, on Ocean Avenue in San Francisco, a young couple named Donald and Doris Fisher set up shop selling records and a wide selection of Levi's, after Donald found himself having some difficulty shopping for a proper-fitting pair. They called their store Gap, after the "generation gap."

The vogue for stylish jeans had been building for some time. Around 1960 a sportswear salesman named Fred Segal went to his bosses with an idea for hip-hugging jeans. "I knew there was a market for tight pants, and that people used to jump in the water with their Levi's on to get them to shrink to their bodies," says Segal, now in his seventies, the founding father of the exclusive Santa Monica boutiques that bear his name. "They laughed at me, so I quit and opened the store myself."

(© Roger Jackson/Hulton Archives/Getty Images)

Flower power

In the beginning Segal sold men's form-fitting jeans for $7.95, an outrageous sum at the time. By the mid-1960s hairstylist Jay Sebring, an inspiration for Warren Beatty in the movie *Shampoo* (and a victim of the Manson murders in 1969), had made Segal's jeans the staff outfit in his salon, which was adjacent to the original Fred Segal store on Melrose. According to Segal, his business took off when Sebring's celebrity clients began clamoring for his jeans. A conceptual innovator, Segal used a red, white, and blue American flag motif decades before Hilfiger and Ralph Lauren, and he dreamed up a tagline for his shop that spoke the language of the emerging Love Generation—"Look See Feel Be Love All." When administrators of nearby school districts in Melrose and Beverly Hills complained that Segal's sexy jeans were an unwelcome distraction, he won them over by explaining that kids wearing his hip-huggers were just "expressing their creativity," which would make them "psychologically healthier." He designed jeans-style pants not just in denim but in velvet, velour, leather, mohair, and wide-wale corduroy, making him the couturier of choice for Jim Morrison, Elvis Presley, Segal's waterfront neighbor Bobby Darin, and other fashion-conscious performers.

By the end of the decade, other entrepreneurs were catching on. In New York, a college graduate named Bobby Margolis had an idea for a stylish, unisex pair of pleated jeans. Macy's, which still sold bolts of fabric, was out of denim, so he went across the street to Gimbel's, where he bought the store's last ten yards. He found a tailor on Fifty-ninth Street who cut the design. Then, prepared to invest five thousand dollars, he took the Metroliner to Philadelphia, where he found a factory that could produce the first lot of A. Smile jeans.

Margolis wanted to put smiley faces on the snaps, but he couldn't afford the $8,700 the button company required for a minimum first order. By the time A. Smile was off and running, the smiley face was on its way out as a pop icon, he recalls. He and his partner, Stanley "Bucky" Buchthal, a former raincoat salesman who lived with Margolis and two other guys in an apartment in Chelsea, cut deals to stock the jeans with their peers, the frizzy-haired young hustlers running the hippie boutiques that seemed to be popping up in every city. Hilfiger was one of their first customers. They did business with Segal in Los Angeles, Alan Bilzerian in Boston, Izzy Ezrailson at Up Against the Wall in Washington, D.C.

"The department store industry pooh-poohed jeans until they realized the business was slipping from them," says Margolis, who is now chairman and CEO of Cherokee, a $2 billion value-channel jeans and apparel company. "In the early days, the retailers would sell out of the boxes. People would line up. When the cash register rings, everything happens. We were chasing demand for years." A. Smile was an early example of a familiar phenomenon in the jeans business today—the independent upstart who takes on the giants of the industry by bringing some novelty to the classic pattern. The company's pleated design won a prestigious Coty Fashion Critics Award in 1973. Other twists included cargo-style pockets and hot pants, both of which Margolis claims to have introduced in America.

"We were in a lot of innovative areas," he says.

For the counterculture, denim fashion was the product of two distinct philosophies. One was aggressive, the other pacifist. The self-styled radicals and outlaws of the underground took their visual cues from biker culture, while the back-to-nature movement saw in jeans a refutation of the country's increasingly disposable consumer aesthetic.

The Hell's Angels Motorcycle Club formed after World War II in San Bernardino, the southern California freeway town also noted as the birthplace of McDonald's. Comprised of military veterans disillusioned by the pursuit of the American Dream, like "Wino" Willie Forkner, the bikers borrowed their name from the Hell's Angels of the U.S. Army's Eleventh Airborne Division. In heavy boots, leather jackets, and jeans, the Angels had little use for neatness. One part-timer described in Hunter Thompson's *Hell's Angels*—a man who wore a blue suit and drove a white Thunderbird to his "straight" job—rode with the Angels in "boots, greasy Levi's, and a sleeveless denim vest, showing tattoos on both arms. He looked like a middleweight Rocky Marciano and talked the same way."

Long after their jeans were torn and frayed, the bikers still wore them, sometimes layering two threadbare pairs. Like the boys aimlessly "dragging the Main" in Aggie Rodgers's Fresno, the bikers, hot-rodders, and other "greasers" wore the effects of the workshop proudly. Their clothing, wrote one observer, was "filthy and soaked in oil, their hair was lank and dirty. . . . Sometimes they would wear cut-down denim jackets so soiled they were gray instead of blue."

Easy Rider, the 1969 cult film directed by Dennis Hopper, who costarred alongside Peter Fonda and Jack Nicholson, forever linked biker bravado with the social dropouts of the hippie scene. This infatuation with lawlessness fed off the emerging idea of the Hollywood antihero. Morals in the new subversive Westerns were not as well defined as black and white hats, and the dusty attire on the complex characters played by actors such as Paul Newman and Clint Eastwood matched this gray area perfectly. Another handsome rogue, Steve McQueen, first came to prominence wearing denim in *The Magnificent Seven*, John Sturges's 1960 ensemble piece about a mercenary band of gunslingers. Years later McQueen, who crafted his own reputation as a fast-driving, hard-living hellion, wore jeans, a plaid lumberjack shirt, and a bushy beard to a black-tie fund-raiser for the injured actor James Stacy. During the event, organized by Frank Sinatra and some of his Rat Pack, McQueen remained seated as "the cream of the crop" of the entertainment world filed past to shake his hand, according to one guest. Clint Eastwood, John Lennon, and Burt Reynolds all stopped by to express their admiration. "They were all in awe of him," the guest reported. "He was not in awe of anybody."

The devil-may-care look had trickled up from the street, all around the world. During the Prague Spring of 1968, student protesters had celebrated their newfound connection to the global youth movement by growing their hair long and wearing sandals and *Texasskis*—their name for blue jeans. One Mexican student leader recalled that America's cultural impact was especially strong on *norteños*, young Mexicans from the northern states near the border. "We were more interested in American culture than our parents," he told journalist Mark Kurlansky, citing the timeless twin bill of influence, *The Wild One* and *Rebel Without a Cause*. "In the fifties students [in Mexico] wore suits and ties. We wore jeans and indigenous-style shirts."

Militant activists, as documented by Tom Wolfe in *Radical Chic & Mau-Mauing the Flak Catchers* (1970), dressed in a style the author called Revolutionary Street Fighter. Their righteous garb, as Wolfe saw it, was a mix of Cuban freedom fighter and dues-paying American prole. It included "berets and hair down to their shoulders, 1958 Sierra Maestra style, and raggedy field jackets and combat boots and jeans." The jeans, Wolfe took care to note, were "not Levi's or Slim Jims or Farahs or Wranglers or any of those tailored hip-hugging jeans, but jeans of the people, the black Can't Bust 'Em brand, hod-carrier jeans that have an emblem on the back of a hairy gorilla, real funky jeans."

Student activism became sitcom fodder on prime-time Saturday nights beginning in January 1971. On CBS's long-running *All in the Family*, Rob Reiner played Mike Stivic, Archie Bunker's live-in son-in-law. Routinely dressed in blue jeans, sometimes with a matching denim shirt, "the Meathead," as Archie famously taunted him, waged an ongoing battle against Archie's closed-mindedness. Like countless intergenerational tussles of the time, their squabbles covered war, politics, God, and bigotry.

Mike, a combative Polish kid from Queens, might have been a likely candidate for utopian commune living had he grown up in, say, Eureka. Surely he would have been familiar with Charles Reich's *The Greening of America*, in which the Yale professor described what he called the "new consciousness," the students' growing aversion to conformity and materialism. Reich's archetype represented the peaceable, idealistic side of the generation. According to his theory of "conversions," huge numbers of conventional middle-class kids were awakening to an alternative lifestyle. The immediate visual evidence of long hair and informal clothes was especially symbolic. Reich devoted several pages to the new generation's dress habits, beginning with its blue jeans.

The hippie tendency toward "drab" colors—faded blues, greens, browns—was a "deliberate rejection of the neon colors and plastic, artificial look of the affluent society," he wrote. "Earthy and sensual," "rough and tactile," the clothes blended well with their natural surroundings. On a practical level, he suggested, "they don't show dirt, they are good for lying on the ground." By contrast, rigid dress codes were a kind of imprisonment of the self. ("A grease spot on an expensive suit," he wrote, "is a social error.") Because durable clothes were suitable for every conceivable activity—working, dancing, sleeping, sitting on the floor, rolling down a hill—they sent a clear message about the self-assurance of the wearer. "It is the same person doing each of these things, not a set of different masks or dolls, but one many-sided, *whole*, individual," Reich declared. The concept echoed Henry David Thoreau's century-old suspicion about costuming. "Beware of all enterprises that require new clothes," the great zealot of simplification had cautioned. The hippies took it to heart.

The carnality of blue jeans, Reich proposed, contributed to a welcome reacquaintance with the body, which had been draped and neutralized by the traditional men's business suit. "Jeans express the shape of legs, heavy or thin, straight or bowed. . . . Sitting across from a man in a business suit, it is as if he did not have a body at all, just a face and a voice." The author, who apparently adopted some of the customs of his young subjects as his own—he is said to have padded around the Yale campus in bare feet—reserved particular affection for the innovation of bell-bottoms, which "express the body, as jeans do, but they say much more. They give the ankles a special freedom as if to invite dancing right on the street." A touch football game played by people in bell-bottoms "is like a folk dance or a ballet," Reich wrote. "No one can take himself entirely seriously in bell-bottoms."

Borrowed from the traditional maritime custom of wearing trousers widely flared at the ankle—thus easy to roll up—denim bell-bottoms were first used by the United States Navy around 1901. When they were introduced to the commercial market in the late 1960s, they were a drastic reversal from the pegged pants of the mod-ish fashion trends of recently retired seasons. By the early 1970s some manufacturers were producing "elephant" flares, with leg holes at the ankles wide enough to cover the entire foot. On the cover of its February 1971 issue, the men's magazine GQ ran an illustration of a dope-smoking, long-haired Uncle Sam wearing bell-bottoms. "I don't want to fade away," sang the prodigious guitarist Eric Clapton—"God," to his most ardent fans—on his song "Bell Bottom Blues," recorded on the 1970 classic *Layla & Other Assorted Songs* with Derek and the Dominos.

The apparel label Seafarer was one of the first to usher the cut into the marketplace, producing denim bell-bottoms cut to navy specifications. Initially intended as surplus items for navy personnel, the pants caught on quickly among young civilians. Another brand that spun off military surplus was UFO, founded by New Yorkers Leo and Evelyn Brody. Leo Brody built a surplus business beginning in the 1940s, adding his own jeans line two decades later. Originally called An-Ev, the jeans were relaunched as UFO in 1967. Licensed in Europe, the brand was an early trendsetter there. In France, a company called Sisley, named in part for the Impressionist painter, got its start by importing navy bell-bottoms and affixing its own label. Later Sisley styles, featuring elaborate stitching details and priced above forty dollars a pair, were considered by some to be among the first designer jeans.

Michael Cohen, a longtime sales rep for jeans lines ranging from Viceroy and Sasson to Todd Oldham, recalls working in the trendy shops on Brooklyn's King's Highway as a teenager in the late 1960s. After growing up in Lee Riders—"We didn't have Levi's in Brooklyn," he says—he became enamored of the Seafarer flare. "It had no outseam. It was a tubular pant," recalls Cohen, who proudly refers to himself, like many industry veterans, as a "jeaner." "We used to split 'em up the middle so they would break on either side of the shoe. We wore round-toed shoes. You'd take downers, you'd wear a peacoat, a nice big scarf, and a pair of Seafarers, and you'd feel like you were melting into the ground. Cooler than words, man."

Cohen's story is typical of the era. After hitchhiking to San Francisco in 1970, he walked into Changing Faces, one of the hip shops along Grant Street in the old Beat enclave of North Beach. The owner "was getting off the phone with a salesman who'd apparently just gotten busted and had to leave town," recalls Cohen, who was hired on the spot. Later, after studying photography at the San Francisco Art Institute, he returned to the apparel business, opening a showroom along Market Street, where he stayed for years. Today he operates a premium denim showroom in downtown Los Angeles; his daughter runs another one in the same building. "My grandfather was a piece-goods guy, and my great-grandfather was a furrier who came over from Russia," Cohen says. "I just fell into it because I loved fashion."

Across the country many of Cohen's peers were participating in the protest movement. During the Vietnam War the navy struggled with this association with the counterculture, temporarily discontinuing its use of bell-bottoms. The move "ended up being very unpopular with sailors," says Mark Weber, director of education at the Erie Maritime Museum, and the so-called Crackerjack uniform—named for the boy in the sailor suit on the snack food logo—was reinstated. The jaunty look of the Crackerjack, with its neckerchiefs, V-neck jumpers, and sailor's caps, was part of a long tradition of institutional swagger. Navies around the world have historically taken a more lax approach to uniforms than their counterparts in other armed services, Weber says, in part because identifying the enemy is easier at sea than on the battlefield. Three decades after Vietnam, the United States Navy recently discontinued bell-bottoms once again, replacing them with the neater silhouette of a Dickies-style work trouser. The practicality of bellbottoms, notes Weber, no longer applies.

"Nobody is swabbing the deck anymore," he says. "They've got a high-pressure hose for that."

In addition to jeans, peasant blouses, fringe jackets, and other hallmarks of the period, many of the independent shops carried an assortment of drug paraphernalia. "We sold costumes, furs, soapstone pipes, and jeans," says Izzy Ezrailson, who opened his first Up Against the Wall shop in Washington, D.C., in 1969 and now operates a regional chain of twenty-three clothing stores. For hippies, these stores were like alternative chambers of commerce. A newcomer could pull into town and instantly identify his peer group. Ezrailson recalls meeting one jeans designer because "his original partner and mine used to buy hashish off the same guy." The retailers in this underground were, not surprisingly, a colorful lot. "They were a bunch of pirate-type characters," Ezrailson says.

Many of them, such as Barry Perlman and Gene Montesano of Miami's Four Way Street chain, founded in 1972, stayed in the business. After working for Guess and then founding Bongo, a popular juniors' line in the 1980s, Montesano reunited with Perlman. Together they launched Lucky Brand jeans in 1991. Though they sold 85 percent of the business to Liz Claiborne for well over $100 million in 1999, the partners have not strayed far from their roots. Lucky Brand advertising often features nostalgic paisley patterns and a very shaggy photo of the founders' younger selves. "Would you buy jeans from these guys?" the caption reads.

Ezrailson worked for a time as a salesman for apparel manufacturers such as Viceroy. Though he jokes that he is loath to admit it, he credits a rival of the time, Atlanta-based Male jeans, with introducing the super-low-rise look. Male was gimmicky, introducing the "screwdriver," a pair of painters'-style pants that came with an actual screwdriver, and the "drive-in movie" pant, which had a zipper extending from the crotch around to the back. When Viceroy knocked off Male's low-rise look with Peanuts jeans ("Love Those Peanuts"), which had a three-snap front-fly closure, the rise—the length of material between waist and crotch—had to be low enough for the pants to slide over the hips of the wearer without undoing the snaps. (Clearly, the low-rise vogue of the early 2000s was not without precedent.)

The male anatomy was increasingly on display. Anthea Sylbert was the costume designer on Hal Ashby's *Shampoo*, released in 1975 but set against the backdrop of the 1968 presidential election. She says she approached Warren Beatty's character, a high-end hairstylist with a knack for bedding women, "the way you normally would treat the female." George Roundy was the archetypal '60s playboy, a sensualist who dressed for his own pleasure as well as his admirers'. All of his clothes, from tank tops to billowy silk shirts, had to be tactile, Sylbert says. "Even his leather jacket was the softest leather I could find." She replaced the zipper on the jacket with laces, because "the zipper was stiff, and nothing could be stiff." Seeking an exquisite fit for the star's jeans, she ended up sewing them herself, adding a Lee Jeans label for authenticity. "He was the sex object in that film," says the designer, "and I wanted those jeans to be like a second skin. They were aged in a way to show off his thighs. If you wear jeans a great deal and wash them, they fade in places that project from the body, one of which is your penis." The details, she says, paid off. "Warren once gave me a great compliment. He said he found his character in the fitting room."

The conventional apparel industry soon realized it was squandering a considerable opportunity. On the advice of the staff at a New York head shop, a sales agent for the Boston-based manufacturer M. Hoffman convinced the company to produce a line of bell-bottoms with the equivalent of men's back pockets sewn to the front. These besom, or envelope-style, pockets gave the garment a sleek look. The new division of M. Hoffman, Landlubber, became a familiar fixture of the early 1970s. The line attracted attention for its crab logo and its droll ad campaigns, which featured nearly nude men and women in ordinary settings—on a bike, on a ski lift, in class. "Nothing is better than Landlubber clothes," claimed the slogan. Competitors countered with titillating ads of their own. Sedgefield, for instance, put forth a challenge on behalf of the company's low-maintenance "Do-Nothing" denim. "Don't buy jeans on faith," the ads recommended. "Compare your pants off."

Three hundred fifty million pairs of jeans were sold in 1971. Between 1964 and 1975, Levi Strauss & Co.'s sales rose tenfold, from $100 million to $1 billion. No longer just the clothes of cowboys, sharecroppers, and questionable characters, jeans were ubiquitous. Denim had become another kind of uniform, as Kennedy Fraser contended, and there were few better indicators than the rock and pop stars of the day. Crosby, Stills & Nash wore matching new jeans on the rustic cover of their debut album, having renounced the tunics and other dubious stage costumes they'd worn with their previous groups. Carole King's blockbuster *Tapestry* album featured a photo of the former Brill Building songwriter at home in California, sitting barefoot by the window in her faded jeans, soaking up the sun and working on some needlepoint. The cover of Elton John's fourth album, *Madman Across the Water*, featured the title words arranged against a blue fabric backdrop, like patches on the back of a denim jacket. "Blue jean baby, L.A. lady," he sang on the record's opening track, "Tiny Dancer." (John later had one of his biggest hits with "Crocodile Rock," in which the nostalgic singer, having gone outrageously glam, fritters away his nights "dreaming of my Chevy and my old blue jeans.")

The most influential album artwork of the kind, however, appeared not on the front cover but the flip side. The back of Neil Young's *After the Gold Rush*, which came out in November 1970, featured the singer's own backside, clad in a heavily patched pair of jeans and photographed in extreme close-up. The black-and-white picture was taken in a makeshift Philadelphia dressing room by Joel Bernstein, then a seventeen-year-old kid from the suburbs who had recently struck up a friendship with Young's fellow Canadian songwriter, Joni Mitchell. Bernstein, now Young's archivist, recalls that he took some ribbing when he shot the photo: "Billy Talbot, the bassist, said, 'Hey, man, he's taking a picture of your ass.' " But the textures of the patches were mesmerizing, and the photographer instantly recognized that it would make a striking visual image. The jeans were the work of Young's first wife, Susan Acevedo, who sewed on overlapping sections of upholstery fabric—paisleys, floral prints, Native American–style sunbursts, and geometric patterns. According to Bernstein, many people have told him over the

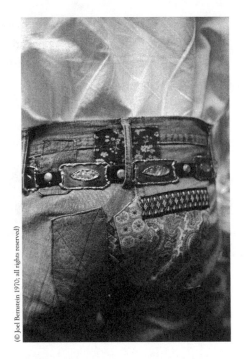

years that the picture was the first time they had seen such de-
tailed artistry on a pair of jeans. "Patches on jeans to that point
were something that people's moms might have sewn on,"
he says.

At the time, Young was living in a redwood house precariously situated on a hillside in Topanga Canyon, a secluded enclave of horse farms and hiking trails in the Santa Monica
Mountains. Topanga was a haven for hippies and outcasts, and
it was an original source of the New West look. Area residents
collected antique patchwork quilts and used animal hides as
rugs and blankets, says Bernstein, who made the exodus to
southern California alongside so many of his peers: "You knew
people who'd gone to Oregon and joined communes. Urban

America in 1969 was something you wanted to get away from."

Bernstein's first West Coast girlfriend, Charlotte Stewart, was once involved with the Doors' Jim Morrison. When friends expressed their admiration for the designs she embroidered on the Lizard King's clothes, Stewart was encouraged to go into business. The Liquid Butterfly sold handcrafted western shirts, jeans, and ponchos. Borrowing from the look of the old frontier and international peasant styles, artisans like Stewart were rubbing out the excesses of the psychedelic era and its "*Alice in Wonderland* panoply of costume," as Bernstein puts it. (Stewart would go on to play Miss Beadle on *Little House on the Prairie*, network television's interpretation of Laura Ingalls Wilder's old-timey pastoral aesthetic.)

The look of the New West soon infiltrated country music. Despite its deep roots in traditional, unaffected American folk song, by the 1960s country was effectively saturated with a splashy show-business mentality, with performers wearing fancy fringed costumes and embellishing their songs with heavy orchestration. The so-called "outlaw country" movement, led by Willie Nelson, Waylon Jennings, and Kris Kristofferson, preferred a stark approach to the music and tilted geographically toward free-wheeling Texas, rather than the recording hub of Nashville. These performers as often as not looked all the way west to California for their cues and attitudes, aligning themselves with rockers such as Young and actors such as Eastwood. "Instead of shining heroes, cowboys were renegades, with long, tangled hair, dirty jeans, and dusty boots," wrote Holly George-Warren and Michelle Freedman in their costume history, *How the West Was Worn*. The style of the modern singing cowboy eventually settled into suburban communities across the country: "By mid-decade, a Western shirt worn with blue jeans and cowboy boots (frequently made by Frye) had become practically a uniform for those attending rock concerts."

Of course, this "natural" look was a conceit like any other. "The biggest pretense was the idea that wearing jeans was not really dressing at all, merely a value-free decision not to be naked," as one critic has written. Rhinestones, pearl snaps, and other adornments could make denim glitter like alligator boots at the Grand Ole Opry. Girlfriends became adept at customizing spangled dude wear for their men, who were more likely to be straddling a chopper or piloting a Volkswagen bus than saddling up a filly.

Publishers issued a wave of books on the fad, among them *The Jeans Book, The Jeans Scene, Make It in Denim,* and *Native Funk & Flash.* The author of *The Jeans Book,* a how-to describing a variety of custom designs, showed off her "autobiographical" pair, with patches including musical notes, a starfish, and a dripping ice cream cone. "My jeans are never finished," she wrote. "I keep adding to them as my life takes its changing course."

Rock 'n' roll groupies such as Pamela des Barres became well known for their flair for alterations. In Connecticut, a fifteen-year-old girl named Pleasant Gehman got her name in a big *Saturday Evening Post* story on the "Blue Jean Revolution" when she started a business called Bottoms Up, "embroidering cuffs, studding seams, and retreading derrieres," as the *Post* reporter observed. (Gehman later became an early member of the Los Angeles punk scene, where jeans reached an altogether different level of permutation.)

Also in Connecticut, in 1973, Wesleyan College mounted

(© Time Life Pictures/Getty Images)

Hitchhiker, Sunset Strip

a show of artistically embellished denim called "Smart Ass Art." The campus newspaper sent a reporter under the alias Wrecks Wreed, who judged the show "cheeky." A few years later Manhattan's Serendipity 3 hosted "Rebirth of the Blues," which featured denim curiosities such as Cher's micro-miniskirt and David Bowie's sequined jockstrap. Articles from the show were donated to the Costume Institute at the Metropolitan Museum of Art, whose curator, Stella Blum, graciously accepted the gift dressed down in a denim jacket. "We have a good collection of peasant clothes," she said at the press preview, "and jeans really are the closest modern equivalent."

Meanwhile Levi Strauss & Co. paid tribute to the ingenuity of its loyal customers, sponsoring its own Denim Art

Contest. Amid the kaleidoscope of stitchery, quiltwork, buttons, and studs were some truly eccentric originals. One entry, a denim shirt, had sleeves layered with white glove fingers to look like angels' wings. Another, a shredded pair of jeans covered in grommets, had one knee patched with the button-fly crotch section of another pair. The fashion designer Rudi Gernreich, inventor of the topless swimsuit, and the photographer Imogen Cunningham were among the judges. The winners' work was exhibited in an eighteen-month tour of American folk art museums, opening with the Museum of Contemporary Crafts in New York. "Denim has transcended *uniform* now," wrote John Burks and Baron Wolman, who published the contest's *Catalogue of Winners*. "For the new Levi's pioneers, it has become a canvas for personal expression."

Wolman, *Rolling Stone*'s first staff photographer, was one of the founders of a short-lived magazine, launched in 1970, about hippie style. It was called *Rags*. For its sixth issue, which featured a maniacally grinning Bethlehem Steel worker on the cover alongside the headline "The Hardhats Are Watching," the staff prepared several features on work clothes, "the universal wardrobe" of stoners and steelworkers alike. In a deadpan spoof on *Consumer Reports*, a team of reporters and photographers compared the durability of nine pairs of blue jeans ranging in price from $7.50 a pair down to $3.79, from top-of-the-line bell-bottom Levi's to Lee Riders, Frisko Jeens, and JCPenney's Ranchcraft. The "*Rags* Road Test, No. 1" subjected the clothing to a number of novel experiments, in which each pair of jeans was frozen, dragged around a parking lot with a brick tied into one leg, and soaked in "a large, outdoor-class urethane polyester bag, commonly known as a 'trash can liner'" for forty-eight hours in a putrid mix of two gallons of

Gallo Paisano Red Country table wine, one pint of Cream of Kentucky bourbon, and three quarts of Regal Select light beer.

The centerpiece of the *Rags* survey was the "Pull Test," an Aquarian version of that antiquarian standby in the blue jeans business—the labeling claim of superior durability featuring an illustration of a tug-of-war. In the Pull Test, each pair of pants was roped between the back bumpers of two late-model Volkswagen Beetles. With one driver setting the emergency brake and the other slowly pulling away, the test conductors documented the length of time it took for the pants to rip, noting whether the tear appeared along the crotch seam or in the fabric itself. Levi's did not fare especially well, lasting just two and a half seconds, bettering only a pair of Maverick Hondos and a sample from Sears.

No longer found predominantly at the bottom of the peasant's laundry pile, jeans were increasingly appearing under glass, and under a microscope. One old pair of Levi's had already been confirmed as an authentic part of American history, entering the collection at the Smithsonian Institution in 1964. In 1971, Levi Strauss & Co. was the recipient of a Coty Award; honors from the American Fashion Critics and Neiman Marcus followed.

"High society swells were wearing them now, just like the Hell's Angels," noted the publishers of the *Denim Art* catalog. As early as 1968 *Vogue* had featured a fourteen-page spread on denim skirts. The following year Yves Saint Laurent became perhaps the first designer to showcase denim on the Paris runway, unveiling a long topcoat with matching boots. England's Princess Anne wore jeans on the morning of her wedding, while having her hair done. Hollywood royalty such as Elizabeth Taylor and Ava Gardner made appearances in denim suits, and Givenchy designed an entire line in denim for his longtime muse, Audrey Hepburn. The Birmingham Ballet League sponsored a Denim and Diamonds reception. One Washington socialite attended an elegant party wearing overalls. "Her purse," reported *Time*, "was a tool kit."

"Jeans represent a rip-off and rage against the establishment," as the zeitgeist thinker Marshall McLuhan told *Newsweek*. In truth, jeans had successfully upholstered the establishment. In January 1977 *The New York Times* reported that Chip Carter, twenty-six-year-old son of the president-elect, planned to wear a denim tuxedo to the Inaugural Ball. An Atlanta formalwear retailer had originally designed a denim tux for Jimmy Carter, showcasing what he called "the most important fabric of the decade." Although Carter, the celebrated peanut farmer, declined to wear the suit, he declared himself one of Levi's best customers, lamenting that his new job would require him to dress more formally. Each successive president since Carter (with the exception of the patrician George Herbert Walker Bush) has made a conspicuous display of wearing blue jeans.

As brand-name recognition for Lee, Levi's, and Wrangler expanded, the country's biggest jeans manufacturers diversified wildly. Each company produced not only western-style shirts and sheepskin-lined jeans jackets but also corduroys, plaid polyester slacks, skirts, dresses, and all sorts of accessories. In the early 1970s Lee introduced the first leisure suit, a double-knit ensemble made of Dacron polyester, with broad collars and flap pockets on the jackets. Today, Lee makes light of its role in conceiving one of the most enduring symbols of 1970s taste. The company was simply "ministering to the whims of a fickle public," it says in an official history, "and should not be blamed for this trend."

Denim was spreading not only into fashion accessories—boots, handbags—but some less fashionable categories as well: umbrellas, notebooks, theater seats, directors' chairs, Christmas ornaments. A *Blue Denim Bible* sold seventy-five thousand copies. Volkswagen produced a limited-edition "Jeans Bug" in 1973, followed by American Motors, which offered a denim interior specially designed for its Gremlin by Levi Strauss & Co. The car featured a Levi's pocket affixed to the side of the driver's bucket seat. The jeans giant, having tenaciously guarded its company trademarks for years, now licensed its logo for products such as clipboards, address books, and aprons.

Some aficionados weren't thrilled. "When you mass-produce," complained the custom-decorating author of *Native Funk & Flash*, "you divide the power of your statement into as many pieces as the items you manufacture." In truth, however, denim production was just getting started.

★

EIGHT

The Diffusion of Glamour: Designers in the Mass Market

It was a godforsaken time. The 1970s had little in the way of good news. Inflation, corruption, crime, poverty, nuclear meltdowns, and international terrorism were relentless worries. Faced with such dour circumstances, ordinary citizens did the only rational thing—they went dancing.

Desperately craving diversion, they found it in the diffusion of glamour. With the arrival of disco, anyone could stake a claim to specialness. The nationwide nightlife carnival that clubs such as New York's Studio 54 begat was an extended stage for exhibitionism. For some, that meant body paint; for others, maybe a see-through wedding dress. But the quickest route to feeling like a star was a status-conscious wardrobe. From the beginning of the decade designers were learning that people would pay a premium for a commonplace item like a pair of blue jeans—provided the garment was stamped on the behind with a fashionable name. "Now everybody can get into Studio 54," the advertisements winked when the velvet-rope nightclub licensed its name for its own line of designer jeans.

The concept of the discotheque did not simply spring up from the ground beneath Studio 54, a former CBS soundstage in midtown Manhattan. It was a cumulative set of ideas reaching back to Berlin cabaret, the groovy futurism of swinging London, and the hedonistic resorts of the international jet set. If exclusive disco was depicted as the antithesis of gritty punk, the other mid-1970s lifestyle concoction, the two had more in common than many participants realized. Each movement in its own way was a reaction to the failed utopianism of the

(© Getty Images)

Fourth of July, 1975

counterculture, which had been quashed time and again by gloomy reality. Both cultures bred a Felliniesque underworld of outlandish alter-egos. Both promoted a kind of unexamined nihilism, a "why not?" that barely bothered to ask why in the first place. Punk was the down-market version of this attitude. Disco was all ambition. Both were dressed in denim.

The Ramones, four unrelated street urchins from the unglamorous neighborhoods of Queens, epitomized punk anti-fashion with the scrappy look they unveiled on the cover of their self-titled 1976 debut album. "It was perfect; classic," said Danny Fields, a music-business operator who was also a veteran of Andy Warhol's Factory scene. "What's better than jeans, a black leather jacket, and a white T-shirt? . . . It's the way you face the street. It's male, it's beautiful, it's tough, and it doesn't date." If Neil Young's wife painstakingly repaired the holes in his jeans with a beautiful patchwork of fabric, stork-like Joey Ramone simply let the holes fester and grow. It was the difference between what suddenly felt like the old guard in rock, who cared so much, and the new, who were way beyond caring.

In England, where an acute economic crisis fed a pervasive punk subculture, the Sex Pistols incubated in Vivienne Westwood's Sex boutique. The shop had gone through previous incarnations as Let It Rock and Too Fast to Live, Too Young to Die, reviving the classic surly-boy look of *Rebel Without a Cause* and Kenneth Anger's 1964 homoerotic biker film *Scorpio Rising*. Punks on both sides of the Atlantic wore battle-ready clothing—big boots, army-surplus coats, ripped T-shirts, and shredded jeans. The stark punk look was especially compelling to the future fashion designer Marc Jacobs, who recalled being entranced at the impressionable age of fifteen by a scenester named Robert Hawkins. With his dramatic hair "colored bright flaming red," Jacobs recalled, Hawkins "was dressed in a small but stretched-out T-shirt and the skinniest black jeans. He looked like a matchstick with its head set on fire. He looked beautiful."

Disco had its own incandescent characters. Some wore tuxes and gowns, others King Tut or Statue of Liberty costumes. Some, like the men who escorted Bianca Jagger and her white horse into Studio 54 on her birthday, wore nothing at all. A generation of onetime political activists, beaten down by the mounting chaos of the outside world, barricaded themselves inside and found the passageway to oblivion through mood-altering substances and all-night dancing. As newspapers scrambled to be the first to report on the latest nocturnal wanderings of Margaret Trudeau, Grace Jones, and fashion icons such as Halston and Yves Saint Laurent, mindless gossip saturated the common discourse. "'Liberation' went mainstream as 'fun,'" wrote Anthony Haden-Guest in *The Last Party: Studio 54, Disco, and the Culture of the Night.*

Just as the work clothes business boomed with the rapid industrialization of the late nineteenth century, apparel companies fell over themselves in the rush to market during the fashion flood of the 1970s. If the public was willing to pay thirty dollars, or forty or fifty, for a pair of jeans, well, there were plenty of opportunists who were perfectly willing to produce them. The Murjani Group, a huge player in the international ready-to-wear market, galvanized the industry when its American division president, Warren Hirsh, set about creating a line of upscale jeans. After designers such as Pierre Cardin turned him down, Hirsh tried another tack. He wanted a name that would connote American royalty. His first choice was

Jackie Onassis, the former first lady. When she declined, Hirsh approached Gloria Vanderbilt.

Vanderbilt, great-great-granddaughter of the nineteenth-century steamship and railroad magnate Cornelius Vanderbilt, was famous for her social status and had been married to the conductor Leopold Stokowski, the film director Sidney Lumet, and the writer Wyatt Cooper. Ever the bon vivant, she was the inspiration for Holly Golightly in her friend Truman Capote's *Breakfast at Tiffany's*. A painter and collage artist, in the late 1960s Vanderbilt became a designer for Hallmark. It was the first venture in a brand-name enterprise that would eventually include cosmetics, luggage, and other signature goods. After showing her artwork on *The Tonight Show*, she was offered a deal to design prints for home furnishings. Her next undertaking, a line of dresses, was short lived.

"Fashion is a will-o'-the-wisp," she wrote in her memoir *It Seemed Important at the Time*, "a gaggle of red balloons held together by strings of gold. . . . Well, as it turns out, my red balloons were being yanked from the strings due to production problems, and my Seventh Avenue dress business was going belly-up." As she recalled, the day the dress venture tanked was the day she met Hirsh. To Vanderbilt's mind, it was a collaboration. "We came up with the idea of branching out into blue jeans that copied almost exactly the expensive ones I had found at Fiorucci's, only priced to 'fly out of the store,' as we say in the rag trade." The heiress accepted the Murjani proposal, and Gloria Vanderbilt jeans were introduced with an ad campaign that ran in select cities during the 1976 Academy Awards. The high-waisted jeans were made to flatten stomachs and "really hug your derriere," assured their namesake.

Despite her acknowledgment that her own jeans were a

direct copy of the Italian designer Elio Fiorucci's, history has bestowed credit for the first designer jean on Gloria Vanderbilt. But if fashion was "a gaggle of red balloons," there were plenty of balloons already in the air. Sasson, Sisley, and the European import Mustang were just a few of the upwardly mobile competitors already established. Veteran sales rep Michael Cohen speculates that Vanderbilt and Calvin Klein have been widely credited with being the "inventors" of designer jeans because of their name recognition, which was already well established by the time those names were stitched to denim. "You couldn't call Paul Guez [of Sasson] or the Nakash brothers [of Jordache] designers then," he says. "Nobody knew who they were."

The transition from the specialty shops of the counterculture to the sudden dominance of designer jeans in the department stores—Macy's, for one, rushed to open a Status Jeans Shop—was indicative of a larger cultural swing. Yet "the boutiques and head shops were still buying the cool things," Cohen says. "There was a strong delineation between them and somebody wearing Calvin Klein and Gloria Vanderbilt, which represented the establishment. That's the stuff that evolved into the department store brands in middle America. The people on the coasts, in the trenches, were not even looking that way."

David Mechaly is one designer who will gladly nominate himself as the originator of designer jeans. "We were the first in the world" to make them, says Mechaly, who created a European sensation with his boutique brand, MacKeen, beginning in 1970. A Frenchman who grew up in Casablanca—his grandfather, a merchant, was the first importer of Levi's in Morocco after World War II—Mechaly stood out there as a kid in his blue jeans and Converse sneakers. In fact, he says, still speaking with a heavy French accent, the way his family dressed him "made a kind of complex" for the boy. After college, he visited New York. It was the late 1960s, and he was excited by the hip jeans the Americans were wearing. He altered a pair of Levi's for himself, lowering the rise and narrowing the thigh. Back in France, his friends all asked for a pair, and he decided to go into production.

He chose the name MacKeen simply for the sound of it, to imply a connection to the dynamic youth culture spanning the Atlantic from the United States to the United Kingdom at the time. (In fact, the jeans featured the Union Jack on the label.) "Like when California started to do wine, they gave French names to their wine," explains Mechaly, who now runs Blue Cult, Sacred Blue, and other premium denim brands with his wife, Caroline Athias. "Let people think it's the real stuff." In France, MacKeen jeans initially sold for about sixty francs a pair, compared with twenty francs for imported Levi's.

Rock and pop promoter Jerry Brandt was an early influence on the discotheque scene with the Electric Circus, an East Village live-music venue of the early 1970s. Always looking for an angle, Brandt later recalled that he was on vacation in Saint-Tropez when he noticed that the locals were all wearing Mechaly's wonderfully flattering jeans. Tracing the jeans to an alley shop near the city's shipping port, he called an investor friend in New York and asked for fifty thousand dollars, which he promptly took to the store. "I put a big bag of cash on the table," Brandt recalled. "I said, 'Pack up the jeans.'"

Upon returning to the States, he and his partners, Jerry and Reva Hart, opened the French Jeans Store on East Sixtieth Street, where they did brisk business for a time selling Mac-Keen jeans for sixty-five dollars apiece. Brandt, who dropped out after the initial investment, told author Anthony Haden-Guest that he "sold the patterns to Calvin Klein, to Jordache, to Sasson, at fifty thousand bucks a pop." By 1976, "French" jeans were a pop phenomenon. In *The Bad News Bears*, the prepubescent pitcher Amanda, played by Tatum O'Neal, agrees to play for Buttermaker (Walter Matthau), the hapless Little League coach, as long as he promises to buy her a pair of French jeans.

When Mechaly opened his own storefront in Los Angeles, he sold a pair to one of the stars of *Charlie's Angels*, though he can't recall which one. Soon all three Angels were wrapping their famously leggy bodies in MacKeen jeans on the set. That kind of celebrity endorsement, so often a crucial piece of blue jeans marketing, has been a particular boon to Mechaly and Athias. When Blue Cult launched in 2000, Gwyneth Paltrow's unsolicited enthusiasm helped the line get off the ground. Later, the label created a line called the Gwyneth.

"I had a handlebar mustache, the long hair. I was a real freak," says Billy Kolber, a hard-partying kid from Philly who remembers giving two Quaaludes to everyone at the door at a promotional party he once threw at a roller-skating rink. "Forget about it," he says with a laugh, declining to go into further detail about the debauchery of the time. "Let's just say that every one of my fantasies came true."

Kolber was selling fitted men's sweaters—"hot as a pistol"— when he hooked up with two brothers from suburban Boston who had made their money in the wig business. The brothers, Michael and Jimmy Shane, "took the wig machines they used and ended up making jeans in the same factories," says Kolber.

Launching in 1972, they called the company Faded Glory. Kolber claims that they were one of the first to push bleached denim. "Kids would go to the beach and run out in the salt water, then sit in the sand and have the sun dry the jean to their bodies." Some used speedboats, he recalls, to break down the color by dragging their new denim clothes in the water. Bleaching achieved a similar effect. Faded Glory was also one of the first boutique jeans companies to promote complementary lines of clothing. "Outfits, tops and bottoms, mix and match," says Kolber, who now oversees a juniors' line called Tyte, working out of a Manhattan showroom. "We were creating a lifestyle."

The three partners worked their connections to gain shelf space in Merry-Go-Round, one of the first hippie-style shops to build a cross-country chain. "We did sixteen million dollars our first year in business, fifty-four million the next," says Kolber. "In 1975, I think we did seventy-eight million. Today that would be like a five-hundred-million-dollar company. It was unbelievable." The Seattle startup Brittania, he claims, borrowed liberally from Faded Glory. "Everything we made, they copied their first year in business. That's how Brittania was born." The difference, he says, was that Brittania went into the department stores—and did $200 million within four years. "We believed in the specialty stores." Today, ironically, the Faded Glory label has been revived as an in-house brand for Wal-Mart.

Cliff Abbey, an Oregonian who grew up riding horses, says he recognized the fashion potential for blue jeans in the early 1960s, while he was still an undergraduate at Oregon State—where jeans had been an undergrad fad as early as the thirties. His entrepreneurial instincts were piqued when Walter Haas visited the campus on an extended tour of school districts, lobbying for dress-code reform. After repping for Van Heusen shirts and A. Smile jeans, Abbey was ready to funnel his experience and instincts into his own venture. At a trade show in San Diego, he couldn't help but overhear the effusive chatter about Brittania, the stylish (and pricey) new jeans line out of Seattle. It was 1973, and fancy jeans were starting to inundate the business. Abbey enlisted the help of a pattern maker, designed a zigzag pocket stitch knocked off from another trendy denim line, France's Sisley, and sat down to come up with a name for his product. After struggling for days, he happened upon a copy of the Rolling Stones' *Sticky Fingers*, with its notorious album cover designed by Andy Warhol—a male crotch shot affixed with a working zipper. "I thought, oh my God! It's an epiphany," recalls Abbey, who has launched several jeans brands over the years and now operates a Napa Valley vineyard with his wife, Clare, granddaughter of Henry and Clare Boothe Luce. "I got on the trademark bandwagon as fast as I could."

In more ways than one, it was a period of anything-goes in the jeans business. Following deep-rooted tradition in the apparel industry, everyone kept a close eye on the other guy's line. What worked for one was sure to work for the next. If Kolber harbored any resentment for his competitors at Brittania, it doesn't show in his voice. Little innovations gave each company a boost: "We had the double zipper. Brittania had the 'waffle' jean. Viceroy had Peanuts." At the time, he says, it took long enough to knock off someone else's idea that the originator could at least get a decent head start. "Today, if I have a hot style, I've got it for thirty seconds," he says.

Faded Glory tried plaids on its back pockets. "We were the first ones to put a label on the inside of the zipper," says Kolber.

"We did all the right things." He left Faded Glory in 1979, clearing out of a fraternal dispute between the Shane brothers. He became president of Bon Jour, the "action" jeans, quickly building the business to $50 million in annual revenue. Then, when Sasson "made me an offer I couldn't refuse," he jumped, catching that brand—makers of one of the earliest designer jeans—on the back end of its arc. By the end of the 1970s, newcomers to the jeans business had to hold on tight for all the giddy ascensions and violent plunges of the proverbial roller coaster. Billy Kolber was just one of many who were addicted to the wild ride.

Cutting an imperial path through all this street-level activity, Calvin Klein emerged as the first bona fide celebrity designer to embrace the blue jeans business. Born in The Bronx and schooled at the Fashion Institute of Technology, Klein was already a name—having won consecutive Coty Awards in 1973, '74, and '75—when he had his first false start with jeans in 1976. A garment-industry consultant named Peter King button-holed the young designer at Studio 54 and convinced him to license his name. The first Calvin Klein jeans appeared that year at Bloomingdale's. At fifty dollars a pair, however, they were not a success, and the designer abandoned the idea after producing one small lot.

Soon after, however, Klein and his financial partner and childhood friend, Barry Schwartz, were persuaded to try again, this time affiliating themselves with the dress manufacturing giant Puritan Fashions. Founded in 1912 in Boston, the company was a powerhouse. In the 1950s Puritan produced an affordable line of Givenchy dresses, priced under fifteen dollars; in the 1960s it was a pioneer in the lucrative merchandising of Beatles fashions. Carl Rosen, son of the company founder, was known throughout the business as "the King." Identifying the Klein brand as a potential Goliath of its own, he cut an unprecedented deal, granting Klein and Schwartz $1 million cash up front, plus another million each year for the duration of the contract. The partners secured one other concession—a one-dollar royalty on each pair of Calvin Klein jeans sold. The deal was announced in June 1977.

For inspiration, Klein looked to the acknowledged classic, Levi's 501s. He cut them apart and studied them. He lowered the rise, then trained his gaze on the posterior, accentuating and drawing attention to it. Puritan manufactured these women's jeans in its seven Texas plants at a cost of $7.50 per pair. Calvin Klein had more publicity than he could have hoped for the week that his jeans were shipped. Not only was the product an instant success, but his daughter, Marci, was briefly kidnapped and held for ransom. The attention, however unfortunate, put the designer's name on the tip of the country's tongue. In one week, the company sold two hundred thousand pairs of pants at thirty-five dollars apiece. Klein, with his daughter returned to safety, decided he wanted to experience the retail mayhem in person. A Saks Fifth Avenue executive advised strongly against it. "They'll tear your clothes off," he said. "It will be like Elvis showing up."

Puritan scrambled to keep up with demand. The company shuttered one division and sold off another to raise the capital for more production. Calvin Kleins for men were introduced in 1979, spiking Puritan sales again. Fellow designers were full of contempt. "Only a pig would put his name on blue jeans," sniffed Halston, who presumably saw more than his share of designer jeans during his nightly visits to Studio 54 and other New York discotheques. The traditional denim industry was equally dismissive. "It's said there are forty million pigeons in the U.S.," said Levi Strauss & Co. spokesman Bud Johns. "Thirty million are birds, and the rest are buying designer jeans." His numbers might have been a little spotty: With fashion figureheads such as Anne Klein and Bill Blass unveiling their own denim, designer jeans were attracting more than just pigeons. Of $10 billion worth of jeans purchased in 1979, $1 billion were designer jeans—a huge slice of a dominant American industry for such an overnight sensation.

Just as Warren Hirsh had envisioned, denim was turning former *shmatte* peddlers and other opportunists into ersatz royalty. The heady realm of designer jeans had a faint whiff of Old World air, with Milan's inventive Fiorucci and Brussels-born Diane von Furstenberg (who married a prince) among the eminent Europeans producing American-style trousers. Ads celebrated the exotic kitsch of the brands, from Sergio Valente's "Uh-oh, Sergio!" to Sasson's "Ooh-la-la, Sasson!" Chic, Bon Jour, Dolce & Gabbana—the quintessential American product was soon soaked in continentalism. "Blue jeans are the most beautiful things since the gondola," the fashion editor Diana Vreeland told *The New York Times* in 1980. It had been a long journey from the mine shafts of the frontier to the canals of Venice.

Jeans for women had been designed for decades, but only in fits and starts. The vast majority of "women's" jeans were simply men's jeans worn by women. "Work clothes looked designed by fiat," fashion critic Anne Hollander has written, "and therefore perfect for expressing antifashion sentiments on the part of both sexes." Although Levi Strauss & Co. had introduced Lady Levi's all the way back in the 1930s, in the early '80s the company was still running ads with sizing charts for

Cher, Studio 54

women, defending the old shrink-to-fit method. But when the marketing department at Lee Jeans determined that 30 to 40 percent of all men's jeans were bought by women, the company resolved to fill the void. Lee's London Rider was "a little fuller fashion jean," says Len Larson, a product development executive who has worked for the company since 1970. "It was still a five-pocket jean, but it was more flattering to a woman's body." Using its huge network of production facilities to keep supplies replenished—a crippling problem for arriviste brands manufactured by contractors—Lee established such a strong reputation among women that several key employees were lured away by competitors such as Bugle Boy, Larson says.

The pursuit of the perfect fit, the obsession of the designer jeans period, was not entirely new. In the 1950s and '60s Wrangler established its niche by offering a slimmer cut and introducing a broken twill, which addressed the old problem of leg twisting, a particular nuisance to cowboys. Later, the drainpipe silhouettes of the mid-1960s and the elephant flares that followed convinced even the most traditional jeans manufacturers of the necessity of heeding trends. What was new was the pronounced emphasis on the female customer.

With the influence of haute couture in steady decline, the ready-to-wear industry was making fashion accessible to ever greater numbers of middle-class women. The country was moving toward a "fast-food" era in apparel marketing, as one magazine put it. And men, no longer constrained by rigid blue-collar and white-collar notions of attire, were becoming newly attuned to the cycles of fashion. These developments had a profound and lasting effect on the look of the American lifestyle. The hierarchy of fashion was collapsing. As elite designers began looking to the street for revitalization, clothing once considered to be merely functional—not just jeans, but athletic wear, the T-shirt, and other casual basics—grew increasingly expressive. Such changing tastes had a democratizing effect. No longer could a person's age, profession, or social standing be determined simply by looking at their clothes. Blue denim blanketed this vast middle ground.

Yet designer jeans were inherently transient. In an industry based on tradition and constancy, they were something startlingly new and different. As John Fiske noted in his 1989 essay, "The Jeaning of America," designer jeans represented leisure, as opposed to the work ethic that had defined jeans for a century. Fashion jeans represented the city, not the country; the East, not the West; culture, not nature. These polarizing qualities made Jordache, Calvin Klein, and other brands the object of some scorn. To the critic Hollander, the term *designer jeans* took on its negative connotations "when it became clear that somebody is designing everything that's made, and constantly modifying the design for profit motives." By 1983, *Advertising Age* was reporting a slackening demand. "There was a guy in school today wearing Calvin Kleins and he was embarrassed," one suburban Chicago high schooler told a reporter. "Guys aren't supposed to get into fashion," a sixteen-year-old boy from the Denver area declared.

Yet although designer jeans are sometimes recalled as a fad that suffered an abrupt demise, the truth is the sophistication of blue jeans has escalated ever since. Ostentation, seemingly at odds with all the old notions of jeans, has become a major part of the blue jeans mystique. "People are going to be prone to spend money," says Joe Ieraci, a former trend forecaster for Burlington who now runs a denim consulting business called the Blue Hound. "The question is, does the name warrant the dollar?"

For better or worse, designer jeans encouraged the consumer to look at premium products not just as an extravagance but an investment. From the perfect-fitting pair of jeans, we now live in a designer era in which the average middle-class family shops for name brands across the entire spectrum of consumer goods. We buy Martha Stewart hampers and shower curtains, Newman's Own popcorn and pasta sauce, George Foreman grills. Every accoutrement of the American lifestyle has been branded, and it started with the brands on our behinds.

NINE

★

"Thought Abhors Tights": Sex in Advertising

C alvin Klein leased an enormous billboard high above Times Square in 1978. The sign once blew smoke rings for Camel cigarettes. Where there was smoke, there would be fire.

For the ad campaign a photographer named Charles Tracy, who worked in-house for Saks Fifth Avenue, took some pictures on spec of a Queens-born model named Patti Hansen wearing a pair of Calvins. Dissatisfied with the results, he suggested the model drink a little vodka to loosen up. "All of a sudden she got on all fours and threw her head back and I said, 'That's it!'" he recalled. "It was like magic was happening in the studio." The tigress shot, enlarged to seven hundred feet, titillated Times Square tourists for four years; Hansen went on to become the wife of Rolling Stones guitarist Keith

Richards. It was a defining moment for Klein's fast-growing marketing machine. "Women Against Pornography said I put her in a submissive position," Klein told *Playboy* in 1984. "I think they're ridiculous, but they're entitled to feel however they choose."

But few propositions in the history of advertising have had the long-term implications of the spare commercials Klein began airing in 1980. Fifteen-year-old Brooke Shields already had plenty of experience as an underage seductress when she came to Calvin Klein. The daughter of a onetime model and a cosmetics executive who were divorced shortly after her birth, at ten she posed for a series of bathtub portraits by photographer Garry Gross, which later became the subject of a lawsuit and a Manhattan gallery show. At twelve she starred in her film breakthrough, playing the title character in Louis Malle's *Pretty Baby*. A period piece set in Storyville, New Orleans's notorious turn-of-the-century red-light district, the movie featured the young actress playing the daughter of a hooker. "I'm not going to grow up to be a prostitute," she assured *People* magazine when it explored the controversy upon the film's release in 1978.

In 1980 Frank Shields, the young actress's father, was in the process of suing Klein and his business partner, Barry Schwartz. Briefly employed as an executive vice president selling Calvin Klein fragrances, Shields had been dismissed. Over lunch with his daughter, Frank Shields told Brooke that he was suing the famous designer. She replied that she already knew— she had just agreed to work for Klein herself, as a model for his blue jeans. Nothing, not even family, could come between her and her Calvins.

The infamous Brooke Shields ads set off a war of words

between Klein and his competitors. "I think it's disgusting," said Dick Gilbert, president of Zena Jeans. "It's getting to be who has the most lascivious commercial." (By 1986, one Zena print ad would feature a model with an exposed nipple.) Paul Guez, cofounder of Sasson, joined the chorus: "You have to be desperate to do this—put sex into jeans commercials," he said.

"I like sex," Klein responded in the press, nonplussed. "What's bad about sex?"

Americans had been asking themselves that question since long before little Nathaniel Hawthorne could identify a scarlet A in his alphabet primer. Sexual suggestion was being used to sell consumer products a century before the designer jeans up-roar, when tobacco companies advertised their cigarettes with underdressed, sometimes completely disrobed women in "clas-sical" poses. Through the years the female form has been de-picted in sales pitches for brewers, flooring companies, and automobile manufacturers, not to mention more obvious fields such as the lingerie business. But it was the dramatic success of designer jeans that pushed innuendo in advertising to the brink of soft porn.

Before Klein, other jeans manufacturers were already emphasizing the body. Italy's Jesus Jeans, unpopular with the Vatican from its inception in 1972, drew the wrath of the Archdiocese of New York three years later with its billboards and posters. The picture showed a pear-shaped behind stuffed into a very skimpy pair of hot pants. "He who loves me, follows me," read the caption. Responding to what *Advertising Age* de-scribed as the archdiocese's "strong-arm tactics," Blooming-dale's canceled its entire spring 1976 order with Jesus Jeans after planning an in-store boutique specially devoted to the line. Other department stores, however, ignored the church and kept selling the popular jeans. (The name continues to provoke. In late 2003, a European licensee reviving the Jesus Jeans brand was denied trademarks in Germany, China, and the United Kingdom, where the patent office called the application "morally offensive.")

Given their emphasis on the body, jeans ads were fast becoming a moral lightning rod. N'Est-Ce Pas? portrayed a topless man and woman wearing its product. Bon Jour was shamed into taking down a few hundred posters from Chicago buses after receiving complaints about a model's partially unzipped jeans. A company executive accused the critics of having "dirty minds." "We are in the business of dressing people," he said, "not undressing them. I think she is zipping the jeans up." Gloria Vanderbilt was questioned for an ad in which a man became sufficiently flustered while admiring a woman's backside to spill his vanilla ice cream cone. Even Wrangler was censored when CBS rejected a commercial featuring a rodeo cowboy patting a female colleague on the ass—to point out the brand label, the company insisted.

By this time, however, much of the public was becoming inured to so much pelvic thrust. One Boston-area network representative noted in 1980 that complaints about late-night jeans ads were "not half as many as we get about female products—sanitary pads and douches."

On television, Jordache was the acknowledged originator of what one *Adweek* writer would later call *"cinéma derrière."* Jordache was founded by three brothers from Tel Aviv, Josef, Ralph, and Avi Nakash. Josef, the oldest, arrived in the United States in 1962 with twenty-five dollars in his pocket, sleeping in subway stations while searching for work in the garment district. By the mid-1970s the brothers were running a Brooklyn storefront together. When the store was looted during a black-out, they invested two hundred thousand dollars of their insurance settlement on a manufacturing operation. With production in Hong Kong barely under way, they cut a television commercial, a mood piece featuring an evidently topless woman riding a horse through the surf, soon joined by a man showing a similar amount of bare flesh. Accompanying the footage was a seductive jingle: "You got the look I want to know better." Though the networks rejected the ad, it ran independently in the New York area, creating an overnight sensation. "Psychologically, it looked like there was a big company behind Jordache," Joe Nakash told *Time* magazine. "The strategy worked." Within a year, the company was doing sales of $75 million.

By 1980, thanks in large part to its unabashed ads, Jordache was up to $120 million. The well-known ad director Jerry Della Femina, for one, was unhappy with the direction his business was headed. He told *Forbes* magazine, "In advertising we say that there was the year of the Lips and the year of the Eyes. Well, 1980 is the year of the Ass." He blamed the trend in sexy ads for "some of the worst advertising ever, ever done. The heavy symbolism is everything that people think is wrong with advertising. It's embarrassing, manipulative, and ugly." Howard Goldstein, a creator of the Jordache ads, scoffed at the criticism. "If that's tacky," he said, "then our society is tacky."

Opinions like Della Femina's were common. But while the Jordache models were unknowns, Brooke Shields was a star—and the public was already well aware that she was an uncomfortably youthful star, thanks to the outcry against *Pretty Baby*. Her Calvin Klein commercials were directed by the late Richard Avedon, the acclaimed portraitist and fashion photographer and the inspiration for the 1957 film *Funny Face*, which starred Fred Astaire as the photographer and Audrey Hepburn as his muse.

Avedon had just taken Shields's picture for *Vogue*, and he chose her for the typically stark Klein shoot. With the model featured against a white "limbo" backdrop, the camera seductively panned her long figure. While inarguably preoccupied with the body, the intention, Avedon said, was to impart a certain classiness on the product. He wanted to wed "the Calvin Klein image to jeans, not a jeans image to Calvin Klein." The commercials' memorable monologues—plainspoken pronouncements of Shields's absolute devotion to her favorite blue jeans—were written by Avedon's assistant Doon Arbus, daughter of the late photographer Diane Arbus. "I've got seven Calvins in my closet, and if they could talk, I'd be ruined," Shields tells the camera in the spot named "Teenager." "Whenever I get some money," she coos in another ad, "I buy Calvins. And if there's any left, I pay the rent." Having earned five hundred thousand dollars for the ads, she couldn't have been scrambling for rent money.

The crowning achievement, however, was the commercial entitled "Feminist II," in which the lanky model poses a question. "You know what comes between me and my Calvins?" she asks. The infamous answer—"Nothing"—was simple, yet riddled with suggestion. Whatever the statement implied (her abstinence? her lack of underwear?), its consequences were clear. Calvin Kleins were being sold with Brooke Shields's body.

Network affiliates in several major markets balked at the

ads, which began airing in mid-1980. Stations in Chicago and Los Angeles backed out. In Boston they were moved into the late-night rotation. Soon thereafter, New York's WNBC banned "Teenager" and "Feminist." Klein was taken to task in the press and by advocacy groups. An observer for *Advertising Age* called the ads "pantiless jailbait," complaining that "there's no more shock value to exploit and no more dignity to lose." But the ads also elevated Klein to the level of superstardom. By January 1982, when the designer appeared on the cover of *People* magazine, romping with Shields on his shoulders, Calvin Klein jeans were the acknowledged front-runners in the highly competitive designer jeans market. (Klein himself estimated that he had more than two dozen rivals at the time.) The magazine reported that he was selling "an incredible" four hundred thousand pairs of jeans each week. His personal income for 1981 was said to be $8.5 million.

After a bit of soul searching, Klein shrugged off the episode. He hired Pat Caddell, a former pollster for ex-president Jimmy Carter, who reported that the complaints were coming from well outside Klein's target audience. "It was mostly an older group who objected," Klein told *People*. "It was someone who couldn't even relate to why anyone wears jeans, which is a very sensual thing to begin with. It just went over the heads of many people."

The rest of the public was fast becoming blasé about sex in advertising. As more parents clung to vestiges of their own youth, the generation gap was eroding. Blue jeans now belonged to the young and the privileged alike, and casualwear had grown ubiquitous among all but the eldest Americans. For the baby boomers, tight jeans were not an entirely new phenomenon. Clingy jeans worn by women, wrote the sociologist Paul Fussell, had been a source of libidinal excitement for both sexes in the 1950s: "The tight seam in front could delineate, even through the thick fabric, the labia majora and similar attractions."

By the late 1970s, however, skintight jeans were no mere underground phenomenon. The *San Francisco Chronicle* began a 1977 article on the subject by quoting an old French saying, *"Il faut suffrir pour être belle"*—"one must suffer to be beautiful." A generation of women "who wouldn't dream of wearing a girdle" were suddenly willing to wedge themselves into blue jeans "as tight as anything Playtex ever produced," wrote the reporter. The look, she noted, signaled a renunciation of flares and bell-bottoms in favor of tapered legs, "the better to fit into their Frye boots." There were potential health hazards, the newspaper warned. Chafing could lead to infections and rashes, as could increased perspiration. "The vagina is particularly vulnerable," wrote the intrepid reporter, "because it is a warm, dark, moist place where bacteria can grow."

A 1978 article in *Playboy* also examined the extent to which women were willing to wedge their lower limbs into restrictive jeans. At Fiorucci and the French Jeans Store in New York, two models posed for a series of pictures as they squeezed into designer jeans. The magazine learned that in special cases, women were obliged to lie down so the staff could help tug the pants on. They used pliers on the zippers, occasionally "shearing away pubic hair in the process." Once zipped, the client typically performed a few sets of deep knee-bends as attendants sprayed her backside with water to help stretch the material. "Your eyes should bulge when you first put these on," one fitter

(© akg-images/Gunter Rubitzsch)

German fashion, 1978

told them. Tight jeans enthusiasts, the writer reported, routinely subjected themselves to "the rearranging of lower-torso internal organs," shortness of breath, and "puckered crotches."

These writers weren't the only ones to notice the irony in the sudden fashion tyranny of jeans, the supposed antifashion. "Thought abhors tights," wrote the Italian semiologist Umberto Eco in his witty essay "Lumbar Thought." Entering middle age, Eco went through a long spell of not wearing jeans while battling a weight problem. After trimming down, he bought himself a new pair. Thus sensually reacquainted with denim, he was surprised to discover that he was more self-conscious of his clothing, and his body, than ever before. "A garment that squeezes the testicles makes a man think differently," he wrote.

For Eco, the clothes had a profound impact on his nature. "I assumed the exterior behavior of one who wears jeans," he wrote. "I assumed a *demeanor*." One who wears jeans is acutely aware of the language of clothes, Eco suggested, and his jeans— far from being the magic liberating factor we often imagine them to be—were in fact a kind of armor. "It's strange that the traditionally most informal and antietiquette garment should be the one that so strongly imposes an etiquette," Eco wrote. Women, he argued, were inherently familiar with this sensation "because all their garments are conceived to impose a demeanor—high heels, girdles, brassieres, pantyhose, tight sweaters." The imposition of jeans was all the more surprising to Eco when he considered the recent history of fashion, in which style after style had been outmoded because they constricted movement: "The Victorian bourgeois was stiff and formal because of stiff collars; the nineteenth-century gentleman was constrained by his tight redingotes, boots, and top hats that didn't allow brusque movements of the head. If Vienna had been on the equator and its bourgeoisie had gone around in Bermuda shorts, would Freud have described the same neurotic symptoms, the same Oedipal triangles?"

"Where Have All the Sissies Gone?" asked a 1978 article in the gay press. Gay men were dressing butch, emulating lumberjacks and construction workers. The "uniform of the moment," the author noted, included "cheap plaid flannel shirts and jeans, or if it is really warm, just overalls, and boots or construction worker's shoes." As invariable as it was, the style was quickly labeled the "clone" look. Gay men saw an image of themselves in the campy dance-pop group the Village People, whose costumed members included a hardhatted construction worker in jeans and a Brandoesque biker in quasi-military leather and denim.

The campy lumberjack style could be traced back to the earliest work of the erotic illustrator Touko Laaksonen, better known as Tom of Finland. His first published drawing, a heroic pair of shirtless, blue-jeaned lumberjacks effortlessly balancing on logs rolling down a river, appeared on the cover of the spring 1957 issue of the American magazine *Physique Pictorial*. The magazine concealed its gay theme from postal inspectors by claiming aspirations to the Greek ideal of body sculpting, much as advertisers depicting nude and near-nude women in "classical" poses had been doing for years. Tom of Finland, who grew up in awe of the mountain men and strapping farmers of his Nordic homeland, first discovered a furtive gay underground in Helsinki as a lieutenant in the army during World

War II. His comic-book-style drawings, which emphasized absurdly muscular men, many of them in uniform—sailors, bikers, cops—had a distinct influence on the international gay subculture, which was until then stereotypically defined as effeminate, "limp wristed."

Like the working-class men they emulated, the clones' style of dress was no style at all. The look wrestled the notion of the macho man away from men who were interested only in women. "The gay rockabilly look and the flat top and the 501s, the sort of James Dean-y kind of thing . . . It was butch and it was cute," recalled one scenester. "It was unisex; boys and girls did it."

The clones' classic blue jeans contrasted sharply with the flamboyance of glam rock and disco. "It is no coincidence that the drag queens and drag kings who express themselves through the artifice of cross-dressing do not use this sincere garment," one critic has written. Yet jeans themselves had emerged as a kind of cross-dressing. Women were free to examine the "masculine" physicality of denim, wrote the sociologist John Fiske, while men were encouraged to explore the more "feminine" role of sexual display. Many argued for less rigid definitions of gender and sexual orientation. John Lennon, who had renounced his pop stardom for the domestic life of raising a child, questioned whether it wasn't time to "destroy the macho ethic." A onetime student of the iconic tough guys of the 1950s, he declared that he no longer wanted "to go through life pretending to be James Dean or Marlon Brando"—posturing male role models who were, ironically, both rumored to be bisexual.

While many of the designer jeans ads reflected an emerging sexual awareness, they weren't always acceptable to the publishing establishment. Studio 54's jeans brand, for instance, was irreparably damaged by its advertising troubles. In 1978 Steve Rubell and Ian Schrager, the impresarios behind the nightclub, cut a licensing deal with Landlubber and ordered an eye-catching ad campaign. The original Studio 54 jeans ads featured two nude models, one male, one female, each bent at the waist and strategically covering themselves, each pulling on a pair of jeans. Both *New York* magazine and *The New York Times* refused to run the artfully provocative pictures. (The *Times* later accepted the ads, after some retouching.) Although the brand's coinciding television ads were nominated for the advertising world's Clio Awards even before they aired, Landlubber was unnerved by the negative publicity and backed out of the television campaign, dooming the venture. "I'm as proud of these ads as of anything I ever did," said veteran advertising man Peter Rogers. "The whole thing was a fiasco." Studio 54 did manage to sell a lot of posters for its jeans.

Guess jeans had much better luck. The four immigrant Marciano brothers, rooted in Morocco and raised in the south of France, left behind a dozen boutiques on the Côte d'Azur to come to America in 1981. Sephardic Jews, they were part of an ethnic lineage that had a long history selling *serge de Nîmes*. Yet their entrée in the business was more happenstance than inheritance; their own father was a rabbi. Upon arriving in the Los Angeles area, the Marcianos sold brother Georges's unique stonewashed jeans, zippered at the ankles, in personal visits to department stores such as Bloomingdale's. They created an instant sensation. By the late 1980s, they were just as famous for their advertising as their clothing. Their high-profile models were known as the "Guess Girls," many of whom, such as

Claudia Schiffer and Anna Nicole Smith, would become celebrities in their own right. (Smith, for instance, was chosen *Playboy*'s "Playmate of the Year" in 1993.) The company, while often aiming for the wholesome appeal of an old-fashioned roll in the hay with its signature farm-girl fashion shoots, was no stranger to bluntness. Its ads were often framed around a model's cavernous cleavage, and the sessions routinely featured references to Marilyn Monroe. As with Calvin Klein and Jordache, the tactic worked. From humble beginnings in 1981, Guess sales leaped to $400 million in 1988, doubling that two years later. Today the company remains one of the industry's most recognized brands.

Unusual for a designer jeans label, Guess claimed that male customers made up half of the company's business. While the bulk of its ads were clearly aimed at the stereotypical man who lusts after curvy blondes, some were more ambiguous. If the photo showed three well-toned young guys limbering up on a beach, shirtless and in Guess jeans, who exactly was the target audience—men or women? Straight or gay?

Designer jeans ads, already recognized as the most risqué genre of commercial advertising, opened a new chapter when they began objectifying the *male* body. Once again, Calvin Klein was out in front of the trend. When the company debuted its jeans for men, Klein again ran afoul of television censors. One ad featured a shirtless model leaning back with the top buttons of his jeans undone. "A body is only a good-looking place to keep your brain warm," ran the slogan of another. By design, they made some viewers uneasy. "A lot of people blinked at the homosexual stuff," said one advertising executive.

Perhaps even more provocative were Guess's first television

ads, which broke still more new ground. Paul Marciano, the youngest of the brothers, had emerged as something of a marketing genius. (The brothers each took distinct roles in the partnership. Georges, who would be bought out in 1993, was the designer, Armand the production and shipping man, and Maurice the financial planner.) The youngest had an idea for the company's television debut, and it was unorthodox to say the least. Influenced by Paul's recollection of the dusty scenes of Monroe and her beloved wild horses in *The Misfits*, an old pickup truck was filmed rumbling down a desert road. In its tracks materialized the Guess logo, an inverted triangle with the company name across the top and a question mark below. They never showed the pants. A mix of "Anne Tyler and Georgia O'Keeffe and Werner Fassbinder all rolled into one," as one writer described it, it was an evocation, not a direct product pitch; pure branding. Already marketed with appeals to the customer's emotions—his or her sense of freedom, individuality, sexiness—the jeans were now almost beside the point. The connotation, not the product itself, was the thing that mattered. The Guess commercial won a Clio Award in 1985.

The company's masterful image-building was a great source of its success. Behind closed doors, however, Guess was also the home of one of the most sensational episodes in blue jeans history, and the subject had nothing to do with sex. The Marcianos' propensity to stir controversy was already clear; they were once sued by the cartoonist Charles Schulz and his *Peanuts* distributor for the unauthorized use of the Snoopy character on T-shirts. Long before they began to advertise, the Marcianos found themselves strapped for cash and scrambling to keep up with demand. On the advice of a deal promoter named Hardof

Wolf, they accepted $4.7 million, about half their annual sales at the time, from Jordache's Nakash brothers in exchange for half the company stock. The deal was cut in summer 1983.

By the following year, Guess was a $150 million block-buster, the toast of the apparel business. "Anything from Guess is just blowing out of the store," reported a Macy's spokes-person. But the Marcianos and the Nakashes were in no mood to toast each other. Instead, they were filing lawsuits. The Marcianos alleged that the Nakashes were abusing their insid-ers' privilege by knocking off Guess designs at their Hong Kong production plants. The Nakashes countered by accusing the Marcianos of demanding kickbacks from contractors, skimming profits to fund their own lavish lifestyles, and cor-rupting the IRS. Featuring boardroom tussles and ancestral grudges, the sordid case dragged on through the decade, with extensive coverage in *Forbes*, *Time*, and *Newsweek*. The *Los Angeles Times* headlined one of its reports "Dungarees and Drag-ons." "It's like a blood feud," a source told the paper. "These guys on both sides are so intense that it's become a deadly fight."

Finally, in May 1990, the two sides reached an agreement. The Nakashes returned their Guess stock, while the Marcianos granted their former partners two thirds of the dividends that had languished in escrow, approximately $66 million. "The fighting would have gone on forever if we didn't settle," Paul Marciano later told the journalist who wrote a book on the rivalry. In *Skin Tight: The Bizarre Story of Guess v. Jordache*, Christopher Byron noted that in the ancient court of Neb-uchadnezzar, two claimants to the same garment were ordered to settle the matter by grappling over it. The award went to whoever could grip the most cloth in his hands. To many observers, the ugly feud was the clear inspiration for another memorable Guess commercial. This one, shot in grainy black and white, followed a starlet and her escort as they frantically tried to escape reporters and paparazzi stalking them all over swinging London. It was a paranoid fantasy, one that seemed to symbolize the cutthroat business the jeans industry had become.

Symbolically, Klein's relationship with Brooke Shields was at its end. Heading into her junior year at Princeton in the summer of 1985, Shields unveiled her own short-lived denim line, called Brookes. Something had in fact come between her and her Calvins. "I have Brookes now," she said. "Why should I wear anything else?"

By then disco was a relic of the previous decade. The sharp angles and synthetic colors of new wave had replaced it as the pop trend of the hour, but there was also a burgeoning movement back to basic, old-fashioned blue jeans. Within a few years, Calvin Klein was sufficiently anxious about its market share to produce an advertising supplement guaranteed to generate the same kind of outrage that had attended the Shields campaign. A freestanding 116-page publication that was packaged as an "outsert" with the October 1991 issue of *Vanity Fair*, the supplement featured a series of Bruce Weber photos depicting a day in the life of a fictitious rock band. Male and female bodies in various stages of undress were everywhere, including, most notoriously, one male model in the shower, running a wet pair of jeans between his legs. The press was predictably scandalized. *Time* described the supplement as "a jumbled pastiche of naked bodies, black leather jackets, Harleys, and tattoos, with cameo roles by a crying baby and a urinal. . . . Oh yes, there are even a few incidental photographs of jeans, most of which are being wrestled off taut bodies or used as wet loincloths."

Despite the handwringing, and the fact that the million-dollar campaign brought no apparent sales boost to the company, Klein had once again set a precedent. Months later, Request Jeans paid for a racy forty-eight-page booklet to be distributed with *Details* magazine. An *Adweek* commentator expressed her contempt: "Add cleavage, a vaguely threatening storyline suggesting imminent violence, bi- and/or homosexuality, and somebody relieving himself, and voilà, you have yourself an ad campaign."

For the back-to-school season in 1995, Calvin Klein produced a series of television ads featuring young men and women in a wood-paneled basement setting. Off-camera, a dirty old man encourages the models to undress. Shot to look like a grainy home movie, the series struck many viewers as disturbingly realistic. In the ensuing uproar the company pulled the ads, and Klein bought a full page in *The New York Times* to apologize. This time, however, the venture paid off. Sales of CK jeans for the year jumped to $462 million.

While that's a big number, it's a fraction of the multiple billions that the American porn industry reaps annually. What was once a tacit understanding in the world of advertising was made plain on our billboards and airwaves by the jeans industry. Sex undoubtedly sells; sexual arousal and the impulse to buy are inextricably linked. Using sex to sell a commodity, wrote University of Alabama professor Tom Reichert in *The Erotic History of Advertising*, is often "a self-fulfilling prophecy." When young people began wearing blue jeans, they discovered something about their own sexuality. When advertisers began exploiting the connotation, they transferred human emotion onto the product itself. "The jeans become sexy," wrote Reichert, "because they are advertised in a sexual manner." It's as if the industry is chasing its own tail.

TEN

★

Hand-me-downs:
Vintage and
Reproduction

Bobby Garnett has had a storefront here since a homeless shelter was the most conspicuous landmark on the block. Now there are new condominiums, artists' galleries, and loft-style office spaces.

In this mixed-use enclave of Boston's South End, a stone's throw from the Southeast Expressway and the city's never-ending Big Dig tunnel project, the shabby chic of Bobby's shop gives it the feel of an old gentlemen's club. Piled high with vintage American and English clothing—from classic denim workwear to reindeer sweaters and straw hats—it's the kind of place where Ralph Lauren might find some inspiration.

In fact, Lauren is one of many fashion designers, collectors, and dealers who consider Bobby Garnett—better known as

Bobby from Boston—to be a founding father of the contemporary resale business and an invaluable resource in the perennial recycling of classic styles. Garnett has been in the business for more than three decades, first selling his "experienced" clothing, as he likes to call it, to hippie students with a flair for creative dress. In the 1980s, when denim collectibles became big business in Japan, certain savvy dealers beat a well-worn path from Tokyo to Bobby's lair. These days, Bobby from Boston does a lot of his business with Hollywood costume designers. Most recently, he sold thousands of dollars of period clothing to the costumer from the Sean Penn remake of *All the King's Men*.

Set on a refurbished but largely untrafficked courtyard, the Bobby from Boston shop is usually as calm and contemplative as its heavy wood furnishings and comfortable chairs suggest. A magnificent old pool table in the center of the room is piled high with incoming merchandise. The only concession to the present day is the sound system, constantly tuned to a high-energy R&B station. In the back, several big brown boxes are being packed for shipping. They are stuffed with Levi's cutoff shorts, which Lauren's company buys in bulk to stock in its summer-resort stores on Long Island and Martha's Vineyard.

At fifty-five, Garnett still dresses like a college student, wearing faded Levi's, white sneakers, and a gray hooded sweatshirt with a Ralph Lauren Rugby cap pulled down over his brow. He was one of the first of his generation, coming of age in the 1960s, to realize the revenue potential in recycled denim. From the beginning he had a collector's nose for it. Acting on a tip from a friend in the south of France, he once bought a hundred pairs of red-line Levi's—the highly collectible "selvage" denim, made on old, narrow looms—for a dollar a pair. He dug through seventy hundred-pound bales of jeans jackets in a rag yard in Worcester, uncovering many prewar gems. When a regional discount chain accepted a huge shipment of "deadstock" work clothes, unsold goods from old stores going out of business, he drove nine hundred miles in two days, snatching up almost all of it. "I was freakin'!" he says in his heavy townie accent, laughing.

Though the vintage market has waned considerably since its heyday in the late 1980s and early '90s, Garnett still buys "big E" Levi's, those dating before 1971, when the company changed the lettering on its red tab from upper- to lowercase. He still travels extensively in search of old overalls, barn and cowboy jackets, and other pieces made by the Big Three of blue jeans, as well as onetime staple brands such as Big Smith and Sears's Hercules label. His pride and joy, however, is his collection of DubbleWare, denim work clothes made in Boston dating to the years between the wars. The DubbleWare brand was produced by M. Hoffman, the longtime Massachusetts apparel maker.

"The best part is buying the stuff," says Garnett, carefully laying out a pair of hickory-stripe railroad overalls and patting it down. "You can't keep it all, so you have to sell some of it."

"He could have capitalized a lot more," says Glenn Mariconda, a former Bobby from Boston employee who is now a designer for Lauren's vintage-inspired Double RL line. "He likes to keep it manageable. He could easily open a showroom in New York, but he has a different kind of motivation."

The wear and tear that was once considered beautiful only to fanatical denim collectors has long since set a standard for fashionable jeans design. The artlessness of the early workwear brands, their utilitarian nature and utter indifference to the world of fashion, is precisely—and perversely—what idealizes them to designers today. They conjure an image (whatever its accuracy) of a simpler time in America, a time of real industry and resolve.

Collector Jeff Spielberg recently bought domestic and international rights to the old Sweet-Orr brand, once one of the giants of the industry, for a hefty sum. After World War I Sweet-Orr's South Africa division merged with Liverpool-based Lybro, Ltd., incorporating in 1930 as Workwear, Ltd. Concurrent business in South America, Scandinavia, Cuba, and elsewhere established Sweet-Orr as an intercontinental ambassador of American workwear decades before the marketplace went global.

After closing its long-standing plant in Wappingers Falls, New York, and moving its base of operations to Dawsonville, Georgia, in the late 1950s, Sweet-Orr went into irreversible decline, finally grinding to a halt in 1999 after bankruptcy proceedings. "It's an unheralded company," says Spielberg, a Santa Monica entrepreneur and onetime head writer for the quiz show *Jeopardy!*. "They were so big, but they've been out of the public realm the last thirty or forty years."

Scarcely remembered today, in its heyday Sweet-Orr was a widely admired brand—almost certainly better known than Levi's, which were still confined in the 1920s and '30s to the West. Spielberg says the company was, among other things, known for supplying the Boy Scouts and producing the world's best corduroy. And its denim earned the trust of generations of builders and assembly workers. If Levi's came to represent the loner mythos of the American West, Sweet-Orr represented huge teams of construction workers building Manhattan skyscrapers. Its denim work outfits, says Spielberg, are likely the ones pictured in Men At Work, Lewis Hine's classic 1932 photographic study of the Machine Age. Hine's iconic pictures included many documenting the construction of the Empire State Building—hoisters, derrick men, riveters, welders, and "sky boys," often shirtless or in sleeveless T-shirts, and denim.

The best vintage pieces are a kind of folk art, says Larry McKaughan, a Seattle dealer specializing in hundred-year-old denim. (He's the guy who sold the fifteen-hundred-dollar scrap to the partners behind the revived Stronghold brand.) In business almost twenty years, McKaughan has gone through phases scouting and selling niche collectibles such as vintage bomber jackets. But prewar workwear is his obsession—the more obscure the brand, the better. He named his Seattle showroom Heller's Café, after his maternal grandfather's gathering place in Fredonia, North Dakota. McKaughan grew up in Sacramento, where his dad was a machinist for a steel company.

"They closed the plant a year before he got his retirement," he says. The childhood image of his father "coming home tired and dirty" has stayed with him, and he knows it's the reason he feels especially connected to old jeans and overalls. "It's certainly an emotional expression for me," he says.

The irony of his business—searching for clothes his stalwart father might have worn and selling them to fashion designers and obsessive, often eccentric collectors—is not lost on McKaughan. "I hope never to do a hard day's work in my life," he readily admits. "I don't want to do what my father did."

Clothing in America has become virtually disposable. Ever-changing seasonal fashions, combined with the consumer aspirations of the vast middle class, the rise of ready-to-wear and the department store, and the fashion industry's bottomless supply in every price range, have made it so. Signs of fraying, fading, discoloring, are all now, as Charles Reich noted, "social errors." No one darns their socks anymore. We throw them out.

Denim is the exception. We wear out our clothes, but we like our jeans worn in. The more it ages, the more denim becomes personalized.

Part of that process can be attributed to the partnership between the fabric and its companion dye, indigo. Unlike other dyes, indigo's unique properties make it compatible with all textiles: the oversized indigo molecule does not penetrate the fiber but clings to the surface, in layers.

With denim, this relationship results in a gradual change in color as it ages. When the dye is abraded, the layers chip away from the fabric, bit by bit. "You dye denim by building up layers of color," explains Skip Gordon, a dyeing and finishing expert for Cotton Inc. "It's like taking a marble, dipping it in wax, letting it cool." Repeat this process several times, he says, and "next thing, you've got a big ol' marble." Shades of denim are indicated by the number of dips and the strength of the dye vat. Faded jeans result from the gradual abrasion of those layers.

For the past century, almost all indigo used in denim manufacturing has been man-made. Synthetic indigo was first produced for commercial use in 1897, when the German chemical company BASF (Badische Anilin und Soda Fabrik) introduced the dye based on the findings of the Berlin chemist Adolf von Baeyer. Baeyer, who would be awarded the Nobel Prize for Chemistry in 1905, first synthesized indigo at the University of Munich in 1880. BASF called its new product "Indigo Pure."

Other European companies, including dyeworks in France and Switzerland, began producing their own synthetic indigo, and natural indigo soon entered its final, irreversible decline on the international market. By 1900, one BASF executive was calling for India to scrap its indigo production in favor of food crops. Although prohibitively difficult to extract—one hundred pounds of the plant yielded just four ounces of indigotin—natural indigo still did not go without a fight. A debate arose about the relative properties of the two indigos, with some purists arguing that the impurities of organic indigo (such as indigorubin, or "indigo red") gave the color a uniqueness unmatched by its artificial counterpart. But BASF added malodorants to ease the nostalgia of longtime dyers who had grown accustomed to indigo's awful smell, further pushing the plant toward commercial obsolescence.

There was a reprieve during World War I, when American denim manufacturers briefly returned to natural indigo in order to avoid doing business with German BASF. But the United States also greatly improved its own capacity to produce synthetic indigo during the war—while there were just five U.S. factories producing aniline dyes in 1914, two years later there were as many as eighty. Germany responded by forming a merger of its most prominent chemical companies, including BASF, Bayer, Agfa, and Hoechst, anticipating world domination of the market after the war. Though the consolidated operation, IG Farben, was dissolved by the Allies, German industry nevertheless continued to produce the bulk of the world's synthetic indigo, as it has to the present day.

While the development of synthetic indigo was "a grand achievement," as a British government report allowed around the time of the dye's commercial introduction, it was also lamented as "a national calamity" for growers. One of the last substantial markets for natural indigo was closed off in the mid-twentieth century, when China's Mao Zedong banned the dye's importation for use in the famous "Mao suit." Today, only a handful of countries, led by India and China, continue to produce natural indigo in notable quantities, primarily selling to the insistent manufacturing purists who make up a tiny fraction of the global denim market.

There have been strong signs in recent years that China is producing enough synthetic indigo to undercut the market

Indigo dye pits, Kano, Nigeria

and challenge the Germans. In 1997, America's lone surviving manufacturer of indigo, an upstate New York company called Buffalo Color, was still producing the second largest output of synthetic indigo in the world—3,500 tons to BASF's 7,000 tons. Of an estimated global total of 20,000 tons, Bann of Brazil was the only other major player, producing 2,000 tons; the remainder was largely divided among smaller companies in Japan and China. With so few manufacturers, prices for this relatively inexpensive product remained artificially high. Just two years later, however, Buffalo Color was reeling from a sudden influx of cheap synthetic indigo from China. The ailing company filed an antidumping petition with the United States International Trade Commission, which recommended tariffs on China.

In response, China abruptly cut off its indigo supply to America in the third quarter of 2002. "Somebody shut that faucet off," said Lawrence Kaminski, president of Buffalo Color. Almost immediately, another crippling influx of underpriced synthetic indigo surged into the United States, this time from South Korea. Convinced that South Korea had not suddenly become a major producer of indigo, Kaminski suspected China of rerouting its export. By 2004, Buffalo Color was in Chapter 11 bankruptcy protection, barely clinging to life. At one time a robust employer of three thousand, the company had been stripped to a skeleton crew of twenty-four. Its indigo business, once 80 percent of its total output, went dormant.

The saga of Buffalo Color is a cautionary tale for the denim industry in the era of global trade. Virtually all of the synthetic indigo used in making blue jeans is now imported. Over the last twenty years or so, the domestic textile industry has conducted a mass exodus overseas, and "American" clothing companies now move their cutting and sewing operations wherever the cheapest labor can be found. With increasingly rare exceptions, every aspect of the manufacture of the quintessential American product is now accomplished outside the United States. It's enough to make even the most hardened free-market supporter feel a little blue.

For decades, denim mills searched for ways to reduce the natural wear and tear on their product. Customers, they assumed, wanted to keep their purchases looking like new. Many American textile manufacturers were first introduced to open-end spinning machinery at the 1967 International Textile Machinery Show in Basel, Switzerland. Open-end spinning combines three of the early stages of traditional cotton processing, known as ring spinning, into one, rendering the process faster and cheaper. The technique produces a "cleaner" yarn; the designer jeans of the late 1970s were typical examples of open-end denim.

Greensboro's Cone Mills, a longtime industry leader, eventually adopted air jet looms, replacing the traditional mechanics of shuttle looms with a process that blows the weft, or filling, yarn across the width of the fabric. And in the 1970s and '80s the company converted to considerably wider looms, gradually expanding from twenty-eight to thirty-six, forty-five, and finally sixty-six inches. That change spelled the end of "selvage" denim from Cone, in which the woven edge of the cloth, parallel to the warp yarn, is usually visible on the inside of the leg seams. For decades each major company buying denim from Cone could be identified by the colored thread along the selvage—white or green for Lee, gold for Wrangler, red for Levi's.

But jeans makers, inspired by the burgeoning collectibles market, soon grew nostalgic for the relative imperfections of the ring-spun process. Ring-spun denim is more durable, has a softer hand, and wears more dramatically than open-end denim, and its flaws are now treasured by designers seeking distinguishing traits in a highly competitive business that revolves around a basic, universal product. Designers and customers now want "whiskers" in their jeans; they want abrasion and aggressive fading; they want slubs.

For a time the demand for imperfection bewildered many industry veterans. "We spent most of our careers trying to make it smooth," says Ralph Tharpe, a longtime Cone front-office man who is currently director of product development. "And now we've spent another hundred thousand dollars to add an attachment to try to make it look screwed up."

Today, whole stretches of Cone's vast White Oak facility, where raw cotton is cleaned, spun, dyed, and woven into denim, are monitored by computer. You can walk the equivalent of two or three football fields, amid the ceaseless din of the machinery, before reaching another human being. From 2,900 employees in 1977, the workforce has been pared down to about 1,200.

Having moved much of its denim production to a plant in Coahuila, Mexico, to compete with the lower labor costs of Asian mills, Cone filed for bankruptcy protection in September 2003. The following spring the company announced it had been acquired by Wilbur L. Ross, the financier best known for his investments in another troubled American sector, the steel industry. Ross had already purchased Burlington Industries, Cone's major Greensboro competitor, out of its bankruptcy. He consolidated the former rivals, naming the Cone-Burlington merger the International Textile Group.

Cone veterans, while bracing themselves for a long, hard struggle with their increasingly tough overseas competition, note that they remain one of the world's largest producers of denim. "We're making as much as the whole Japanese market is making," says Tharpe.

Scott Morrison, founder of the premium brand Earnest Sewn and the onetime conceptualist behind Paper Denim & Cloth, describes the appreciation of worn, flawed denim in terms of the Japanese notion of *wabi-sabi*, in which the natural decay of the physical world is not to be lamented but admired. Rooted in ancient Japanese poetry, the tea ritual, and Zen Buddhism, *wabi-sabi* finds serenity in "the beauty of things as they are, at this very moment," as one student of the philosophy has written. It is the patina on a copper roof, the weathered finish on an old wooden bench, or the weather-stained walls that Leonardo da Vinci urged his students to study. A beautifully weathered pair of blue jeans, says Morrison, is the epitome of *wabi-sabi*.

It's such an appealing concept that designers have become impatient with the natural aging process. They now collapse time by degrading new denim with increasingly scientific techniques. In 2001, Levi Strauss & Co. historian Lynn Downey won a furious last-minute bidding war on the auction Web site eBay for the oldest known pair of Levi's in existence, a miner's pair of buckle-back waist overalls produced sometime in the 1880s. The price: $46,532. (The bid eclipsed the company's previous record, $25,000 paid in 1998 to the owners of the New York vintage store What Comes Around Goes Around for a pair of 201s traced to 1893.) Nicknamed "Nevada" after the state in which they were discovered, dug from a garbage dump in an old mining town, the $46,000 jeans were meticulously replicated by Bart Sights of Sights Denim Systems in Henderson, Kentucky, a leader in vintage denim effects. A limited run sold for four hundred dollars a pair. In 2003, Sights produced another replica for Levi's, this one based on a pair from 1917. Heavily patched on the knees and thighs, the pants were painstakingly reproduced in a fifty-two-step process and sold as the "Celebration" jean. Honoring Levi Strauss & Co.'s one hundred fiftieth anniversary and the one hundred thirtieth anniversary of the company's rivet patent, the edition sold for $501 apiece.

From chlorine and enzymes to golf balls, tire treads, and lasers, blue jeans have been treated with a laundry list of aids, abrasives, and additives. The first step was to soften the denim as it softens naturally. François Girbaud has sometimes been credited as the first to experiment with washes, in the 1960s. He entered the clothing business in mid-decade, working without pay at Western House, the cowboy-themed boutique first hatched at the Paris Flea Market in the late 1950s by enthusiasts Madeleine and Maurice Szpira, who sold westernwear imports to nouvelle vague French youth smitten with American culture. When Girbaud and his wife, Marithe, began designing on their own, they washed their jeans four or five times, then sandpapered the product to add texture.

Around the same time Japan's biggest jeans makers were also prewashing, including Big John, the country's traditional workwear brand. Japanese prewashing was a direct result of consumer demand. Aficionados were accustomed to the soft hand of the used jeans left behind by American GIs from World War II. The popularity of that resale business inspired the rise of Japan's own blue jeans industry in the early 1960s.

Lee Jeans was the first major American manufacturer to institute prewashing—"wet process"—around 1973. Prior to that, most garments in the industry were "what we called 'raw' denim," says Len Larson, who started at the company as a pattern designer in 1970. When a vice president of merchandising suggested softening the denim, Lee hired a local Kansas City laundry service to put some jeans through the cycle. "Retailers absolutely loved it," says Larson.

By the early 1970s, some boutique labels were toying with novel finishes. Adriano Goldschmied, often called "the Godfather of Denim" (or "the Goldfinger of Indigo") for his work with Diesel, Replay, Gap's 1969, his own AG label, and dozens of other lines, was a ski bum with hopes of going pro when he opened his first shop in the Italian Alps resort town of Cortina d'Ampezzo in 1972. "I was looking for an excuse to tell my mother I was busy and doing something good," he recalls with a laugh. A friend offered the use of a storefront, and Goldschmied, despite having no experience, began making clothes. To his bewilderment, his jeans-style trousers in fancy fabrics— brocades, velvets—were an instant success.

Within a year or so, he began working with denim, which was, he says, "at the time a little boring—nobody was washing. We started bleaching the jeans, making big spots, creating a kind of fantasy. We had a big bowl in the garden with a fire, and we were making the bleach very hot, very aggressive to the jean." His little black dog, always underfoot, was usually bleached as well.

Goldschmied wasn't alone. Cone Mills, for instance, had a brief success in 1969 selling its flukey "Pinto Wash" denim with bleach streaks—actually a big batch of denim that had been damaged in a flood. But that was a salvage operation. The industry still expended most of its energy on changing silhouettes (flaring or tapering the legs, as the seasonal trend dictated), and pocket stitching. By the mid-1970s, however, the fast-growing ranks of jeans makers were scrambling for ways to distinguish themselves.

Just as John Wayne tied his jeans in a bundle and sank them in the ocean, jeans lovers had long used a variety of primitive tricks to break in a new pair. The famous Hollywood westernwear designer Nudie Cohen—the real "Rhinestone Cowboy," born in 1902 in Kiev—may have been the first to do professional stonewashing. Cliff Abbey is one advocate of the theory. Peddling his Sticky Fingers jeans around 1973, Abbey dropped in on the tailor in his Lankershim Boulevard store. "He took me in the back of the store and said, 'You have to see this,'" Abbey recalls. "He had a gigantic washing machine with pumice stones in it." Whenever Nudie was called upon to clothe an "authentic" cowboy for the movies, he would run the actor's jeans through the stonewash cycle. With the tailor's blessing, Abbey began putting his own jeans through the process. Retailers, he says, were slow to appreciate the results: "In those days, people either rinsed the jeans or bleached them, and that was it. The problem with retailers was they thought kids were not going to pay the money for a beat-up pair of jeans."

Although stonewashing caught on soon enough, the

technique took a circuitous route to the mainstream. The route, oddly enough, wound through the lawn and garden supply business. After graduating from Iowa State, where he set records as a championship wrestler, Mark Emalfarb joined his father in the family's Chicago-area firm in the late 1970s. They furnished stone for landscapers, decorative garden rocks with names that sound like gourmet ice cream—Alpine White, Coral Crush, Arctic Rainbow, Western Sunrise. With shipping by train growing increasingly cost prohibitive, the young businessman began looking into the possibility of importing large quantities from overseas.

He started scouting for volcanic rock by picking locations, including Italy, Greece, the Canary Islands, and the Azores, out of a Time-Life volume on volcanoes. On one of his missions Emalfarb visited Iceland, where he learned that local quarries had just started supplying pumice stone to apparel manufacturers in England. Lee Cooper, the British workwear company founded in 1908, had been a consistent early adopter of styles and techniques, selling bell-bottom "hipsters" in 1963 and, briefly, a line of prefaded denim in 1965, as well as miniskirts and hot pants in the early '70s. The company was among the first major producers to use pumice stone to soften denim. (The Japanese company Edwin claims it introduced stonewashing in 1975, though it kept the process a secret until 1979.)

Emalfarb hadn't heard of stonewashing, and he sensed an opportunity. He began importing Icelandic pumice and selling it to denim companies. One of his first customers was Girbaud; another was Guess. He found industrial laundries in Virginia, Houston, Los Angeles, and elsewhere that were willing to learn the technique, and he began demonstrating it for potential customers.

"I remember running a trial in the basement of Levi's, showing them how to wash jeans, coming up with new fashions and finishes," he says. He named his new company Dyadic. His father, Seymour, the son of a Russian-Ukrainian immigrant, was baffled. "My father basically thought I had rocks in my head," the son recalls with a laugh.

Collaborating with Levi Strauss & Co., Lee, Wrangler, and Guess, Emalfarb was soon trafficking three hundred ocean containers of lava rock each month. Customers quickly became accustomed to finding rocks in the pockets of their new jeans, and they wanted them "softer, softer, softer," he says, "kind of like toilet paper." Designer jeans, with their deep dyes and sharp creases, were on the way out. Stonewashing was such a success by the mid-1980s—virtually all of Guess's product, for instance, was heavily stonewashed—that it naturally led to further experimentation. On one trip to Europe Emalfarb learned about a new chemical method, and he began giving lessons in how to soak pumice in chlorine bleach or potassium permanganate ("purple salt"). The jeans were then tumbled with the stones in heatless dryers. The technique, pioneered by the Italian brand Rifle, was called acid wash. The end result of "snapping off the blue," as Emalfarb describes it, created a marbling of deep indigo and white, a look which inspired such names for the fad as "snow," "ice," and "electric" wash. For a few years the hottest look in fashion, acid wash was also a prolific source of controversy. It sparked several rounds of proprietary lawsuits involving some of the biggest names in the business, as well as product recalls in which the technique was sometimes found to diminish the tensile strength of the garment. And the misleading name of the process, which didn't actually involve acid, helped feed panicky health rumors about skin rashes, even cancer. The Food and Drug Administration eventually determined that acid-washed jeans were a health hazard only if eaten.

All these new developments created "instant millionaires," Emalfarb recalls, as industrial launderers in the Carolinas, Texas, southern California, and elsewhere could charge three or four dollars to wash a single pair of jeans. Fashion jeans by now were hovering in the thirty-dollar range, with hot companies such as Guess commanding more than twice that. The process was predictably hard on washing machines. With stonewashing, says Lee's Len Larson, eroded pieces of pumice got caught in the drains. "We had a horrible problem of cleanup," he says. And the chemicals used in acid wash created a disposal problem.

Stonewashing was so popular that one entrepreneur marketed something called the "Authentic Stone," individual pieces of pumice wrapped in "beds of denim." He sold tens of thousands of these novelties in department stores for six dollars apiece. But increased competition soon drove down prices in the pumice market. From a high of thirty-two cents per pound, Emalfarb says, it sank to about six cents. By the end of the 1980s Emalfarb turned his focus to developing his own enzymes, which had replaced chlorine as the favored catalyst in the acid wash process.

With the fall of the Berlin Wall, Emalfarb hired hungry scientists out of Moscow State University and other Russian institutions. By 1994 they had developed superior, yet cheaper, cellulases. In an effort to identify a fungus that could produce a milder enzyme, the team from Dyadic stumbled upon a remarkable find. They discovered that the microorganism they drew from an alkaline lake in remote eastern Russia can "read" a gene, reproducing its protein. The discovery has opened new avenues of research in food and energy, and Florida-based Dyadic has been working with various partners on protein therapeutics, a fast-emerging class of the pharmaceutical industry.

"From jean to gene," Emalfarb says. "We're looking to develop better, more affordable drugs, all stemming from the stonewash business. Hopefully, cures for diseases that have plagued mankind for millennia will be made from our technology. And I didn't even take a biology class in college."

The introduction of the "designer" mentality to jeans in the late 1970s and early '80s set off a symbolic skirmish over the nature of consumer culture. Hippies, punks, and metalheads had all been wearing ripped jeans for years, collectively renouncing the concept of upward mobility. "If 'whole' jeans connote shared meanings of contemporary America," wrote the sociologist John Fiske in his essay "The Jeaning of America," "then disfiguring them becomes a way of distancing oneself from those values." Ripped jeans were interactive, a transformation of a purchased good rather than a passive acceptance of it. They were also a gesture of refusal, a declaration that the wearer had opted out of one aspect of the cycle of consumption— buying a new pair as soon as the old ones wore out.

For some, such an avowal had a historic connection to spiritual, impoverished figures. Christ, of course, dressed humbly. Omar, successor to the prophet Mahomet, preached in tattered

cotton. For many, however, ripped jeans represented no kind of faith but a distinct lack of it. They were a fashionable form of nihilism.

In the ceaseless power struggle between consumer and capitalist, the torn jean was a kind of guerrilla warfare on the part of the underdog—until the inevitable, that is, when big business co-opted the look, mass-produced it, and sold it back to the public. By the 1980s runway designers such as Vivienne Westwood, Katharine Hamnett, and Dolce & Gabbana were scavenging punk culture for their shredded denim trousers, and the look quickly trickled down to ready-to-wear. Cliff Abbey produced batches of a line he called Agnelli jeans with a staggered grid of two-inch horizontal razor cuts, a process that required the full-time efforts of dozens of Filipino factory hands. A Chattanooga, Tennessee, company offered a limited run of "shotgun" denim, jeans used as target practice. Each pair came with a spent shotgun shell.

By 1991, with the success of grunge, the hardcore-influenced rock of Nirvana and a thousand copycat bands, torn jeans were ubiquitous, stretching from junkie alleyways to bejeweled boulevards. Thurston Moore of the band Sonic Youth, a forerunner of the grunge groups, recalled encountering Nirvana and its ragtag leader, Kurt Cobain, for the first time in 1989. He compared them with the "demonic hick kids" in the shlock horror film *Children of the Corn*—"you know, long, stringy hair, ragged flannel, and ripped dungarees." When the Seattle music scene became the mecca of aspiring rock stars, a Sub Pop Records employee made rock 'n' roll history when she duped a *New York Times* reporter into believing the "grunge lexicon" she made up on the spot. "Wack slacks" were those ubiquitous tattered jeans; a "lamestain"—an uncool person—was presumably someone who wore jeans with a crease.

While Nirvana's ratty jeans were a reminder of the band members' penniless origins, those of the couturiers often looked scarcely different. Some in the haute monde were not amused by this flagrant slumming. The high-end New York boutique Charivari, where Marc Jacobs once worked as a stockboy, hung billboards that read: "Ripped Jeans, Pocket Tees, Back to Basics. Wake Us When It's Over." Yet torn jeans, flaunted by the groundbreaking Italian brand Diesel in the late 1980s and early '90s, have since been featured by such mainstream lines as Lee and Gap.

On the first day of the February 2005 Magic Marketplace, the retail fashion industry's gigantic semiannual trade show, a middle-aged man stood in the middle of the teeming lobby of the Las Vegas Convention Center's North Hall. For a moment he seemed to be the only person among thousands who wasn't moving. With well-trimmed salt-and-pepper hair and a certain fatherly quality about him, he looked expertly cast as a midlevel executive. He wore a light-colored sports jacket and a crisp new pair of premium blue jeans.

His jeans had a near-perfect slot along the right thigh, just below the front pocket. Big enough for a silver dollar, the cleanly frayed opening was clearly the work of a professional. This man, it was safe to assume, did not pack a pair of accidentally torn jeans for his business trip.

Despite their longevity, ripped jeans still have subversive power. In a 2004 60 *Minutes* segment on the celebrated Russian soprano Anna Netrebko, the singer took correspondent Bob Simon on a shopping excursion down Haight Street in San Francisco. Dressed in a pair of thigh-hugging Dolce & Gabbana jeans with considerable gashes in the knees, she explained that they cost $1,200.

"For twelve hundred dollars," Simon grumbled, "you'd think they wouldn't have holes in them."

Like "distressed" denim, prewashing remains a constant in the denim industry in one form or another. After years of variations—resins, incense—some designers have become enamored of a new treatment, one with the potential to sweep the industry in the coming years. Some jeans are now washed in ozonated water, using equipment patented by a company called FiberZone. "It actually really cleans the fabric and brings out the whiteness of the cotton. It has a slight greenish tint, too, more true to the cast of the original looms," says Jason

Ferro, designer of the boutique brand Los Angeles Denim Atelier (LADA). Ferro, whose background includes stints with Guess and Levi's, was the talk of Project, the mostly denim premium-brand showplace that ran concurrent to the Magic trade show in Las Vegas.

The athletic-looking Ferro, a fine arts major who had never designed clothes when he took his first job with a surfwear startup, was introduced to ozone treatment at Sights Denim during his period with Levi Strauss & Co. After guiding Guess through its urban/hip-hop phase of the mid-1990s, Ferro defected to Abercrombie & Fitch, where he helped launch the "Hollister" jean, one of the popular basics that transformed the former outdoor supplier into a fixture of the mainstream youth market. "That's when Levi approached me with the golden ticket back home (to the West Coast), to work for the king of denim," Ferro recalls. "I jumped at the opportunity." After building his reputation there, he returned to the Guess fold; LADA is bankrolled by the Marciano brothers.

In ozone treatment, compressed air is submitted to electrolysis, creating ozone gas. The ozone is then bubbled into water, which becomes ozonated. In the wash, the temperature must be kept below one hundred degrees or the ozone will break down. "From an environmental standpoint, it's low energy, and it naturally biodegrades easily," says Cotton Inc.'s Skip Gordon. "The beauty of it is that it purifies the water. Most bottled water is ozonated." It appears that the process is more gentle on the fabric than many of its predecessors, and designers such as Ferro are excited about its end result. "I don't know of any negatives at this point," says Gordon.

Ferro, as laid-back as his surfing background suggests, is nevertheless quite protective of the details of his work with ozone treatment. In the ongoing one-upsmanship of premium denim design, innovations can be used to fend off competing brands—provided, that is, they aren't stolen. LADA's access to the private wash facilities at Guess has been invaluable, says Ferro. "You can't go to a laundry and show your washes out in the open," he says. "If a wash guy walks in and sees it, he'll have it in his line. The business is becoming very secretive."

In an industry that sometimes seems stuck in an endless loop of rehashed ideas, the appearance of newness is critical. Even JCPenney is savvy enough to market its in-house brand, Arizona, with a variety of exotic-sounding washes including Voodoo, Petrol, and Vapor. Many contemporary brands now use labor-intensive, uniquely hand-designed touches such as sand-blasting and whiskering. And the emphasis on hand-crafting is balanced by the never-ending search for improved technology. A Cincinnati company called TechnoLines recently took out thirteen patents on laser-printing machinery that can burn images—logos, pinstripes, flower patterns—onto the surface of denim without damaging the cotton fibers. "You could burn the Mona Lisa onto your jeans," says Claire Dupuis, a trend forecaster for Cotton Inc.

"We make new stuff in new ways every day," says Andrew Olah, a New York–based agent for leading international denim mills including Japan's Kurabo and, until recently, Italy's Legler. Olah compares the specialization of the denim world to the upscaling of the neighborhood grocery store. Originally from Toronto, he remembers when the Canadian chain Loblaws was struggling mightily some years ago. The company began diversifying its own product line, augmenting its sale of plain old ketchup, for instance, with dozens of ethnic specialty sauces.

Aggregate sales of the sauces, Olah says, soon trounced what the chain had been selling in ketchup alone.

It's an apt, if belated, cautionary tale for the denim world, where resistance to change contributed heavily to the downward slides of giants such as Levi's and the dominant North American mills, Olah says. The blue jeans equivalent of all those little specialty sauces has succeeded in cultivating a substantial market of denim connoisseurs who are now willing to pay top dollar for top-shelf product.

Shadowy figures are shopping furtively in the dark. Each keeps his distance from the others, hoping to cut a fresh path through the maze of vendors. Trundling laundry carts or oversize duffel bags on wheels, they are digging for vintage denim in the pre-dawn murk at the Rose Bowl Flea Market, a massive monthly event held in a sprawling lot at the foot of the ninety-thousand-seat coliseum in Pasadena.

At the front gates the jaunty, overamplified sound of ragtime piano seems hopelessly festive at such a brutal hour. Inside the fences, the music quickly dissipates, leaving the flea market to unfold in relative silence save for the hum of generators. A little later, some dealers will turn on their boom boxes or car speakers, creating a jumble of moods with their classical stations, their punk and ska CDs. Right now, however, the early birds are mostly wordless—faceless, too, under the slate sky. In February, it's cooler than most southern Californians are accustomed to, and their hooded sweatshirts and bundled layers only add to the uneasy sense that secrets are closely guarded here.

For well over a decade, the Rose Bowl Flea Market has been an internationally recognized pilgrimage site for serious denim collectors. Just as some of the first customers for overall pants plumbed the riverbeds of the Sierra Nevada foothills for gold nuggets, the buyers and sellers of vintage blue jeans today are essentially in the excavation business. Here, daylight is for dabblers. Any article of workwear worth real money will be sifted and packed away inside the market's opening hour.

At the far corner of the lot, past row upon row of dealers selling the usual flea market fare—antique kitchen tools, chipped pottery, clown paintings, grubby baby dolls with fluttering lashes—dozens of rag traders fill the equivalent of a football field. By the light of the moon they open van doors, lay down tarps, roll out pipe racks jammed with clothes. They unload huge piles of old sneakers, small mountains of army fatigues. They hang T-shirts commemorating Live Aid, bygone Rolling Stones tours, *Mary Hartman, Mary Hartman.* Then there is the denim. Most of it is Levi's. Prime quarry are the "big E" Levi's. A good-condition pair of big E Levi's currently sells in the $250 to $300 range at the Rose Bowl, marked up to $500 or so upon resale in Japan. A decade ago, the same pair might have fetched $1,200.

Special display is reserved for one-of-a-kind items. One dealer showcases a bleach-stained, custom-sewn jeans skirt, cut open along the inseam and fitted with denim panels. Its maker, maybe a small-town girl whose boyfriend worked at the body shop, carefully decorated the piece with store-bought patches—Budweiser, Goodyear, Platt Electrical Supply. "We Install Confidence," reads one. An aisle or two over, another vendor hangs a pair of Hercules overalls, made by Sears and dating perhaps to the 1940s or 1950s. Deadstock, it still has the retailer's cardboard hang tags, touting the garment's San-forized nine-ounce denim and "a crotch that will let you bend."

The recycled denim clothes being bought and sold at the Rose Bowl are as evocative of an older America as a boxcar diner or a Craftsman bungalow. But the collectible market-place for old American work pants was created by foreigners, and they still dominate it. Language is a perpetual barrier among the French and Italian designers, the German collectors, and the Thai and Japanese suppliers who comprise the bulk of the participants at this end of the flea market.

It was the Japanese who instigated the bidding wars that made the vintage denim market so volatile in the late 1980s and early '90s. With their economy flush, they spent, invested, and collected with impunity. After World War II the Japanese grew enamored with the swaggering style of the occupying GIs in their bomber jackets, Hawaiian shirts, and dungarees. "In the fifties, American soldiers were like gods in Japan," says Jeff Spielberg. "They were big guys with money, and they were friendly. They were wearing Levi's, carrying Zippo lighters, lis-tening to Elvis and dressing like him. That became iconic in Japan—that kind of cool, that power." When Japanese apparel companies such as Big John and Edwin & Co. began making denim clothing in the early 1960s, they held up the can-do spirit of classic workwear as their ideal.

By the time Levi Strauss &. Co. broke into the Japanese market in 1970, the company fretted that it was competing with dozens of Japanese startups. Some of those continue to thrive today. Big John began as the Ozaki Clothes Company, with its namesake selling imported American jeans door-to-door on his bicycle. Like Levi's in America, Big John is some-thing of a legend in Japan. For years many Japanese believed that the company created the original denim work trouser. Also like Levi's, Big John was once scorned for its lower-class appeal, dismissed by some older Japanese as "hobolike slacks." Yet the company still specializes in work clothes today.

Edwin, on the other hand, has transformed itself to compete in the premium market, partnering with Fiorucci and enlisting Brad Pitt for an ad campaign. Evisu, a much younger brand formally launched in 1991, took a number of liberties in paying homage to Levi's. Originally known as Evis, the company added the *u* after pressure from its American counterpart. It also discontinued its copycat version of the red pocket tab. Today Evisu is recognized as an international trend leader, producing a wide variety of fashions identified by the company's trademark "seagull" pocket swoosh. Founder Hidehiko Yamane got his start as a vintage clothing importer, and his nose for profit is epitomized by the name he chose for the company— Evisu is the name of the Japanese Buddhist god of money.

American blue jeans are just one of the collectible markets driven by the Japanese, whose thirst for Western pop culture has boosted vintage T-shirts, sneakers, and many other categories. The country's young adults can afford to be fashionably adventurous because many of them live at home with their parents until they get married, says Claire Dupuis of Cotton Inc. "They have no cars," she says. "They don't have to think about bills." Dupuis travels to Tokyo, London, and other metropolitan areas taking photos of trendsetters in imaginative streetwear, which she uses in presentations to clothing manufacturers. The most style-conscious Japanese, she notes, tend to gravitate to historic subcultures, some dressing like original punks, others like colorful hippies—most of them in denim of some sort.

At the Rose Bowl, a couple of prearranged phone calls lead to Hitoshi Yamada, a thirty-four-year-old full-time denim "picker" who limits his buying to prohibitively expensive items, some of them as much as $25,000 apiece, coveted by his tiny clientele of collectors. Though Yamada comes to Los Angeles every month for the flea market, these days he rarely brings anything home. The last time he bought something at the Rose Bowl, he thinks, might have been six months ago. His collectors are discriminating in the extreme. Two of them are designers—one European, one Japanese—on the never-ending quest for inspiration. Another sells real estate. A fourth, surprisingly, is a thirty-four-year-old Tokyo mailman. Hitoshi, whose English is choppy at best, grins broadly. The guy is apparently indebted to his employer. "He always asking the post office, 'Let me borrow,' " Hitoshi says with a laugh.

On this day Hitoshi himself is wearing thousands of dollars of denim. His jacket is a United States Navy–issue parka from the 1940s, a hooded, placket-front denim pullover. It looks brand-new; its indigo dye is mesmerizingly deep. While the average passerby might not take a second look—especially given Hitoshi's very ordinary-looking heavy socks and Birkenstocks—wearing such an outfit at the Rose Bowl Flea Market is "the equivalent of a woman strolling down Madison Avenue in her Chanel," as one collector puts it.

Besides delving through flea markets and thrift stores, Hitoshi sometimes goes ranch hunting for old jeans. He'll learn about a dwindling western town, one in which the local mines are closed or the farms are waning. Then he'll advertise in the newspaper, offering perhaps fifty dollars a pair for unwanted jeans. One recent excursion resulted in a bonanza when a farmer unpacked about two hundred pairs of Wranglers from the 1950s. "Pieces of shit," says Hitoshi. "Not good shape, but cool for designers." Hauls like that sometimes go to Hitoshi's friend Tee, a twenty-six-year-old Rose Bowl regular who has been in the business since he was sixteen.

Tee Komol was born in Bangkok. He came to Los Angeles to join his older brother, James, who was working here as a rag-picker. James went back to Bangkok to open a vintage store, for which Tee, a slender guy with a warm smile and a feathery quiff of black hair, is now the supplier. At the Rose Bowl, he is also a vendor, setting up a small lot each month specializing in vintage western shirts, cowboy boots, and denim. Today he brought a few dozen pairs of big E Levi's, all priced around three hundred dollars. He also has a few Levi's jackets lined with sheepskin—a tough sell in southern California, certainly, but even more so in Bangkok, where the average temperature is in the eighties.

Having made five thousand dollars by nine in the morning, Tee asks his mother to watch the stuff. Strolling off to look around, he comes back a few minutes later with two pairs of Levi's—lowercase *e* on the tab, but with a single stitch across the inside of the back pockets, indicating they were made before the early 1980s, when Levi's went to double stitch. He also has a great-looking "sawtooth" western shirt from the 1950s, made by Levi's. Other than a tear just inside the right pocket, it's in beautiful shape. Tee paid $150 for it, and he might get three hundred from someone in Thailand. "When this stuff was really popular," he says, jamming his hands in the pockets of his gray sweatshirt, "maybe eight hundred."

"Better than saving money," says Hitoshi, admiring the shirt. But the prices for vintage have tumbled considerably.

Just as new Levi's are now shunned by many school-age kids in favor of Lucky or Abercrombie, vintage Levi's are not quite the cult status symbol that they were a decade ago. Most of his customers are over twenty-five, says Tee.

"The new generation, they don't buy 501s."

ELEVEN

Wrapped in the Flag: "America's Gift" in the Global Era

Levi Strauss & Co. is headquartered in Levi's Plaza, a cluster of buildings along the Embarcadero at the foot of Telegraph Hill in San Francisco. The lobby of the main office bisects the building up to the seventh floor, providing views of administrators padding through the halls several floors above. Visitors enter the lobby past a museumlike time line of Levi's history. A darkened kiosk serves as a viewing room for an endless loop of the brand's archival television commercials.

"People love our clothes and trust our company," reads the inscription along the wall by the security desk. "We will make the most appealing and widely worn casual clothing in the world. . . . We will clothe the world."

They came awfully close.

For decades blue jeans have been recognized around the globe as a symbol—perhaps *the* symbol—of Western culture. The product is like "a magnificent flag that says 'USA' to the world at large," as a president of the Denim Council once put it.

As the idealism of the American youth movement spread overseas, sales of blue jeans in Western Europe rose from $8 million in 1968 to $100 million in 1972. "The World Is Blue-Jean Country Now," *Life* magazine declared that year, noting that American students "have been known to finance their entire summer European travels by selling off extra Levi's." And not just in Europe either: "Moscow and Tokyo youths often offer to buy jeans warm, right off an American tourist's anatomy," reported one wire service.

The quintessential "American" product, of course, has its ancestry in European workwear. Foreign influence has been considerable since the designer jeans era, which can be traced in part to early 1970s French labels such as MacKeen and Sisley. And the premium fashion leaps of recent years are largely rooted in the innovations of Italian brands like Diesel and Replay. Yet the creation myth is so powerfully American that few bother to challenge it. When Johnny Hallyday, the "French Elvis," endorsed a new jeans line in the late 1980s, he called it Western Passion.

"It is true that historically the two European cities of Nîmes in France and Genoa in Italy represent the places where denim was born," writes Renzo Rosso, the founder of Diesel, in an e-mail. "But for me it's from the fifties to the seventies in America, with James Dean and the flower-power movement,

that our culture of denim and the idea of freedom come from." When the Berlin Wall came down in 1989, blue jeans symbolized the arrival of Western-style democracy—and commerce. No longer did they have to be smuggled. One Italian company introduced a line called Perestroika jeans. Another, Rifle, opened a store in Red Square, and a brand called Cimarron put an image of Mikhail Gorbachev on its hang tags. There is "more power in blue jeans and rock and roll than the entire Red Army," as Régis Debray, the French guerrilla philosopher and comrade of Che Guevara, once said.

Like the nation it represented, the Levi's brand was now seen as the reigning global superpower. Its impeccable authenticity made it the gold standard, both at home and on the international underground. Trucks delivering Levi's were frequent targets of hijackers. By the time LS&CO. signed its first licensing deal in Eastern Europe in the late 1970s, black-market Levi's were selling in Hungary for the equivalent of one hundred dollars apiece. A decade later, just before the fall of the Iron Curtain, smuggled Levi's were worth at least twice that much in the USSR. Counterfeiting, too, has been a constant bane of the company. In Italy in the mid-1970s, the number-two brand of blue jeans, after Levi's, was imitation Levi's. Company security officers, working with the Italian government, identified and closed two plants that were turning out the fakes.

By the late 1980s, Levi Strauss & Co. was the envy not only of the garment world but branding experts everywhere. The manufacturer had instilled its own story into American history, perfecting a product that was familiar to a wildly disparate cross-section of the population. Perhaps no commodity of any kind has benefited more from the imprimatur of Americana. In 1984, the year Levi's was the official outfitter of the United States Olympics team, one of the biggest-selling albums of all time featured a cover image of the artist, Bruce Springsteen, facing an American flag. Shot from behind by the celebrity photographer Annie Leibovitz, Springsteen's backside on *Born in the USA* is flying the little red flag—Levi's red tab.

As designer jeans waned in the mid-1980s, consumers surged back to basics. It was a windfall for Levi's, which capitalized by adopting some of the new tricks of the trade—namely, the claim to sex appeal. With Levi's, as often as not the object of desire was male, as the company's pivotal commercials "Bath" and "Laundromat" attest. In the former, a shirtless man submerges himself in a bathtub, shrinking his 501s the old-fashioned way. In the latter, a young man doing his laundry strips to his boxer shorts, stuffing his jeans into a washing machine as fellow patrons gawk. Both ads ran in slightly different versions in England and America. In England, they were a phenomenon. The original versions of the oldies songs that accompanied the commercials, "Wonderful World" and "I Heard It Through the Grapevine," both reentered the pop charts. Nick Kamen, the model in the washing-machine spot (retitled "Launderette"), became a celebrity, a pop singer whose online fan clubs still swoon over the ad today.

But the massive, decades-long growth of Levi's was beginning to show signs of erosion. The "Bath" and "Laundromat" commercials were so popular, even competitors benefited; Lee jeans claimed a marked increase in sales. *Levi's* had been a generic term for blue jeans for decades by this point, and that generic quality, coupled with the universality of the classic five-pocket jean design, made success in the field a distinct possibility for anyone who entered it. Growing at an annual rate of 24 percent in the 1970s, LS&CO. was disinclined to make many concessions. But a hint of future troubles could be gleaned from a comment made by Robert T. Grohman, then the company's chief operating officer, in a *Forbes* cover story in August 1978. "We've been running without time to catch our breath," he said, explaining the reluctance to chase trends. "Fashion jeans just weren't important. You can't have the kind of growth we had in basics and also develop fashion."

It was a harbinger. In the coming years, the venerable San Francisco clothier would remain fiercely committed to its core product, resisting innovations as fleeting fads. The behemoth of the industry gradually developed an unfortunate reputation as the garment world's Johnny-come-lately. Ideally suited for the momentary return to basics of the late 1980s, it was reluctant to acknowledge the baggy jeans phenomenon of the early 1990s. And it was slow to respond once again when low-rise would dominate the racks a few years later. Though still the world's largest purveyor of blue jeans, Levi's has tumbled from a record-high sales volume of $7 billion in 1996 to just over $4 billion in 2004. Observers and competitors, many of whom are unabashed fans, agree that blame for the company's woes can be pinned on its methodical approach, its tendency to stand apart from the changing marketplace. With the aging of the baby boomers and the maturation of Generation X, Levi's—for decades the tribal uniform of the young—had become yesterday's news to the prime jeans-buying market of eighteen- to twenty-four-year-olds. "They are like an oil tanker, so big, so tough to move," says Mark Emalfarb, who recalls that the company held out as long as it could on the stonewashing trend.

"Levi ain't used to somebody telling them what they got to do," says Bill Hervey, retired president of Wrangler Menswear, who minces no words when it comes to his lifelong rival. "Their arrogance, their lack of consideration for the consumer—it's mismanagement of the whole brand. I mean, it's two hundred years old," says this dapper Southern gentleman, rounding up a little, "and they're killing it."

In the midst of the designer era Wrangler received an unexpected boost. The suburban zeal for fancy cowboy boots, mechanical bulls, and beer in long-neck bottles that swept the nation in the wake of the 1980 movie *Urban Cowboy* greatly profited the company, the most cowboy-identified brand of the Big Three. "You have no idea how it set this country on fire for western. We expanded like crazy," says Hervey, who maintains an office at Wrangler headquarters in Greensboro. Employees there still call him "Mr. Wrangler."

In 1986—a year in which *Life* magazine reported that thirteen pairs of jeans were sold every second—VF Corporation, which had bought H. D. Lee in 1969, engineered a friendly merger with Blue Bell, Wrangler's parent company. The combined enterprise claimed 25 percent of the then-six billion jeans market. VF, which began in 1899 as a Pennsylvania glove and mitten company, later becoming Vanity Fair Intimates, today calls itself the largest publicly traded apparel company in the world, selling Lee and Wrangler, Chic, Gitano, Brittania, and Earl Jeans, as well as Nautica sportswear, Vans sneakers, and many other brands.

VF wasn't the only emerging Goliath to bank on jeans. In the late 1970s the clothing chain of San Francisco–based Gap Inc. had grown to more than two hundred stores, and the company was phasing out its once-total reliance on Levi's. By 1980 Levi's accounted for just 35 percent of sales in the stores as Gap introduced its own private labels such as Foxtails, Monterey Bay, and Durango. One of Gap's big breaks from its San Francisco neighbor involved a joint venture cut in 1978 with Ralph Lauren.

Lauren, born Ralph Lifshitz, was a onetime necktie salesman with a flair for the dramatic—he had a showroom in the Empire State Building—who launched his own clothing line, Polo, in 1968. A decade later, he had become well known for reviving aristocratic fashion, having cleared the way for the preppie explosion of the 1980s with his stylized costume work on *The Great Gatsby* (1974) and Woody Allen's *Annie Hall* (1977).

For Gap, Lauren made his first foray into jeans with Polo Western Wear. Once called "the apotheosis of the self-made man," Lauren was more at home in tweeds and tennis sweaters than work pants. In an unauthorized biography by Michael Gross, the author quoted a former neighbor who recalled a visit the young designer paid to his mother: "Once, Ralph drove up in a sports car, wearing jeans. Frieda was horrified. Jeans were a mark of being poor. She gave him hell. 'If you want to see me, you dress properly.' He came the next week in a suit." But by 1978, jeans could confer considerable status, and Lauren saw a way in. He would appropriate the American tradition of the rugged individualist as part of his own growing range of lifestyle offerings. "I made westernwear very important," Lauren once said. "I pioneered it." (To which a former associate supposedly replied, "Yeah. He invented horses too.")

The Polo Western Wear showroom on 54th Street in Manhattan featured suede furniture and huge boulders trucked in from the Southwest. Despite the elaborate trappings, however, there was something about the line that was not quite right. "We all tried on the pants," recalled one salesperson, who had been obliged like the others to wear cowboy boots. "They didn't look good on anyone who wasn't long legged and thin." The jeans, concluded a Gap executive, "didn't fit the asses of the masses." Only half of the $50 million wholesale order for 1979 was actually manufactured and delivered, and Gap pulled the plug in February 1980, writing off $5.8 million. "It was the first, but not the last, time that Ralph would fail with blue jeans," noted Gross.

Not until the 1990s did Lauren confirm himself as a player in the jeans business. After enduring another setback with the underwhelming launch of his Double RL jeans, a weathered-looking line named for Lauren's Colorado ranch and retailing for $78 a pair, he finally found his audience with the launch of Polo Jeans Co. Priced under fifty dollars and more youthfully appealing than other Lauren designs, Polo Jeans were licensed to El Paso's Sun Apparel, which had prior history with Sasson, Code Bleu, and other upscale denim companies. Lauren himself had taken to affecting a leisurely denim look, influenced in part by his on-again, off-again relationship with the actor Robert Redford, who began marketing his own lifestyle gear through his Sundance catalog in 1989. "Ralph never wore jeans and boots until he came under the influence of Redford," said one fashion editor.

Lauren has worked hard over the years to infuse his denim lines with a certain gravity, a sense of history to rival the American flag's. Polo Jeans, for instance, featured a flag logo with little "RL"s in place of the stars. In July 1998 Lauren effectively purchased the archetypal American flag, paying $13 million for the restoration of the enormous banner that flew over Baltimore's Fort McHenry during the War of 1812, the flag that prompted Francis Scott Key to write the poem that would become "The Star Spangled Banner." Some saw Lauren's act of philanthropy as a power play aimed to undercut another flag-fixated designer, Tommy Hilfiger, whose own jingoistic jeanswear provided stiff competition for Lauren beginning in the 1980s.

Hilfiger, the onetime bell-bottomed, shag-cut shopkeeper out of Elmira, New York, was all but unknown when his initials went up on a Times Square billboard in the mid-1980s. The ad audaciously declared him to be one of the "Four Great American Designers for men," alongside "RL," "CK," and "PE" (Perry Ellis). Having served as a freelance designer for Jordache, Hilfiger was handpicked by Murjani to be the face of the company's all-American line, a counterpart to Lauren. At first the boyish upstart was ridiculed as an impostor, likened to the Monkees. But his steady apparel sense, carving a middle ground between Lauren's upward striving and Calvin Klein's fountain of eternal sexuality, calmly settled into its niche. The niche quickly expanded. From 1990 to 1992, following a break with the financially troubled Murjani, Tommy Hilfiger Corp. quadrupled its sales to $107 million. An initial public offering raised $46.9 million.

By the middle of the decade an unlikely phenomenon was under way. Hilfiger's boldly branded jeans and oversized jerseys had become a status symbol for young African-Americans. Tommy's younger brother, Andy, was in the habit of giving away Hilfiger clothes to performers in his job as a music-industry lighting technician. LL Cool J was one of the first prominent rappers to wear Tommy onstage, adopting the red, white, and blue jumpsuit that Hilfiger had designed for the Lotus Formula One auto racing team. "I never pushed for them to wear Tommy onstage," said Andy Hilfiger, "but you know, when you give away clothes, somebody's going to wear them *somewhere* where they will be noticed." His brother's business was virtually transformed when Andy delivered a few striped rugby shirts for Snoop Dogg on the eve of the budding superstar's 1994 appearance on *Saturday Night Live*. Snoop wore one of the shirts on national television, conspicuously displaying the designer's name—"Tommy" on the front, "Hilfiger" on the back. The designer did not squander his golden opportunity. He hired Kidada Jones, daughter of the musician Quincy Jones, who modeled Tommy clothes and dressed Michael Jackson in them for a cover photo shoot for her father's *Vibe* magazine. With rap groups such as A Tribe Called Quest and Mobb Deep soon extending shout-outs to "Tommy Hill" ("He called me his nigga!" Hilfiger gushed to *Playboy*), the designer had the urban buyer in his hip pocket. It was only a matter of time before suburban white kids, who made up the bulk of the hip-hop audience, followed suit.

By 1999, the kid from Elmira was piloting a $1.7 billion juggernaut, and contending with the usual dilemmas such huge growth attracts. With thirty divisions, including footwear, fragrances, golf outfits, and home furnishings, Tommy Hilfiger designs were both bold and domesticated, urban and preppy. Amid the identity crisis, one thing seemed certain. When the company tried to scale back its trademark oversize logos, loyalists balked. The logos quickly returned to prominence. Whatever the product, the customer wanted it loudly branded.

It hadn't always been the case. Hip-hop's original architects, working underground in The Bronx in the late 1970s, often dressed in "gang mode," as Nelson George has called it. They wore dungaree jackets turned inside out, often emblazoned with gang names or graffiti tags. The hooded sweatshirts that went underneath concealed identity and provided protection from the chain-link fences of the subway yards, where graffiti taggers lurked. "A true hip-hop spirit doesn't need—or want— a designer label on his jeans," argued Sally Flinker in a 1985 essay. "His own name, or his tag, is the only commodity to promote, and it's borne proudly on the backs of denim jackets, huge nameplate necklaces, and belt buckles."

"Don't want nobody's name on my behind," rapped Joseph Simmons, better known as the Reverend Run, on the groundbreaking 1984 debut album of the rap group Run-DMC. Yet in the next line of "Rock Box" he betrayed his own name-brand bias: "Lee on my legs, sneakers on my feet." If the jeans were Lee, the sneakers were undoubtedly Adidas, the German company that enjoyed a huge bounce from another Run-DMC song, "My Adidas," eventually signing the group to an endorsement deal worth more than $1 million.

"We always bought into logos," the hip-hop impresario Russell Simmons—Run's brother—told Vogue in 1996. "The reason for it is that it represents all the shit we don't have." Simmons, the cofounder of Def Jam, the record label that helped push hip-hop into the mainstream with Run-DMC, Public Enemy, and the Beastie Boys, was one of the first rap figures to go national with his fashion ideas. Launched in 1992, Phat Farm still sells what it calls "classic American flava," a blend of "the hip-hop culture of the streets and the preppy culture of the Ivy League." Labels such as Phat Farm and FUBU—"For Us By Us," a line of urban gear started as a home business by Queens native Daymond John—helped spread the extreme look of baggy jeans, the ubiquitous street fad of the early 1990s. The baggy look implied a familiarity with prison life, where inmates, denied the right to wear belts, often wore pants that hung loosely off their hips. Gang members and would-be gangstas popularized the trend, passing it along to suburban kids eager to telegraph their own petulance.

At first, achieving the look simply meant buying jeans that were several sizes too big. Soon, however, retailers were selling jeans with extra-roomy legs and trimmer waistlines. Brooklyn-ite Carl Williams, known in the business as Karl Kani, was one of the first designers to emphasize the extra-baggy look around 1991. His collaboration with the West Coast Cross Colours brand, known for its baggy overalls with a prominent red, yellow, and green logo, emphasized its origins. "We want it

(© Getty Images)

understood that only Cross Colours is made by true brothers from the 'hood," read the ads, marking turf against super-baggy interlopers such as Girbaud, which had stumbled onto urban-market success after being licensed in America by the casual-wear giant VF Corp.

Though Cross Colours went bankrupt in 1996, by then Kani's reputation was set. The following year he did $50 million in sales, making his new line the largest black-owned apparel manufacturer in the country at the time.

In New York in the late 1980s, when the baggy look was just catching on, a young college student and Brooklyn native named April Walker was often on the scene among the high-roller crowd cruising Harlem's legendary 125th Street. She was especially drawn to Dapper Dan's, the twenty-four-hour custom tailor shop frequented by friends ordering Gucci and Fendi knockoffs, velour sweatsuits, mink coats, and oversized denim ensembles.

"There was a lot of money," recalls Walker, who has been compiling footage for a documentary on the rise of urban fashion. "Porsches, Mercedes, all these cars double-parked outside late at night, with people having these elaborate outfits made. It amazed me."

Near the stately old mansions of Brooklyn's Clinton Hill, Walker opened her own tailor shop, Fashion in Effect, "on a shoestring budget." The storefront was short-lived; a Christmas Eve robbery convinced her to work by appointment only. By then, however, she had built a following among many of New York's up-and-coming rap stars, who began hiring Walker to style their photo shoots, their videos, and album covers. She designed for MC Lyte, Naughty By Nature, Queen Latifah. Soon she had West Coast customers, too, including Tupac Shakur and Snoop Dogg. And she quickly grew accustomed to working with oversized patterns—one regular was the rotund Christopher Wallace, aka the Notorious B.I.G., and another was the basketball superstar and sometime rapper Shaquille O'Neal.

WalkerWear, as she called the line, consisted at first of a few simple items—a sweatshirt, a T-shirt, a baseball cap, and a denim "hookup," a baggy matching top-and-bottom set she called Rough and Rugged, available in blue, black, and oatmeal. Heeding a suggestion from her friend Jam Master Jay, Run-DMC's DJ, she sewed huge pockets on the jacket. During a New York apparel trade show she rented a nearby hotel room and invited ten buyers from some of the country's most influential urban clothing chains, including Merry-Go-Round, Up Against the Wall, and Dr. Jay's. "I didn't know what my response would be," she recalls. "Surprisingly, they all bought."

Walker became a fixture at the music awards shows, inviting rappers up to her suite for fittings, and her clothes were all over MTV and on CD covers. "That was my way of competing," she says. "I didn't have ad dollars." Although the baggy jeans phenomenon was handed down from prison culture, "prisonwear was not my thing," Walker says. "I was trying to transcend that, actually." Though she cut deals with national department stores, she quickly grew discouraged. "People didn't even understand what the urban market was," she says. "I stumbled on it, and I loved what I did. When it became such a big business, I didn't love it anymore. I love being creative, but I don't like the business. Mass producing—that's not fashion." Today she runs a nonprofit program in Brooklyn for young designers, arranging mentorships with FUBU, Phat Farm, and other successful urban labels.

The odd affinity between the hip-hop status seekers and department store fixtures such as Hilfiger and Lauren created a ready-to-wear version of the country's old melting pot ideal. Just as the designers gleaned ideas about fit and branding from their new urban customers, hip-hop labels including Phat Farm and FUBU, followed by Sean John, Rocawear, and Ecko, set overarching goals like Tommy's and Ralph's. They, too, wanted to be total lifestyle providers. The two sides fed off one another, and the traditional jeans manufacturers took note. Lee and Wrangler soon rolled out their own baggy and "relaxed" fits.

Levi Strauss & Co. was less enthusiastic. After posting record sales of $7.1 billion ($1 billion in profit) in 1996, the company tilted into its slow, steady decline. By 1999, the venerable institution was starting to panic. Ignoring the trend toward baggies had been a mistake, management conceded. "Loose jeans is not a fad. It's a paradigm shift," Sean Dee, Levi's jeans' new brand director, told *The New York Times Magazine*. The company's decades-long domination of the basic five-pocket jean business was no longer a lock. JCPenney, which premiered its private denim label, Arizona, in 1990, had a $1 billion success on its hands by the end of the decade. Sears, Roebuck, another longtime Levi's partner, unveiled its own label, Canyon River Blues. Malls across the country featured young-adult-oriented chains such as American Eagle and Abercrombie & Fitch, which relied heavily on private-label denim sales. With so many competitors biting into its business, Levi Strauss & Co. began a seemingly endless cycle of layoffs, and it set out in search of leadership from the outside. When Peter Jacobi resigned as president and chief operating officer after just two years in 1999, he told a group of textile executives that the company had been asleep to the scope of its problems.

"The alarms were going off," he said, "but frankly, we hit the snooze button a few too many times."

Like the jeans themselves, Levi Strauss & Co. has always been staunchly independent, a kind of lone wolf in the apparel business—a bit of a rebel. It is also a straight shooter in an industry prone to flash and artifice. In order to raise capital to keep up with the dizzying growth of the 1960s, the company had made its first public offering in 1971. Seven years later *Forbes* reported that LS&CO. stock was a solid, if not spectacular, investment. "In going public, as in selling blue jeans," the magazine wrote, "the Haas family sold the public an honest product at an honest price."

But the family never warmed to the idea of answering to Wall Street, and in 1985 it engineered a $1.6 billion leveraged buyout, at the time reportedly the largest in history. The move paid off almost immediately, inspiring a return to basics after flirtations with such far-flung products as down parkas, warm-up suits, and briefcases. The successful launch of Dockers chinos, the company's solution for the professional customer who had outgrown the jeans of his youth but was still averse to the well-pressed formalities of his father's wardrobe, would not have been possible were the directors beholden to stockholders, claimed then-president Thomas Tusher. "There's no way we could have spent ten million dollars on advertising like we did to get the name established," he told *Fortune* magazine in 1990.

If Levi Strauss & Co. was by nature honest and independent like its jeans, the company could also betray a much thinner hide than the durable work pants it gave to the world. It did not take criticism well. In the 1970s then-patriarch Walter Haas Jr. sought the advice of a religious ethicist to help institutionalize the sense of morality and fair play under which the company had operated for decades. That ideal surfaced in the company's commitment to its domestic workforce, even as the rest of the apparel industry began its long, steady exodus overseas. When LS&CO. began closing some of its American plants in the late 1980s, it did so with obvious anguish and defensiveness. The angry demonstrations of more than a thousand employees of a shuttered San Antonio factory were a particular embarrassment. At one point members of the so-

called Fuerza Unida ("United Force") protesters chained themselves to the doors of Levi's headquarters in San Francisco.

Oddly, a very similar scenario had unfolded decades earlier at
the Amoskeag Manufacturing Company, once the world's
largest producer of denim, and the exclusive supplier to Levi's.
When Amoskeag management instituted a 20 percent pay cut
in 1922, its once-loyal employees struck. The crippling stand-
still lasted nine months. The strike proved to be an omen for
the mighty company. Cheap labor was driving the textile business elsewhere, as newer mills in North Carolina and other
southern states capitalized on their proximity to the cotton
fields and a hungry labor pool. The cost of modernizing the
company's suddenly antiquated equipment was simply too great
a burden. The fickleness of fashion was a factor, too, as one of
Amoskeag's longtime staples, gingham, fell out of favor after
the turn of the century.

Ultimately, it was the company's own "giantism" that led
inexorably to its collapse. In a bitter end, Amoskeag filed for
bankruptcy but was denied the right to reorganize. Instead, the
court ordered the company to liquidate in 1936. Rather than
acknowledging the southward shift of the textile industry, Treasurer F. C. Dumaine had stubbornly soldiered on in Manchester,
building one last new mill in 1909 and annexing Amoskeag's
largest local competitor, the Stark Mill, which specialized in
duck cloth, in 1922. The most important lesson to be learned
from the fall of Amoskeag, wrote Dumaine's biographer, is that
"a corporation cannot succeed in accomplishing a socially desirable goal, valiant though it may be, when it is directly opposed

to the dictates of a competitive market." It is a lesson that, three quarters of a century later, Levi Strauss & Co. would also learn the hard way.

Today, the old Amoskeag mill yard reflects the changing façade of business in America, with tenants including a software company, a mortgage broker, and a martial arts gym specializing in "combative concepts." High above one end of the yard looms a neon sign that reads COTTON. It is the name of an upscale bistro serving "American comfort food."

Just as the southern migration of the textile industry effectively killed off Amoskeag, globalization has pummeled the domestic denim industry. Over the past few decades competitive foreign manufacturers have brought giant North American mills such as Cone, Swift, and Canada's Dominion Textiles to their knees. India's Arvind Mills, rooted in a multigeneration family cotton business, has become one of the world's biggest denim manufacturers and the number-one exporter, producing more than 120 million meters annually. Brazil—now the second biggest consumer of *"pantalones vaqueros"* in the world—is home to several huge mills, including Santista, Cedro, and Vicunha Textil. Cedro, a textile mill founded in 1872 by two brothers who supervised the importation of fifty tons of equipment from the United States into the rural Brazilian state of Minas Gerais, now promotes its trend-driven denim and other fabrics out of offices covering Europe, Asia, and the Americas.

By 1997 East Asian suppliers had surpassed the aggregate output of United States mills, producing 1.7 billion square yards. In recent years Turkey has emerged as another aggressor, building at least three massive mill groups. One of them, iSKO, entered a joint venture with Cone in 2002 to supply Levi's Europe (and allow Cone to sidestep the 8 percent import tariff it faced in Europe). "Our brands are international," the CEO of Cone Denim, John Bakane, told *Women's Wear Daily* in 2004. "We're selling to more foreign customers, and all of these people have sourcing offices all over the world— Hong Kong, India, Indonesia, Japan, and Europe. . . . I don't think you're going to see any solely domestic companies left in developed countries. The surviving companies have to be international in scope."

More than ever in the garment business, "Made in the USA" simply means the product was cut and sewn here, using imported materials. For many contemporary jeans brands, Italian mills such as Legler, Candiani, and Montebello and Japan's twin pillars, Kurabo and Kaihara, make some of the most desirable denim in the business. Yet rapid technological improvements have given newcomers the ability to compete with long-established textile companies, both domestic and overseas, in terms of quality and innovation. Mexico, for instance, has become such an industry force that both Cone and Swift have moved much of their production south of the border. With mills around the world making exceptional denim products, insisting on the denim of a particular country—American or otherwise—now makes little sense, says Andrew Olah, the denim mills agent who represented Legler for twenty-five years and has been with Kurabo for fifteen: "It's like saying, 'I only eat Italian food, or French.' "

Held up to disproportionate scrutiny, Levi Strauss & Co. remains justifiably proud of its legacy. The company had insisted on operating integrated facilities in the South in the 1950s and '60s, sometimes in the face of harsh local opposition. By the late 1970s, 44 percent of its employees were minorities. Philanthropy and social conscience had been major initiatives from the days of Levi Strauss himself, setting standards across the corporate world. Benefits were always exceedingly generous. And employees were considered part of the family, always welcome at the table. Bob Haas recalls visiting his father at the old Battery Street headquarters while he was still in high school and being regaled by an elderly salesman named Joe Frank. The last living employee to have personally known Levi Strauss—he still carried the old man's wallet—Frank kept a desk until his death in his mid-nineties. Once upon a time he had delivered jeans by horse-drawn carriage. Now he was content to bend the ear of the boss's teenage son, who was obliged to listen.

Sitting at a round, blond-wood conference table in his corner office, Haas gazes out the floor-to-ceiling window, past the Ansel Adams prints and his top-floor patio, to the spectacular San Francisco Bay. Dressed in a crisp new pair of Levi's and a stylish brown leather shirt, the sixty-two-year-old heir to the company speaks warmly and chuckles easily. Harvard-trained but initially reluctant to go into the family business, Haas has weathered occasional criticism over his stewardship of the world's biggest blue jeans manufacturer. If this tall, slightly stooped man in round wire-rim glasses has endured the consequences of some of his decisions, he nevertheless carries an air of eternal optimism and gratitude for his family's good fortune.

"Arguably, no single U.S. corporation has done more to establish the moral high ground for social responsibility in business," wrote Karl Schoenberger in *Levi's Children: Coming to Terms with Human Rights in the Global Marketplace*. But loyalty was proving to be an increasingly burdensome yoke around the company's neck. Beginning in the 1970s, it had cut deals with overseas manufacturers, but only for its international markets. Two decades later, the apparel industry's race to the bottom would finally force the all-American brand to move all its production, including production for its domestic market, abroad. Workers at the San Antonio plant had been making six dollars an hour; their replacements in Costa Rica received six dollars a day. Appeals that flag-waving competitors such as Ralph Lauren and Tommy Hilfiger had fled the country years prior— if in fact they had ever produced substantial quantities of their product in North America—went unnoticed. LS&CO. had made integrity the root of its identity, and now the perception was that its integrity was subject to revision. In 1998, the same year President Clinton awarded Bob Haas the first Ron Brown Award for Corporate Leadership, the company quietly announced it would close another eleven domestic plants and trim its white-collar staff of five thousand by 20 percent. Having operated sixty-three United States plants in the early 1980s, Levi Strauss closed the last two, both in San Antonio, on January 8, 2004. From paying thirty-seven thousand global employees as recently as 1996, the company had downsized to twelve thousand.

Competitors faced the same challenges. When Mackey McDonald, a former Lee executive, became CEO of VF Corp. in 1996, he began closing Blue Bell factories around the country. "He's unassuming, yet strong as an acre of garlic," says Wrangler's Bill Hervey. "He foresaw the fact that we couldn't be competitive with sixty to one hundred plants scattered across the U.S. He had the courage to close them. Blue Bell was the only thing in Oneonta, Alabama. It was a disaster for Oneonta."

But Levi Strauss & Co. couldn't win. On one side were the analysts who belittled the company's stubborn adherence to a moral compass when profitability was clearly headed south. On the other were the disenchanted idealists who had hoped Levi Strauss & Co. would "fulfill some sort of quasi-messianic role in shaping the moral universe of big business." Today, the company battles an image of itself in desperation mode. Just as decades ago it stuck with its mom-and-pop retailers long after the department stores had redefined the shopping experience, for years the company resisted moving into the so-called "value channel," the big discounters such as Wal-Mart and Target. Now that the company has developed its cost-conscious Signature line, sewn in low-wage nations and sold in American discount stores, customers can buy a pair of Levi's for less than it would have cost twenty years ago.

"Levi's always had history on their side," says Joe Ieraci, of the Blue Hound denim consulting. "Historically, the customer always came back to Levi. This time they didn't."

"When I think of Levi's, it's kind of like Kleenex," says Len Larson, longtime employee of archrival Lee. "It's hard to imagine a company like that could slip that far." Countless innovators in the business freely admit having learned much of what they know from Levi's, whether as former employees or business partners. And they all have theories about the company's hardships. For some it's the disinclination to adapt; for others it's the watered-down effect of the scramble to improve profit margins with cheaper goods. Many analysts believe it comes down to the company's "touchy-feely management style," as Schoenberger notes in *Levi's Children*: "In other words, Levi Strauss had become exhausted by its ethics, choked into laggard inefficiency by political correctness."

For Jason Ferro, the rising designer who now has his own premium line, LADA, the biggest disappointment is his former employer's inconsistency in upholding itself as the industry's gold standard. In recent years, he says, the company has become "notorious for starting something so fresh, so good, and then ditching it right when it's about to peak." Tentative sojourns into the premium jeans market with limited-edition vintage reproductions have sometimes seemed more like public relations moves than sustained moneymaking ventures. Customers wonder whether the company represents value-priced jeans at Wal-Mart or pricey, heritage-laden limited editions in SoHo boutiques. "I think there's room for both," says Ferro, "but they keep on ditching the top end. They don't really go after it like they should."

"We can produce anything the customer wants," said Grohman, the former chief operating officer, in that 1978 *Forbes* article. "We're not a one-product company. You can't relate our future to the future of denim jeans."

In more ways than one, he might have gotten it just right.

TWELVE

★

Bottoms Up:
Blue Jeans at
a Premium

Like factory workers everywhere, the machinists who print our paper money are partial to wearing blue jeans on the job. At Crane & Co., the fine Massachusetts paper-making company that has supplied the United States Bureau of Engraving and Printing with all of its circulating currency paper since 1879, Vice President Tim Crane would love to join them, but he wears slacks and ties to work. While there is a casual-Friday policy in effect in the administrative offices, jeans are still considered a little too casual at this deeply traditional firm.

"I'll dress down as quickly as anybody will let me," says Crane, a sixth-generation descendant of founding father Zenas Crane, "but I don't wear denim in the office."

He does, however, buy plenty of it. Americans spent more

than $14 billion on jeans in 2004, and every piece of the paper money exchanged in those transactions featured a familiar ingredient—the cast-off scraps of the jeans industry. For roughly fifty years now, Crane & Co. has incorporated pulped denim remnants into its recipe for money paper, the company's signature product. Founded in 1801 in the Berkshire Hills of western Massachusetts, the firm's moneymaking history is as much a part of American lore as Levi's jeans—Zenas Crane's father, Stephen, once sold his paper to an engraver named Paul Revere, who printed the colonies' first banknotes with it in 1775.

Denim, says Tim Crane, is no more or less durable for moneymaking than any other cotton weave, but it has one distinct advantage: There's a lot of it. The company claims it has used millions of pounds of denim scraps over the years. Crane & Co. makes its paper from cotton, not wood. As the company legend goes, Zenas Crane launched his business by asking local homemakers to set aside their household rags for him. "We've always been reliant on waste product," says Tim Crane. "Nobody grows cotton to make paper. It would be horrendously expensive."

Denim constitutes between 20 and 30 percent of each bill Americans spend, and its near purity as a cotton product makes it well suited to the moneymaking process. Only the synthetic indigo dyestuffs must be removed. (In comparison, plain white T-shirt trimmings are actually more problematic, Crane says, due to the fluorescent additives that act as "optical brighteners.") Removal of the indigo is outsourced to an Ohio company that can handle the waste by-product. Pulped denim arrives at Crane & Co. in the form of thick, cardboardlike pressings.

To source its denim, Crane & Co. works with specialized

middlemen, waste haulers under contract with denim-cutting factories. They sort the scraps, identifying those of sufficient quality and designating the rest for industrial uses such as mattress filling, or, barring that, landfill disposal. The garment industry's infatuation with polyester during the 1970s put a scare into the papermakers. "We were concerned that you wouldn't be able to find a one-hundred-percent-cotton garment," says Crane. "That prompted us to use more denim."

In recent years, with cutting factories moving overseas along with the rest of the apparel industry, Crane & Co. has been obliged to follow the emigration, chasing denim scraps from the American South into Mexico, the Caribbean, and Asia. "The shipping costs go up when you have to source in Asia," he explains, "but the actual cost of the scraps may be going down. If there's a place in Bangladesh doing rag sorting, you can imagine they're not paying their workers a lot."

Reusing unwanted rags, Crane & Co. has always touted its cotton paper goods as environmentally friendly products. Environmental concerns, in fact, helped inspire one of the company's more unusual ventures. In the early 1990s, Crane's cut a deal with Levi Strauss & Co. to relieve some of its cutting plants of their excess denim and recycle it as blue denim paper. The paper was then sold back to LS&CO. as company stationery.

Tim Crane credits the idea to a New Mexico papermaker named Stefan Watson, who pioneered the process in the 1980s and presented it to the blue jean behemoth. Watson's small operation couldn't produce the quantity LS&CO. wanted, so he turned to Crane & Co. for help. For a time the companies had hopes of selling the paper as a branded Levi's product, but cost cutting at LS&CO. soon put an end to the collaboration—at about a dollar a pound to produce, the paper was much too expensive. It did, however, inspire Tim Crane to come up with an idea for recycled stationery made from shredded paper money removed from circulation. And it gave the socially conscious jeans maker a nice bit of press coverage.

"They had a great green-marketing story to tell," says Crane. "It would've actually worked if it wasn't so damn expensive."

If Peter Lang Nooch had his way, he'd be the next Levi Strauss. The jeans he makes with his independent Glendale, California, company, Farmer, are a top-shelf interpretation of traditional workwear. "We want to be known as Levi, Lee, Wrangler, Farmer," he says. "I would love to be on the same shelf as Levi's." But Farmer's relaxed-fit styles, low-slung on the hips and a little saggy in the seat—ideal for the kind of bar-hopping urbanite who wears a wallet chain (or a strand of pearls that hangs like a wallet chain)—are priced near the top of the fashion-denim scale.

The five-pocket jean is a time-tested concept, essentially unchanged over more than a century. Today, with improved technology, the construction of a $40 pair of jeans isn't drastically different from that of a $99 pair, or even one that costs $185. The prime difference is in the perception. The rapid rise of the $200 blue jean can be attributed to an industry-wide mastery of the art of brand identity. Even a brand that consciously shuns brand identity—Farmer, for instance, which stands out for its defiant *lack* of labels—can sell for a premium, perversely, by stressing its aversion to elitism.

"It is this purchasing of *identity*—of meanings as opposed to materials—that many critics find so irrational and unpleasant about brands," wrote the authors of *Nation of Rebels: Why Counterculture Became Consumer Culture*. But most consumers, they argued, are savvy enough to know the difference between meaning and material. "More often than not, we don't care about the quality of the material in our shirts, the stitching in our jeans, or the alcohol in our bottles. What we care about are the identities conferred by Tommy Hilfiger, J. Crew, and Absolut Vodka," they wrote. Consumers "know that they are drinking the ad, not the booze, and wearing the label, not the jeans."

Conspicuous consumption, of course, is the whole objective in Las Vegas, where Lang Nooch is due to arrive for a trade show. Everything sparkles in the futuristic rotunda of I Bar, the main lobby lounge at Mandalay Bay, the sprawling casino-resort. Even the cocktail napkins convey a strong sense of identity. "I am dangerous," the inscriptions read. "I am sexy. I am exciting. I am confident."

This, presumably, isn't quite Lang Nooch's kind of place. When he walks in and surveys the lights, the mirrors, the showgirl waitresses, he is wearing an unmarked hoodie and a cuffed pair of his own jeans. Glitz and glamour are not the reasons Peter Lang Nooch got into fashion. In fact, he dislikes calling it fashion at all. "There's fashion, and then there's the real deal," he says. Born in Bangkok and raised in Hollywood, where he surfed, skateboarded, rode BMX bikes, and played team sports, he has been at least that active in adulthood. At thirty-seven, he has already had a board shop, a T-shirt line, a digital design firm, an Asian bistro, and a son. He likes to have his say. Sitting down for a late dinner with his assistant, Aida, upon their arrival from L.A., he instructs her to order the aged beef raw.

The Pool show, where Farmer is a vendor, is a kind of rock 'n' roll trade show whose vendors share an irreverent attitude. Lang Nooch is one of the few denim specialists at Pool, which features a wide array of hipster products, from trucker hats and ironic T-shirts to handbags made of old skateboards and vintage automobile upholstery. Many of his premium-jeans competitors are set up next door at Project, in another cavernous showroom in the Mandalay Bay complex. There the aisles are crowded with buyers and sellers chattering about hot brands—Amsterdam's Blue Blood; Henry Duarte and his flamboyant rock-star designs; Yanuk, developed by the daughter of the jeans kingpin Paul Guez. In the high-stakes world of premium blue jeans, Lang Nooch prefers the fringe. "Everyone else broke right, and we broke left," he says.

He once had a girlfriend whose mother, a Thai immigrant, amassed a gigantic pile of selvage denim in her suburban California garage. Anticipating the vintage boom of the late 1980s, she bought the pants at thrift stores for a few dollars a pair and resold them at a hefty profit. Lang Nooch was fascinated. Yet despite his enthusiasm for the deep, rich history of blue jeans—or maybe because of it—he is dismissive not just of his competitors' pretensions but his own talents as well.

"I don't consider it 'designing' when you've got eons of denim to look at," he says. "People act like they invented the shit."

A few years ago, the denim business was hardly eventful enough to warrant its own trade show. In the late 1990s, cargo pants were the casual look of the moment. Big-bellied people who had never been enrolled in a gym were wearing track suits to the mall. Gap had raised the profile of khakis with its ad campaign featuring various icons of cool. And Levi Strauss & Co.'s Dockers brand was holding strong, having reached $1 billion in sales just five years after its mid-1980s launch.

Some observers were actually predicting the demise of blue jeans. The baggy look was no longer a novelty, and LS&CO.'s historic denim business was entering an alarming free fall after its record 1996. The *International Herald Tribune* quoted retailers in England on the downturn. "You always get blips," said one, but "this is seismic. It'll never get back to how it was before."

"It was like denim walked off the edge of a cliff," added a spokesman for a London menswear group.

It was not the first time the fashion industry had prepared a eulogy for jeans. The Denim Council, the consortium of American mills, was formed in the 1950s to address a lull in sales due to the hysteria over teens in jeans. In England in the late 1960s, some analysts saw Lee Cooper's colored jeans as an ominous sign for traditional indigo dyeing. And the introduction of polyester blends in the 1970s precipitated another round of speculation that all-cotton jeans were destined for obsolescence. As with those periods of skepticism, however, the sounding of the millennial death knell for blue jeans was soon smothered by the industry's latest noisy resurgence.

With waistlines slipping down over the hips, the industry began pulling itself up by the britches. Low-rise jeans were the new vogue. Like most fashion "innovations," the low-rise look wasn't entirely without precedent. Historically, men, not women, were more often than not the catalysts. The do-it-yourself fad of folding over and ironing down the waistband, meticulously re-created for *American Graffiti* by the costume designer Aggie Rodgers, gave way to the commercially produced hip-huggers of pioneers such as Fred Segal, Peanuts, and Male jeans. That skintight, ass-grabbing, what's-in-those-trousers silhouette, first flaunted in velours and leathers by sexually charged performers such as Jimi Hendrix and Jim Morrison, helped define the look of the classic rock 'n' roll era. By the early 1970s every lanky young male with a full mane of shaggy hair could dress like a rock star in stylish denim.

While disco-era trends featured higher waistlines designed to flatten the tummy (and invite a more mature socialite to the party), the supremely youthful hip-hugger silhouette has remained a recurring theme in jeans. The Lucky brand, for instance, was founded in 1991 on a retro rock 'n' roll vibe. Italy's Diesel went global in the early 1990s, marketing its adventurous jeans as a core lifestyle accessory with the renowned ad campaign "For Successful Living." At the designer level, Alexander McQueen, sometimes called the "hooligan" of English fashion, sent his models down the runway wearing jeans he called "Bumsters." The pants were cut so low that the cleft of the model's rear end was clearly exposed. "If these jeans were any lower," joked one rep, "you would have to call them chaps." McQueen relished that kind of controversy. British newspapers clucked that during his apprenticeship on Savile Row, he often scribbled "McQueen was here" into the linings of the clothes he sewed, including jackets for Prince Charles. When in 1996 McQueen was appointed head designer at the house of Givenchy, fellow couturiers were predictably outraged.

McQueen's scandalously low-rise Bumsters were an experiment in high fashion; it took a few more years for the concept to trickle down to the retail market. Earl Jeans was founded in

1996 when Hollywood stylist Suzanne Costas's favorite old pair of 501s, which she'd been customizing since college, were stolen from a neighborhood Laundromat. The incident convinced her to begin sewing her own line of low-cut jeans. By 2001 Earl was so popular it was snatched up by Nautica, now a division of VF Corp.

"Earl and Frankie B. were the only two American companies trying to be somewhat Diesel-ish," recalls Earnest Sewn's Scott Morrison. Frankie B. jeans, named for Francesca, the daughter of designer Daniella Clarke, began appearing in such influential Los Angeles stores as Traffic and Fred Segal in 1999. Precariously low slung, they were an instant status symbol among the rich and famous, with curvy celebrities such as Pamela Anderson and Jennifer Lopez professing their devotion to the risqué brand. When the actress Charlize Theron began wearing Frankie B. jeans to movie premieres, Clarke says, she set a new precedent in Hollywood formalwear: "You could now dress jeans up. You put on a pair of strappy sandals and a cute top, and off you go to a premiere."

Clarke, who is married to the guitarist Gilby Clarke, a former member of the rock band Guns N' Roses, says she has been smitten by tight-fitting jeans since she was a kid growing up overseas. Born in Nazareth on Valentine's Day 1969, she remembers her stepfather, a production manager for Lee Jeans in Israel, bringing home presents for Clarke's mother—a jean jacket with embroidered roses on the back, for example. "I'd go crazy," she says.

At sixteen, having relocated to California, where she was working as a model, Clarke was introduced to her future husband. A few years later they were on the road together with Guns N' Roses, the biggest draw in the concert industry at the time. Clarke took her backstage pass around the world, and the audacity of the musicians and their entourages goaded her already provocative fashion instincts. "It just seemed more fun to me to be a little wilder," she says. "There are so many serious things going on in the world."

Customizing her own jeans by taking them apart at the seams and lowering the rise through the crotch—not, she clarifies, simply cutting off the waistbands, as is sometimes reported ("I hated that look!")—she fielded constant questions from admirers about her personal style. The attention gave her the confidence to begin sewing jeans in her garage. In concocting the Frankie B. look, she reached back to her childhood obsessions. She was a big fan of *Charlie's Angels* as a girl. "I had a paper-doll set of them," she says, "and I remember trying to alter the little outfits." And she was especially inspired by Led Zeppelin, whose singer, Robert Plant, wore some of the tightest trousers in the business. The sound of classic rock continues to drive Clarke creatively. "I'll be driving in my car and I'll hear a great Hendrix song. All of a sudden I'll have a whole new idea of what I want to do when I come into the office in the morning."

The fledgling Frankie B. line was lavished with press coverage. When Clarke saw the singer and actress Lopez tugging at her jeans as she rose from her seat at the MTV Music Awards, she knew her brand was a hit. J-Lo's hip-wagging shimmy, rearranging her jeans so they sat just so on her ample posterior without giving too much away—Clarke calls it "the Frankie B. wiggle." Despite the windfall from such unsolicited endorsements, Clarke stuck to her careful slow-growth plan. Sales were a reported $10 million in 2003, and Frankie B. didn't place its first national ads, in *Vogue* and *Elle*, until early 2005.

"This is the first time I've loosened the reins a little," she says. "I knew the death of every company is that they grow too fast. At this point, I finally have the capacity, the knowledge, and the strength to let it grow. I really wanted to keep it special, to make sure it wasn't going to burn out."

If the public eye had momentarily wandered away from jeans by the late 1990s, low-rise was the look that yanked the attention back. More specifically, all eyes were on the suddenly ubiquitous midriff, liberated as it was from the tyranny of seven-inch zippers. In back, clear views of "the other cleavage" were, to some, a provocation, as schools tried to impose regulations on the low-rise trend. For women, the low-cut look was emphasized by conspicuous thong underwear, just as showing off your boxers and briefs had been part of the baggy jeans fad among young men a few years prior. Brash, fast-rising denim brands such as Seven for All Mankind, Citizens of Humanity, and True Religion, the latter symbolized by a guitar-strumming Buddha, were launched with low-rise, and the jeans establishment quickly followed suit. Levi Strauss & Co., mindful of its reputation for being slow on the uptake, quickly unveiled a low-rise variation on the classic 501 accompanied by another of its memorable advertising campaigns, this one featuring a talking belly button.

Despite the widespread use of stretch denim—cotton blended with a small percentage of Lycra—tighter jeans created some health concerns. Publishing in a legitimate medical journal, an Ontario doctor maintained that form-fitting jeans were the root cause of a modern affliction he called meralgia paresthetica—a pain in the "lateral aspect of the thigh" brought on by "compression of the lateral femoral cutaneous nerve." "Now that hip-huggers are back in fashion," he wrote, "physicians can expect to see more patients with tingly thighs."

But the perils of tingly thighs were not much of a deterrent. By 2003, as low-rise broadened its base from would-be models to the juniors market and the wardrobes of soccer moms, commentators were ruing its preponderance. In an article titled "Hello, Moon: Has America's Low-Rise Obsession Gone Too Far?" a *Slate* contributor declared that the country was "in the throes of a crack epidemic." Noting the introduction of a functional jean called Down2There, the rise of which could be adjusted with a built-in bungee cord ("as though adjusting a set of Venetian blinds"), the writer wondered whether the "dark fissures and peek-a-boo undies" of the low-rise cult were "physical emblems of our confessional culture, the sartorial equivalent of the tell-all memoir."

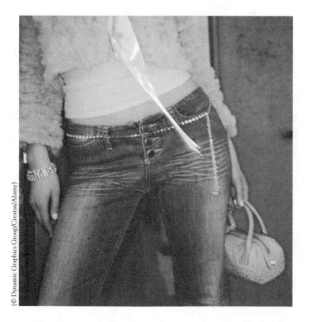

(© Dynamic Graphics Group/Creatas/Alamy)

But it wasn't simply titillation that revived interest in blue jeans. Denim was no longer ghettoized as a novelty at the upper end of the fashion world. When Paper Denim & Cloth debuted in Europe, says Scott Morrison, the jeans were displayed alongside Prada in exclusive boutiques, showcased as America's contribution to couture. Like Charlize Theron's Frankie B.'s on the red carpet, fashionable jeans were now going places where they would once have been frowned upon, or even banned. "In New York, you can go to any restaurant now wearing jeans, or even flip-flops in the summer," says Morrison. "That certainly wasn't the case a few years ago."

And denim's great versatililty gave designers the freedom to experiment. Unlike other garments, jeans are often only partially finished when the sewing is completed. The alchemy of connecting the pants to abstract notions of history and sex appeal has lately been enhanced by real chemical breakthroughs, as designers increasingly rely on superior washes and finishes to distinguish their product. The cost of special washes has risen to as much as fifteen dollars or more a pair, and labor-intensive details such as hand sanding, tinting, and baking have further inflated costs.

"We don't just ask for that kind of money because we're greedy," says Tim Kaeding, creative director at Seven, a company that expected to reach $200 million in sales in 2005. "In today's marketplace, the competition is so fierce and the labor is so intense, that's just what it costs." Denim itself, he says, is a relatively inexpensive fabric, roughly five to seven dollars a yard for good quality. "And the sewing is nothing—five, six, seven dollars. It's all in the wash. If you've got one guy with a piece of sandpaper, and you're paying him by the hour, that's the expense."

Morrison launched the premium brand Paper Denim & Cloth in late 1999 with backing from industry veteran Dick Gilbert. A canary in the price-wars coal mine, Paper Denim soon broke the $150 mark, just as Diesel and Lucky had shown the way to one-hundred-dollar blue jeans a few seasons before. After leaving the brand in 2003, Morrison founded the boutique label Earnest Sewn, where he quickly established a valuable backstory involving a scrupulous hands-on production process. Every pair is signed and dated on an inside pocket lining by the three workers who sewed, abraded, and laundered it. Working with two state-of-the-art finishing facilities, Kentucky's Sights Denim and Italy's Martelli, Morrison doesn't cut any corners. One of his contractors in San Francisco employs several former sewing machine operators from the old Levi's manufacturing plant that doubled as a working museum. "I guarantee you I have the highest production costs in the business," he says.

Once an aspiring professional golfer who was mentored at the University of Washington by Chuck Fancher, a founder of Brittania, Morrison learned a major lesson when he joined Gilbert's juniors' label, Mudd, in the mid-1990s. There he was enlisted to help build Jack Jeans, a premium line positioned to compete with Diesel and Lucky. "It was a complete disaster in everybody's book," says Morrison. "They wanted to produce it out of Mexico with two-dollar piece goods and a four-dollar finish. It was horrible."

Getting Gilbert to support his idea for Paper Denim & Cloth took some convincing, but Morrison's potential as a designer was realized when the line did $18 million in its second year, $40 million the third. The circumstances of his 2003 departure, however, were awkward, with Gilbert telling the press that Morrison got more credit for the success of Paper Denim than he deserved.

"I never would have had the opportunity I did without Dick Gilbert," says Morrison. "It's a real testament to him. He let me make mistakes along the way." At the same time, he feels he deserved a little more respect on the way out: "Hey, I left the guy a forty-million-dollar brand for his kids to run."

A spring 2005 visit to the men's Denim Bar at Barneys New York found almost all of the jeans priced well past the two-hundred-dollar mark. In heavy rotation on the fifth floor of the Madison Avenue retail emporium were Earnest Sewn, Serfontaine, coveted European imports such as Nudie and G Star. Stitch's jeans, with typically rugged names such as the Dakota and the Nebraska, featured leather laces and a promise that the pants were "aged in redwood barrels"; these ran $265 and up. Also showcased were Rogans, made famous by the cast of *Friends*, and Edun, the new label codesigned by Rogan Gregory and U2 singer Bono and his wife, Ali Hewson. Those, too, were priced at more than $250 apiece.

Across the country, at the ultratrendy Ron Herman store in Los Angeles, that was considered the low end. One deep-dyed pair of jeans was lovingly displayed on a glass shelf, like a piece of fine art. At $720, it was priced that way too. The jeans featured an intricate accordion pleat below the waistline in back—"fashion origami," as the designer, Junya Watanabe, liked to call it.

Just a few years after Diesel's previously inconceivable hundred-dollar breakthrough, $200 jeans were suddenly run-of-the-mill. True Religion debuted a $395 line in fall 2004; the following spring, *The New York Times* asked the question that set the industry "all atwitter," as one marketing consultant put it: "Who Pays $600 for Jeans?"

"Right now you could have a pair of jeans that cost a thousand dollars, and people would buy them," said the owner of Pittsburgh Jeans Company. The reporter noted that premium jeans prices were now off "in cloud-cuckoo-land."

For some brands, these superpremium lines aren't expected to be moneymaking ventures. Rather, they serve as status confirmation for the rest of the collection. Joe Dahan, founder of Los Angeles–based Joe's Jeans, explained the idea behind his top-of-the-line Joe's Premium label to *Women's Wear Daily*. "I consider this my advertising dollars," he said. Featuring hand stitching, floral embroidery, and imported Spanish denim, the $250 jeans were expected to bring in just 10 percent of the company's estimated $3 million for the year.

"It's a way to showcase and create a signature piece for the brand," said Marshal Cohen, chief industry analyst at the NPD Group, a New York research firm that watches clothing sales. "It's all part of the marketing budget . . . and for retailers, it's great window dressing. They all want to catch lightning in a bottle."

The deafening buzz surrounding premium blue jeans has drawn a rash of new players in recent years. The cost of entry, says Scott Malone, a former editor at *Women's Wear Daily*, has gotten a lot lower. Years ago, starting a clothing line meant building factories and hiring a labor force. "It was a capital-intensive business," says Malone. Now, with outsourcing, all it takes is a label, a pattern, and an answering machine. In some ways, the incoming opportunists are just following tradition. "The fashion business has always been very entrepreneurial," says Malone. "Calvin Klein, Ralph Lauren, Tommy Hilfiger megaempire, all started on their own. They all went from zero to megaempire. You can't do that in the car industry."

By some accounts as many as sixty new premium brands have entered the jeans world each year since the beginning of the decade. Throw in private department-store labels, discount off-brands, and various overseas lines with little penetration into the United States, and there is little doubt the number of jeans manufacturers has climbed well into the thousands globally.

Yet the more things change, the more they stay the same. The VF Corp., parent to Lee, Wrangler, and Earl as well as such resurrected brands as Chic, Gitano, and Brittania, remains the world's largest collective jeans manufacturer. Levi Strauss & Co., for all its troubles, still sells the most pairs of denim pants of any single brand. And the great majority of jeans sold still cost the average consumer the equivalent of a couple of pizzas, not her next car payment.

As was the case during the designer jeans era, the attention paid to the glittery world of premium denim is inversely proportionate to its actual share of the market. In recent years premium jeans have been said to account for perhaps 3 percent of all jeans sold, at best. It's a small number, yet given the fact that the price of clothing in America has been dropping for ten years due to outsourcing and automation—compounded by the fact that the share of the American wallet set aside for clothing has been diminishing for decades—it's an intriguing number. Art Spar of STS Research, an agency that tracks the apparel industry from textiles to manufacturing and retail, says the category shot upward in 2005: "I wouldn't be surprised if

5 percent of the units and ten percent of the dollars right now are in the premium business."

All these figures can be a bit misleading, cautions the editor Malone, since some analysts consider "premium" to be jeans priced at fifty dollars or higher, while others set the cutoff at seventy-five or one hundred dollars. Whatever the parameters, the premium category affects the industry far beyond simple numbers. Ever more quickly in the age of technology and global competition, the fresh ideas of the fashion leaders are adopted (some would say "stolen") by budget-conscious manufacturers making cutting-edge fashion available to the average consumer in Anymall, USA. The innovative washes of recent years, for instance, have been knocked off repeatedly for a fraction of the cost, says April Walker, the founder of WalkerWear. "They're doing the same washes [as the premium labels] and retailing jeans for fifty bucks," she says. "You can do anything you want now."

Such rapid dissemination of ideas naturally gives even the most stable premium brands cause for concern. It was the question on the tip of every tongue in the industry: Could those heady premium prices continue to rise? "Is the $300-jeans market about to crash?" asked a *Slate* article that warned of a "Denim Bubble." By fall, some overstocked stores were slashing prices.

Some argued that value-priced fashion brands would pry the customer away, forcing the boutique labels to lower their profit margins. Most insiders agreed that a weeding-out process among the premium competition was inevitable, given the ridiculous number of newcomers. But they also believed—they felt compelled to believe—that the cream of the crop is here to stay.

"Everything's so saturated, there has to be some fallout," says Minya Quirk, a cofounder of Brand Pimps and Media Whores, a New York City marketing company that has represented G Star, Howe jeans, and PRPS, a Japanese vintage-reproduction label. "But that oversaturation makes room for a new standard."

"I think it's pretty simple," says Seven's Tim Kaeding. "Seven was one of the first jeans over a hundred dollars. People

were willing to pay that because you look so good in them." In five years, he says, those customers aren't going to decide that they'd rather look "just OK" in a twenty-dollar pair of jeans. "The bar has been set. Will everyone be wearing skirts in five years? I have no idea. No one knows. All I know is that jeans have been around for a hundred and fifty years. They're in every closet in the world."

"Denim has been around so long, I really don't see it going anywhere," agrees Frankie B.'s Daniella Clarke. "I've been wearing it my whole life. It's the first thing when I pack—how many pairs am I going to take? I take my bikini and a few pair of jeans."

Wherever fashion leads, the jean has proven to be as durable as the American myth itself. When *Cosmopolitan* surveyed an earlier incarnation of "The Blue Jeans Craze" in May 1973, the magazine noted that it wasn't the style leaders of New York, Los Angeles, and international café society who were truly supporting the fast-growing category. "The real jeans person . . . isn't *found* among these privileged ones," the magazine determined. Rather, it was the ordinary consumer who "has made jeans much more than the transient hula-hoop of the apparel industry."

Long after the trendsetters have moved on to the next two-hundred-dollar hula hoop, the vast midsection of consumers will be swiveling their hips in the latest permutation of the quintessential American product.

CONCLUSION:

★

The Process

D id they flatten your butt out?"

The moment the customer pulls back the dressing room curtain, the quick-talking shopkeeper peppers her with questions. "How do the jeans fit?" she asks. "Are they tight in the thighs? How do they feel on the hips?"

She's not just trying to make another sale, although at an average of $180 a pair, the high-end denims Leah Eckelberger retails at Jean Therapy, her Boston boutique, every sale is a considerable victory. Eckelberger, twenty-nine and compact as a gymnast, is no master of the hard sell. She'll cheerfully send first-timers who blanch at her prices down to Newbury Street, to the Lucky Brand store, to buy less expensive fashion jeans. She just wants her customers to go home feeling flattered, feeling cared for, as if they'd been to a spa. To Eckelberger, jeans are, in fact, a kind of therapy. They are comforting and familiar, yet they can make you feel sexy and adventurous. Her enthusiasm for her merchandise—enthusiasm, hell!; it borders on pathology—is contagious.

"Leah Eckelberger talks about jeans the way Wolfgang Puck talks about food," read a blurb in in a local newspaper when the store opened in late 2004. "You might not be hungry when you start watching, but you're starving by the end."

Eckelberger likes to say that shopping for jeans brings out the best and worst in us. Customers don't hesitate to announce what they perceive to be their physical deficiencies: "They'll say, 'I'm short,' or 'I have big legs,' " she says. "They're overaware of their bodies, actually. It's crazy." For many women, she says, the act of buying a new pair of jeans has become as intimate, and as anxiety-riddled, as picking out a bathing suit or a prom dress.

That's one reason the store owner believes the recent boom in couture denim is no passing fad. People will continue to pay higher prices, says Eckelberger, as long as the industry does not neglect the needs of ordinary buyers. Right now, she is fixated on the five-year domination of low-rise. A favorite among twiggy model types and school-age Lolitas, the look, Eckelberger says, is flat wrong for just about everyone else. She doesn't mince words, calling the style a "debacle."

"I want to sell something that's relevant to people's lives," she says.

Not long ago, Eckelberger didn't think she'd be selling anything at all. Convinced she was destined to run some sort of nonprofit foundation, working in politics or social services, she took the GMATs for business school. Preternaturally gifted in every endeavor from childhood, she was shocked when she failed miserably.

"It was like Michelle Kwan going for the gold and not even getting the bronze," she says. "It was horrendous."

Friends and family urged her to take the test again, but she knew it was a sign that she'd been on the wrong path. She realized almost instantly what she should be doing.

"I used to sketch clothing all the time as a kid," she recalls. "I was always the one wearing bizarre outfits."

The last of three military brats in a family that moved often—her dad was a two-star rear admiral in the navy—Eckelberger was the only girl, and the only adopted child. Asian by birth, raised in a family of German-Irish heritage, she once attended a Quaker prep school. Aware of her uniqueness at an early age, she flaunted it with her taste in clothing.

She was, in her own words, treated like a princess. But she was also tomboyish, "a little rough-and-tumble." Her favorite clothes were her brothers' hand-me-downs. She wore Chad's old pair of Levi's 501s through high school. They became an ongoing art project, says Eckelberger. "At one point I hacked the bottoms. Another time I sewed flowers on the pocket."

Recalling that passion, she decided she should be selling clothes. "My first words were *Sears* and *Coca-Cola*," she says. "I was definitely meant to go into retail." So she took a continuing education class in small business management. Then she opened her store.

For years the basement space that Jean Therapy now shares with an adjacent bookstore was home to the Rathskellar, a dank punk-rock hovel affectionately known as the Rat. Now stark white and brightly lit, the space has a concrete floor patterned with Jean Therapy's graffiti-style logo, spray-painted with a cardboard stencil. The transformation is telling, a microcosm of urban renewal in America. The yowling nihilism of the dive bar that once was the Rat has given way to the hip Zen of boutique shopping. At Jean Therapy, Leah Eckelberger sells blue jeans with names that imply devotion, names such as Earnest Sewn and Sacred Blue.

In the crook of the store's L-shaped layout sits an old Singer sewing machine on a child-size table. It's a little shrine to Eckelberger's youthful infatuation with clothing. The mall jeans and Salvation Army castoffs she has altered over the years—Diesel, Gap, Liz Claiborne, "things that I've ripped apart, hemmed, studied"—are folded into stacks on the small shelves above.

Eckelberger opened the store with a loan obtained using her parents' retirement fund as collateral. She went through three banks before finding a match, she says, fielding the same question at every one: "Who's going to spend that much on jeans?" But this young entrepreneur knows what the loan officers may not have understood. Jeans, whatever their momentary position on the fashion ladder, are not like other clothes. We are as loyal to a good pair as we are to an old friend.

"There's a perception built into any denim product that says comfort and history," suggests Joe Ieraci, the consultant and former trend forecaster for Burlington. "It's a proven. How do you then make yourself distinct within that market? The fact is, the history of denim is the history of rebellion, and most people play off that image." It comes as little surprise, then, when rappers and rock and pop figures—Jay-Z, Sean "Puffy" Combs, Nelly, Jennifer Lopez, U2's Bono—get into the jeans business. The attitude is inherent in the product, says Ieraci.

"You're almost handed it on a plate. And the question is, do you turn it into steak or meat loaf?"

Thomas George knows a steak from a meat loaf. Owner of E Street Denim in Highland Park, Illinois—on the site of a former Morton's Steakhouse—George has been in the clothing business for thirty years. These days he is recognized as one of the country's foremost denim retailers, always willing to take the lead on a new style or brand. In 1990, flat broke from a previous venture, he opened E Street with five or six dozen pairs of Girbaud jeans, selling them out of the empty brown boxes they came in.

But he hasn't established the store as a premier destination for blue jeans by sheer dumb luck. From his original six-hundred-square-foot boutique in downtown Chicago, George moved out to suburban Highland Park, where he now has twelve thousand square feet stocking fourteen thousand pairs of jeans. An ex-military man and a race-car enthusiast, he never stops thinking about the symbolism of a great pair of jeans. His enthusiasm, like Eckelberger's, is contagious.

"If you're a denim person," he says, "someplace inside you've got heart, you've got respect, you've got appreciation. You've got a conscience." Jeans, he says, represent "the belief of who we can be, not the reality of who we are. You put 'em on, and you walk a little taller."

They feed the imagination, but they're practical too. "You can have two pair," says George. "One in the wash, and one on your ass."

Exactly why do we invest so much—so much meaning, time, money—in something as elementary as a pair of jeans? The answer lies in the fact that jeans are mutable. Each pair changes as it ages, and "blue jeans" in the abstract have changed dramatically over time, evolving from function to form, from drudgery to romance. Like Willie Stark in *All the King's Men*, we have hung our old work clothes on a nail to stiffen with the last of our sweat.

Yet contemporary jeans are an accumulation of history, not a renunciation. Faded, frayed, molded to the peculiarities of our bodies, jeans show the work, even where there may not have been any. "They say, 'Yes, I'm alive!' " says the vintage workwear collector Larry McKaughan. " 'I have life, I have character, I have substance. You can see it. Look, here it is!' "

In his essay "What's 'American' about America," the late critic John Atlee Kouwenhoven wrote that ours is "a concern with process rather than product—or, to reuse Mark Twain's words, a concern with the manner of handling experience or materials rather than with the experience or materials themselves." "Matter," Kouwenhoven wrote, "is no longer to be thought of as something fixed, but fluid and ever changing." His list of a dozen definitive American products included such monuments to change as the skyscraper and the Manhattan skyline, the gridiron town plan, the assembly line, the improvisation of jazz, the ongoing story lines of soap operas and comic strips, and chewing gum, the sole appeal of which "is the process of chewing it." Had Kouwenhoven lived a half century later—in our denim-obsessed time, rather than during the infancy of branding—he would surely have put blue jeans at the top of his list.

America *is* process, he wrote. The country's history is the process of moving into and out of its cities; of moving west, and back again; of moving up and down the social ladder. It is also the process of reconciling contradictions. Americans themselves, Kouwenhoven argued, are "the most materialistic of peoples," and also the most idealistic; "the most revolutionary, and conversely, the most conservative"; "the most rampantly individualistic, and, simultaneously, the most gregarious and herdlike"; the most irreverent toward our elders, yet "the most abject worshipers of 'Mom.' " We've made the process, and those contradictions, inherent in our jeans.

The associations are as bottomless as the color blue itself. In the final analysis, however, jeans define America for the simplest of reasons. The man who saw consumer culture as the great art form, Andy Warhol, recognized that jeans were extraordinary in their very ordinariness. The designer of the infamous zipper cover on the Rolling Stones' *Sticky Fingers* album, a man who once wore a pair of jeans underneath his tuxedo trousers to the White House, Warhol loved what jeans do to the body, and he loved the fact that they are long lasting and machine washable.

"Jeans are so easy," he said.

ACKNOWLEDGMENTS

★

Many thanks to everyone I interviewed, everyone who pointed me in the right direction, and everyone who set me straight.

Thanks to the good Californians at Levi Strauss & Co., particularly Lynn Downey, for her keen eye and diligence, as well as Jeff Beckman and Bob Haas.

Thanks to Susan Downer at Wrangler and Jennifer Johnson at Lee for access to their archives. Thanks to Ralph Tharpe, Raymond Fuquay, and Floyd Nesbitt for welcoming me to Cone Mills.

Thanks to Andrew Olah for his enthusiastic encouragement. Likewise to Leah Eckelberger, who gently eased me into the present day.

Thanks to Jeff Spielberg for his vast expertise in the vintage world, and for showing me the stuff.

Thanks to Jenny Balfour-Paul for her invaluable knowledge of indigo.

Thanks to my agent, Paul Bresnick, for finding me, and for sticking with me. Thanks to Greil Marcus for suggesting me.

Thanks to my editor, Brendan Cahill, for his spot-on suggestions, and for lunch.

Thanks to Billie Porter, my photo editor, for her perseverance and cooperation.

Thanks to Joel Selvin, David Wiegand, David Dayton, and my friends at the *San Francisco Chronicle*.

Thanks to Alan Kaufman for his comradeship.

And thanks to my mother, who never minded the holes in the knees.

NOTES

★

Introduction

Interviews: Michael Cassel and Michael Paradise of The Stronghold.

"The most successful celebrities are products": George W. S. Trow, *Within the Context of No Context* (Boston: Little, Brown, and Co., 1981), p. 48.

Yves Saint Laurent, "I wish I had invented blue jeans": Alice Harris, *The Blue Jean* (New York: PowerHouse, 2002), p. 95.

Bill Blass, "The best single item of apparel": Barbara Fehr, *Yankee Denim Dandies* (Blue Earth, Minn.: Piper, 1974), p. 11.

Charles James, "Blue denim is America's gift": Nancy MacDonell Smith, *The Classic Ten: The True Story of the Little Black Dress and Nine Other Fashion Favorites* (New York: Penguin, 2003), p. 43.

One

For the section on indigo, Jenny Balfour-Paul's *Indigo* was an indispensable resource.

Brigham Young, "Fornication pants": Lynn Schnurnberger, *Let There Be Clothes: 40,000 Years of Fashion* (New York: Workman, 1991), p. 266.

This "barbaric" practice: Diana de Marly, *Working Dress: A History of Occupational Clothing* (London: B. T. Batsford Ltd, 1986), p. 8.

Lord Carlisle, "The gnats in this part of the river": ibid., p. 62.

"At least 100,000 of whom were doomed for life": Philippe Perot, *Fashioning the Bourgeoisie: A History of Clothing in the 19th Century* (Princeton, N.J.: Princeton University Press, 1994), p. 39.

Providence Gazette report: Florence Montgomery, *Textiles in America 1650–1870* (New York: Norton, 1984), p. 216.

Dungri: ibid., p. 228.

"19 peecs Jeines fustian": ibid., p. 271.

"Ribdenims . . . Thicksetts, Corduroys": Perry Walton, *The Story of Textiles: A Bird's-Eye View of the History of the Beginning and the Growth of the Industry by Which Mankind Is Clothed* (Boston: John S. Lawrence, 1912), p. 182.

George Washington, "The whole seemed perfect": ibid., p. 158.

Wassily Kandinsky, "The deeper blue becomes": Alexander Theroux, *The Primary Colors: Three Essays* (New York: Henry Holt and Company, 1994), p. 67.

"It is curious that in English the word *blue:*" Victoria Finlay, *Color: A Natural History of the Palette* (New York: Ballantine, 2002), p. 286.

Blue-dyed cloth used to wrap Egyptian mummies: ibid., p. 319.

Indigo plant soaked in liquid: Simon Garfield, *Mauve: How One Man Invented a Color That Changed the World* (New York: W. W. Norton & Company, 2000), p. 40.

Seven ships representing the Dutch East India Company: Jenny Balfour-Paul, *Indigo* (Chicago: Fitzroy Dearborn, 1998), p. 44.

Trading indigo for slaves: ibid., p. 60.

Woad merchant Pierre de Berny: Michel Pastoureau, *Blue: The History of a Color* (Princeton, N.J.: Princeton University Press, 2001), p. 125.

"Pays de cocagne": Finlay, p. 326.

Stained-glass artisans portray blue devils: Pastourneau, p. 64.

Dutch claim of sexual impotence: Florence H. Pettit, *America's Indigo Blues: Resist-printed and Dyed Textiles of the Eighteenth Century* (New York: Hastings House, 1974), p. 27.

Moroccan dyers' legend: Finlay, p. 338.

Menstruating women forbidden to work with dye pots: Annette B. Weiner and Jane Schneider (eds.), *Cloth and Human Experience* (Washington, D.C.: Smithsonian Institution Press, 1989), p. 150.

Caribbean islands producing more indigo than India by 1640s: Finlay, p. 329.

Eliza Lucas in South Carolina: ibid., pp. 330–332.

England imports five hundred tons from colonies in 1770: Garfield, p. 124.

Gandhi: Finlay, pp. 344–346.

Two

Some research for this chapter took place in the Levi Strauss & Co. archive in San Francisco. The company's self-published history, *This Is a Pair of Levi's Jeans*, proved especially useful. Jeff Spielberg provided helpful historical materials for Sweet-Orr; likewise Jennifer Johnson at Lee. Interviews: Daphne Stevens of Old Sturbridge Village; LS&CO. Chairman Bob Haas and Historian Lynn Downey.

Shortage of goods in gold rush country: J. S. Holliday, *The World Rushed In* (New York: Simon & Schuster, 1981), p. 41.

Lincoln visits Amoskeag: George Waldo Browne, *The Amoskeag Manufacturing Company of Manchester, New Hampshire: A History* (Manchester, N. H.: Amoskeag Manufacturing Company, 1915), pp. 157–158.

Levi Strauss & Co. sues rivals: Ed Cray, *Levi's: The "Shrink-to-Fit" Business That Stretched to Cover the World* (Boston: Houghton Mifflin, 1978), p. 24.

"Merchant Prince" Henry Carter: Roger Carroll, *Lebanon, 1761–1994: The Evolution of a Resilient New Hampshire City* (West Kennebunk, Me.: Phoenix, 1994), pp. 115–116.

"A suit of cloaths": Jane Ford Adams and Lillian Smith Albert, *Pictorial Overall Buttons: A Descriptive Catalog of Pictorial Buttons Worn on Work Clothing, 1900–1935* (Boyertown, Pa.: National Button Society, Boyertown Publishing Co., 1965), p. 4.

Military-issue overalls: Past Patterns No. 910, "One-Piece Apron Front Overalls Circa 1870 to 1901."

Whitman's "caricature of working-class garb": Davis S. Reynolds, *Walt Whitman's America: A Cultural Biography* (New York: Vintage, 1995), p. 363.

"A poseur of truly colossal proportions": ibid., p. 161.

Federal Writers' Project oral history: Past Patterns.

Three

Some research for this chapter took place in the Wrangler archive in Greensboro.

Frederic Remington, "Shall never come west again": David McCullough (Introduction), *Frederic Remington: The Masterworks* (New York: Harry N. Abrams, Inc., 1988), p. 34.

Violence is not the real crux of the Western: Robert Warshow, *The Immediate Experience: Movies, Comics, Theatre, and Other Aspects of Popular Culture* (Garden City, N.Y.: Doubleday, 1962), p. 137–144.

John Muir, "tired, nerve-shaken, overcivilized people": Michael Kimmel, *Manhood in America: A Cultural History* (New York: Free Press, 1996), p. 136.

Buffalo Bill Cody's Wild West: Michael Allen, *Rodeo Cowboys in the*

North American Imagination (Reno: University of Nevada Press, 1998), p. 22.

William S. Hart, "The real cowboy clothes are all made for utility": Holly George-Warren and Michelle Freedman, How the West Was Worn (New York: Harry N. Abrams, Inc., 2001), p. 44.

Betty Rogers on husband Will's style of dress: Richard M. Ketchum, Will Rogers: His Life and Times (New York: American Heritage, 1973), pp. 314–315.

"Wayne hated horses": Garry Wills, John Wayne's America (New York: Touchstone, 1997), p. 15.

Western stars' "elaborate signals worked out through their costume": ibid., p. 19.

Michael Wayne describes father's laundering technique: George-Warren/Freedman, p. 49.

Walter Haas Sr., "We had a ship bringing us two hundred bales of denim": Cray, p. 67.

"One look at him and you know": James B. Twitchell, Twenty Ads That Shook the World: The Century's Most Groundbreaking Advertising and How It Changed Us All (New York: Crown, 2000), pp. 128–131.

Four

Interviews: Peter Lang Nooch of Farmer; Tim Kaeding of Seven for All Mankind.

"The woman shall not wear that which pertaineth unto a man": Deuteronomy 22:5.

Elizabeth Cady Stanton, "The true idea": Catherine Smith and Cynthia Greig, Women in Pants: Manly Maidens, Cowgirls, and Other Renegades (New York: Harry N. Abrams, Inc., 2003), p. 114.

"This woman is a modern pioneer": Penny Colman, Rosie the Riveter: Working Women on the Home Front in World War II (New York: Crown, 1995), p. 63.

Real-life Rosie the Riveters: ibid., p. 21.

George Orwell on tramping attire: de Marly, p. 153.

University of Oregon: Cray, p. 97.

Claire McCardell, "For me it is American": MacDonell Smith, p. 52.

Slim Keith with Montgomery Clift: Slim Keith with Annette Tapert, Slim: Memories of a Rich and Imperfect Life (New York: Simon & Schuster, 1990), pp. 121–122.

Five

Interviews: costume designer Aggie Guerard Rodgers; former head of Jeanswear Communications Norman Karr.

Robert Mitchum, "I'm sorry if my new look doesn't appeal": Lee

Server, *Robert Mitchum: "Baby, I Don't Care,"* (New York: St. Martin's Press, 2001), p. 168.

"If you want to know the good boys": Cray, p. 126.

Baby boomers a $10-billion-a-year industry: Thomas Doherty, *Teenagers and Teenpics: The Juvenilization of American Movies in the 1950s* (Boston: Unwin Hyman, 1988), p. 52.

Levi Strauss & Co. at the end of the 1950s: Cray, p. 131.

Brando at the Russian Tea Room: Peter Manso, *Brando: The Biography* (New York: Hyperion, 1995), p. 175.

"Bowery bum" attire: ibid., p. 250.

Costume designer Lucinda Ballard: ibid., p. 228.

Dean's "defiant stoop and despondent gaze": Donald Spoto, *Rebel: The Life and Legend of James Dean* (New York: HarperCollins, 1996), p. 217.

Henri Cartier-Bresson on Monroe: Fred Lawrence Guiles, *Norma Jean: The Life of Marilyn Monroe* (New York: McGraw-Hill, 1969), p. 360.

Tommy Hilfiger buys Monroe jeans at auction: Harris, p. 111.

PTA Magazine, "The trouble with teenagers": Doherty, p. 42.

"A vast, determined band of blue-jeaned storm troopers": ibid., pp. 51–52.

Johnny Cash and the Tennessee Two: George-Warren/Freedman, p. 159.

William Burroughs on "On the Road": Graham Marsh and Paul Trynka, *Denim, From Cowboys to Catwalk: A Visual History of the World's Most Legendary Fabric* (London: Aurum Press, 2002), p. 80.

Gary Snyder on Neal Cassady: Anne Charters (ed.), *The Portable Beat Reader* (New York: Penguin, 1992), p. 189.

"They look beat up and depraved": Philip Norman, *Shout: The Beatles in Their Generation* (New York: Simon & Schuster, 1981), p. 175.

"Style has become a language": Ted Polhemus, *Streetstyle: From Sidewalk to Catwalk* (New York: Thames and Hudson, 1994), p. 54.

Vince Man's Shop: Shaun Cole, *Don We Now Our Gay Apparel: Gay Men's Dress in the Twentieth Century* (Oxford: Berg/Oxford, 2000), p. 72.

Bing Crosby's denim tuxedo: Cray, p. 198.

Denim Council campaign: Richard Campbell, *Media and Culture: An Introduction to Mass Communication* (New York: St. Martin's Press, 1998), p. 339.

Antifashion "has often simply been the next fashion": Anne Hollander, *Sex and Suits: The Evolution of Modern Dress* (New York: Alfred A. Knopf, 1994), p. 193.

Walter Haas Sr., "It seemed impossible to me": Cray, p. 151.

Six

Some research for this chapter took place at Cone Mills headquarters in Greensboro. Interviews: Cone's Raymond Fuquay and Ralph Tharpe.

"Annual sales of dungarees": David Hajdu, *Positively 4th Street: The Lives and Times of Joan Baez, Bob Dylan, Mimi Baez Fariña, and Richard Fariña* (New York: Farrar, Straus and Giroux, 2001), p. 116.

"Theorists of blue jeans in the sixties": Kennedy Fraser, *The Fashionable Mind: Reflections on Fashion, 1970–81* (New York: Alfred A. Knopf, 1981), p. 93.

"There was a burgeoning awareness": Naomi Klein, *No Logo* (New York: Picador, 1999), p. 7.

"Identity no longer depended on pedigree": John Leland, *Hip: The History* (New York: Ecco, 2004), p. 54.

"To the careful observer": Alison Lurie, *The Language of Clothes* (New York: Owl/Henry Holt, 1981/2000), p. 17.

The Pill: Paul Fussell, *Uniforms: Why We Are What We Wear* (Boston: Houghton Mifflin, 2002), p. 50.

Deneuve/Bailey wedding: Marsh/Trynka, p. 104.

George Harrison on Haight Street: Charles Perry, *The Haight-Ashbury: A History* (New York: Rolling Stone Press, 1984), pp. 226–227.

Abbie Hoffman letter to the *Village Voice*: Jeff Tamarkin, *Got a Revolution!: The Turbulent Flight of Jefferson Airplane* (New York: Atria, 2003), p. 130.

Levi Strauss & Co. in Blackstone, VA: Cray, pp. 127–129.

Country Joe and the Fish: Perry, p. 188.

Seven

Interviews: jeans rep Michael Cohen; Izzy Ezrailson of Up Against the Wall; costume designer Anthea Sylbert; rock photographers Joel Bernstein and Baron Wolman.

Kennedy Fraser, "Apart from the men in business suits": quoted in MacDonell Smith, p. 54.

"He looked like a middleweight Rocky Marciano": Hunter S. Thompson, *Hell's Angels: A Strange and Terrible Saga* (New York: Ballantine, 1966), p. 129.

"He was not in awe of anybody": Marshall Terrill, *Steve McQueen: Portrait of an American Rebel* (New York: Donald I. Fine, Inc., 1993), pp. 281–282.

American cultural impact on students in Mexico: Mark Kurlansky, *1968: The Year That Rocked the World* (New York: Random House, 2004), p. 330.

"No one can take himself entirely seriously": Charles A. Reich, *The Greening of America* (New York: Random House, 1970), pp. 234–237.

"Instead of shining heroes, cowboys were renegades": George-Warren/Freedman, p. 169.

"The biggest pretense": Stephen Bayley, *Taste: The Secret Meaning of Things* (New York: Pantheon, 1991), p. 169.

"High society swells": Baron Wolman and John Burks (Introduction), *Levi's Denim Art Contest Catalogue of Winners* (Mill Valley, Calif.: Squarebooks, 1974), p. 3.

Yves Saint Laurent: Marsh/Trynka, p. 104.

"When you mass-produce": Alexandra Jacopetti, *Native Funk & Flash: An Emerging Folk Art* (San Francisco: Scrimshaw Press, 1974), p. 12.

Eight

Interviews: designer David Mechaly; industry veterans Billy Kolber and Cliff Abbey; Len Larson of Lee; consultant Joe Ieraci.

"It was perfect; classic": Marsh/Trynka, p. 94.

"He looked like a matchstick": Marc Jacobs (Introduction), *We're Desperate: The Punk Rock Photography of Jim Jocoy* (New York: PowerHouse, 2003), unnumbered page.

"We came up with the idea": Gloria Vanderbilt, *It Seemed Important at the Time* (New York: Simon & Schuster, 2004), p. 120.

"I said, 'Pack up the jeans' ": Anthony Haden-Guest, *The Last Party: Studio 54, Disco, and the Culture of the Night* (New York: William Morrow and Company, 1997), p. 139.

First Calvin Klein jeans: Steven Gaines and Sharon Churcher, *Obsession: The Lives and Times of Calvin Klein* (New York: Birch Lane Press, 1994), p. 213.

"They'll tear your clothes off": Gaines/Churcher, p. 250.

Diana Vreeland, "Blue jeans are the most beautiful things": Harris, p. 78.

"Work clothes looked designed by fiat": Hollander, p. 168.

"When it became clear that somebody is designing": ibid.

Nine

Steven Gaines and Sharon Churcher's *Obsession: The Lives and Times of Calvin Klein* and Christopher Byron's *Skin Tight: The Bizarre Story of Guess v. Jordache—Glamour, Greed, and Dirty Tricks in the Fashion Industry* were especially helpful in researching this chapter.

"It was like magic": Gaines/Churcher, p. 257.

History of sexual suggestion in advertising: Tom Reichert, *The Erotic History of Advertising* (Amherst, N.Y.: Prometheus, 2003), p. 13.

Wedding "the Calvin Klein image to jeans": Gaines/Churcher, p. 288.

"The tight seam in front": Fussell, p. 50.

"It was butch and it was cute": Cole, p. 170.

"It is no coincidence that the drag queens": *Artenergie: Art in Jeans* (Milan: Charta, 1997), p. 29.

Jeans as a kind of cross-dressing: John Fiske, *Understanding Popular Culture* (Boston: Unwin Hyman, 1989), p. 3.

John Lennon wonders whether it's time to "destroy the macho ethic": quoted in Kimmel, p. 293.

"The whole thing was a fiasco": Haden-Guest, p. 142.

Sephardic Jews and *serge de Nîmes*: Christopher Byron, *Skin Tight: The Bizarre Story of Guess v. Jordache—Glamour, Greed, and Dirty Tricks in the Fashion Industry* (New York: Simon & Schuster, 1992), p. 47.

"A lot of people blinked": Gaines/Churcher, p. 275.

"Anne Tyler and Georgia O'Keeffe and Werner Fassbinder": Byron, p. 51.

"The fighting would have gone on forever": ibid., p. 312.

In the ancient court of Nebuchadnezzar: ibid., p. 193.

"The jeans become sexy": Reichert, p. 228.

Ten

Interviews: collectors Bobby Garnett, Jeff Spielberg, Larry McKaughan, Seth Weiser, and Gerard Maione; designers Adriano Goldschmied and Jason Ferro; stonewash pioneer Mark Emalfarb; Claire Dupuis and Skip Gordon of Cotton Inc. At the Rose Bowl Flea Market: Hitoshi Yamada and Tee Komol.

BASF in 1900: Garfield, p. 151.

German industry and synthetic indigo: ibid., p. 161.

"A national calamity": Balfour-Paul, p. 81.

Wabi-sabi described as "the beauty of things as they are": Robyn Griggs Lawrence, *The Wabi-Sabi House: The Japanese Art of Imperfect Beauty* (New York: Clarkson Potter, 2004), p. 10.

"If 'whole' jeans connote shared meanings": Fiske, p. 4.

Vivienne Westwood, Katharine Hamnett, and Dolce & Gabbana: Marsh/ Trynka, p. 109.

New York boutique Charivari: Teri Agins, *The End of Fashion: The Mass Marketing of the Clothing Business* (New York: William Morrow and Company, 1999), p. 11.

Eleven

Interviews: Diesel founder Renzo Rosso; Wrangler's Bill Hervey; designer April Walker.

Counterfeit Levi's in Italy: Cray, p. 231.

"Once, Ralph drove up in a sports car": Michael Gross, *Genuine Authentic: The Real Life of Ralph Lauren* (New York: HarperCollins, 2003), Gross, p. 94.

"He invented horses too": ibid., p. 221.

"It was the first, but not the last, time": ibid., pp. 191–192.

"Ralph never wore jeans and boots": ibid., p. 178.

Tommy Hilfiger likened to the Monkees: Agins, p. 102.

Andy Hilfiger, "I never pushed for them to wear Tommy": ibid., p. 112.

Gangs wearing dungaree jackets turned inside out: Nelson George, *Hip Hop America* (New York: Viking, 1998), p. 157.

Russell Simmons, "We always bought into logos: Agins, p. 111.

Karl Kani and Cross Colours: George, p. 163.

"The alarms were going off": Agins, p. 276.

"A corporation cannot succeed in accomplishing a socially desirable goal": Arthur M. Kenison, *Dumaine's Amoskeag: Let the Record Speak* (Manchester, N.H.: Saint Anselm College Press, 1997), p. 8.

Wages in San Antonio, Costa Rica: Karl Schoenberger, *Levi's Children: Coming to Terms with Human Rights in the Global Marketplace* (New York: Atlantic Monthly Press, 2000), p. 49.

"Some sort of quasi-messianic role": ibid., p. 128.

Levi's Signature line: Ted C. Fishman, *China Inc.: How the Rise of the Next Superpower Challenges America and the World* (New York: Scribner, 2005), p. 4.

"Levi Strauss had become exhausted by its ethics": Schoenberger, p. 160.

Twelve

Interviews: Tim Crane of Crane & Co.; Scott Morrison of Earnest Sewn; Frankie B. founder Daniella Clarke; former *Women's Wear Daily* editor Scott Malone; marketing guru Minya Quirk.

"It is this purchasing of *identity*": Joseph Heath and Andrew Potter, *Nation of Rebels: Why Counterculture Became Consumer Culture* (New York: HarperBusiness, 2004), p. 211.

Consumers "know that they are drinking the ad, not the booze": ibid., p. 212.

Conclusion

Interviews: Leah Eckelberger of Jean Therapy; Thomas George of E Street Denim.

America *is* process: John A. Kouwenhoven, *The Beer Can By the Highway: Essays on What's American About America* (Garden City, N.Y.: Doubleday & Company, 1961), pp. 39–73.

INDEX

⭐

Note: Page numbers in italics refer to illustrations.